101

EXPLOSIVE BENEFITS OF FASTING

GLENN AREKION

Faith House Publishing

ISBN 978-1-943282-09-8

faithhousepublishing.com

CONTENTS

Dedication

∽

I dedicate this book to Thomas C Duddy.

A friend, brother in Christ and prayer partner.

Gone home to be with your Lord too soon.

Loyalty was your asset.

You had your flaws but the greatest virtues
were persistent prayer, relentless fasting,
a voracious appetite for the Word and
a wacky sense of humor.

You are missed but we will see you
on the other side of glory.

∽

INTRODUCTION

I have been preaching and teaching on fasting extensively for the last ten years. This book is a product of an intensive fast where I fasted for one year and during that one year I experienced so many breakthroughs. It was through this fast, that the Lord gave me the 101 explosives benefits of fasting which we aired on national and international TV. We have sold thousands of these messages and people have been blessed by it. I deem it important to put the information in book form. Since it aired on television, many are using the 101 benefits of fasting to their advantage. Some have even used the messages and put them out as their product and research. I believe the information in this book will radically change your life.

If you crave the supernatural edge in your life, church and ministry then the information in this book will challenge and motivate you to contend for it. Our Lord Jesus, whose ministry epitomized the supernatural, was a man of fasting. He is our example. Please understand that fasting has nothing to do with your salvation and sanctification as that can only be the result of grace and grace alone. Fasting simply gives you the supernatural cutting edge, making you effective and your Christianity adventurous.

WHEN IT COMES TO SUPERNATURAL DEMONSTRATIONS
WE HAVE THE MENTAL BELIEF BUT WE DO NOT HAVE THE
PHYSICAL MANIFESTATIONS AND THAT IS BECAUSE WE
LACK SPIRITUAL POWER

CHAPTER 1
THE CURSE OF POWERLESSNESS

IT is my every intention to move you to tap into the power and privilege of fasting. Nowadays, access to fast and high-quality food has become a normal indulgence for most people around the world. The idea of fasting is viewed as archaic and irrelevant. Our lives seem to revolve around the food table. This is seen especially within the Christian community in the USA, where restaurants understand that there are major profits to be made on days where church services are held: our bellies are satisfied yet our 'inner man' is yearning for the miraculous. There is a supernatural dimension missing in our lives. Many ministers – as well as believers – have relegated the subject of fasting to the back burner. It is somehow considered old fashioned, for the old-timers or early-church fathers but not relevant to us in this hi-tech world in which we live.

Many churches rely heavily on modern technology for an effective church service, with dazzling lights, special effects, professional music for praise and worship, video and audio aid for a well organized service, yet untold millions leave services Sunday after Sunday with their needs unmet. Of course, great efforts have been made by many ministers to be studious to give the faithful attendees a solid word on Sunday, with many going deep into the Hebrew and Greek meanings. While this is commendable and we love all those mentioned above, all these methods cannot heal the sick nor deliver the oppressed from wicked spirits. In the last few years, great emphasis has been placed on healing, however it is not on physical healing but emotional healing or inner healing. While this is needful there is something missing in all of this. Where is the raw power that expelled sicknesses and demons out of the lives of oppressed people like we read in the Bible from the ministry of Jesus, Peter and Paul?

The ministry of Jesus was and is the epitome of what a ministry should look like today. We find that Paul and Peter, among others, in the New Testament fashioned their ministries after that of Jesus. This is why they had so many saved, healed and delivered. While many Pentecostal, Spirit-filled and Charismatic churches profess to believe in the supernatural power of God, few see the manifestations of the raw *dunamis* power of God. Why? Because when it comes to the supernatural, we have the mental belief but we do not have the physical manifestations because we lack spiritual power. There is a plague of powerlessness running rampant in the modern church. Sooner or later we will have to face the fact that we are not fulfilling the words of our Master, when he said, '*Verily, verily, I say unto you, He that believeth on me, the works that I do shall he do also; and greater works than these shall he do; because I go unto my Father*' (John 14:12). Where are the healing evangelists who graced our world in the twentieth century? Did you notice these words, '*the works that I do shall he do also*'. The believer is supposed to do the works of Jesus and in fact the Lord went even further telling us we will do greater works. So we need to find out:

§ **What were the works of Jesus?**

§ **What are the *greater works*?**

WHEN IT COMES TO THE SUPERNATURAL WE HAVE THE MENTAL BELIEF BUT WE DO NOT HAVE THE PHYSICAL MANIFESTATIONS BECAUSE WE LACK SPIRITUAL POWER

These days the *greater works* have been rationalized to simply mean that we should lead people to Christ, to the born-again experience. Indeed, this is the truth but not the whole truth! We still have to explain why we are not doing the works of Jesus. What were they exactly? Let's allow Jesus and the Bible to answer this question.

And as Jesus passed by, he saw a man which was blind from his birth.
And his disciples asked him, saying, Master, who did sin, this man, or
his parents, that he was born blind? Jesus answered, Neither hath this
man sinned, nor his parents: but that the works of God should be made
manifest in him. I must work the works of him that sent me, while it is day...

JOHN 9:1-4

Jesus and the disciples saw a man blind from birth. The pitiful case of
that man provoked them to ask Jesus a question, 'Master, who did sin, this
man or his parents, that he was born blind?' The disciples ascribed this
man's sad state of affairs as due to either personal or parental sins. In their
mind someone had sinned but they did not know whether the guilty party
was the man or his parents. They were expecting a pre-anticipated and a
preconceived answer but Jesus gave them an answer that ruined their little
theology:

Jesus answered, '... neither hath this man sinned, nor his parents: but that
the works of God should be made manifest in him..."

The man didn't sin therefore he was **not** the guilty one.

His parents did not sin therefore they were **not** the guilty party either.

We need to know who or what was the cause of this man's miserable
state. If neither him nor his parents were guilty then **who** or **what** was the
cause behind this man's dilemma? Don't foolishly assume that God was
the cause of this man's blindness. Let's analyze the answer of Jesus, which
was threefold in nature:

❖ The man did not sin.
❖ The parents did not sin.
❖ The works of God should be made manifest in Him. *I must work the works*
  of Him that sent me while it is day.

The puzzle is solved in the third part of Jesus' statement and the key words are **works** and **manifest**. Jesus emphatically expressed that He was commissioned to do the works of the Father:

*For this purpose the son of God was **manifested**, that he might **destroy the works of the devil**.*

1 JOHN 3:8

Bear in mind the key words are **works** and **manifest**. John informs us that Jesus was manifested to destroy the works of the devil. Therefore, Jesus' manifestation was the works of God destroying sickness and the works of the devil. With this in mind, permit me to give you my rendition of Jesus' answer: '*The man didn't sin, nor did his parents, but this blindness is the work of the devil and I am here to destroy his work with the works of my Father.*' Healing, deliverance and power over the works of Satan are the works of God. Peter tells us that, '*God anointed Jesus with the Holy Ghost and power who went about doing good and healing all those oppressed of the devil*' (Acts 10:38). From the mouth of Jesus, in Luke's first treatise to Theophilus (Luke 4:18) he unveiled his works:

* Preaching the good news to the poor.
* Healing the sick.
* Delivering the oppressed.
* Casting out devils.
* Recovering of sight for the blind.
* Healing the lame and the crippled.

Are we walking in the reality of these works? While we believe God can heal, many of us would identify more with the disciples who could not deliver the lunatic boy – brought to them by his father to receive healing – than we would with Jesus. That is the plague of powerlessness rampant in the church. We need to realize that powerlessness is the blight of the modern church. We have technology and eloquence but not much demonstration of power. We have too much Cosmetic Christianity and not enough Authentic

Christianity. You see, Cosmetic Christianity is Christianity without power and manifestation of the Spirit. A lot of what we call *manifestation of the Spirit* today is at best emotionalism gone wild without changing lives. Let us scrutinize the event with the father and the lunatic son more closely.

WE NEED AUTHENTIC CHRISTIANITY
NOT COSMETIC CHRISTIANITY

And one of the multitude answered and said, Master, I have brought unto thee my son, which hath a dumb spirit; And wheresoever he taketh him, he teareth him: and he foameth, and gnasheth with his teeth, and pineth away: and I spake to thy disciples that they should cast him out; and they could not. He answereth him, and saith, O faithless generation, how long shall I be with you? how long shall I suffer you? bring him unto me. And they brought him unto him: and when he saw him, straightway the spirit tare him; and he fell on the ground, and wallowed foaming. And he asked his father, How long is it ago since this came unto him? And he said, Of a child. And ofttimes it hath cast him into the fire, and into the waters, to destroy him: but if thou canst do any thing, have compassion on us, and help us. Jesus said unto him, If thou canst believe, all things are possible to him that believeth. And straightway the father of the child cried out, and said with tears, Lord, I believe; help thou mine unbelief. When Jesus saw that the people came running together, he rebuked the foul spirit, saying unto him, Thou dumb and deaf spirit, I charge thee, come out of him, and enter no more into him. And the spirit cried, and rent him sore, and came out of him: and he was as one dead; insomuch that many said, He is dead. But Jesus took him by the hand, and lifted him up; and he arose. And when he was come into the house, his disciples asked him privately, Why could not we cast him out? And he said unto them, This kind can come forth by nothing, but by prayer and fasting.

MARK 9:17-29

The man brought his son to the disciples. Why did he do that? Well, if you look at the Gospel of Luke which recorded the same scenario with the man and his son, you will notice some eye-opening details.

Then he called his twelve disciples together, and **gave them power and authority over all devils, and to cure diseases...** *And they departed, and went through the towns, preaching the gospel, and healing every where...* **And the apostles, when they were returned, told him all that they had done. And he took them, and went aside privately into a desert place belonging to the city called Bethsaida.**

LUKE 9:1, 2, 6, 10

From the two portions of Scripture above, I want to draw out **seven** important points as we observe the sequence of events that took place,

1. *He gave them power and authority.* This means He gave them 'dunamis', translated as 'explosive power and ability', as well as 'exousia', meaning 'the right to exert power over all devils and diseases'. This is seen in the first verse and second verses where He commissioned them.
2. *They departed and went through town, preaching the gospel and healing everywhere.* This means the healing virtue of God was manifest as they preached the Gospel. This is evident from the sixth verse.
3. *When they were returned, told him all that they had done.* This means they could do what Jesus sent them to do. This is in verse ten.

Now look at the following verses:

And it came to pass, that on the next day, when they were come down from the hill, much people met him. And, behold, a man of the company cried out, saying, Master, I beseech thee, look upon my son: for he is mine only child. And, lo, a spirit taketh him, and he suddenly crieth out; and it teareth him that he foameth again, and bruising him hardly departeth from him. And I besought thy disciples to cast him out; and they could not.

LUKE 9:37-40

4. *I besought thy disciples to cast him out and they could not.* This means the disciples tried but the result was not there. The effort was there but the effect was not what they desired. The willingness was there but the work was not executed. The purpose was there but not the power. They rose up to the challenge but unfortunately came down deflated to a devastating outcome. This is in verse forty. Here is the point I am endeavoring to get you to see. In the sixth verse they had the power to get results, in the tenth verse they testified they had results and then in the fortieth verse they could not produce what they produced in the sixth verse. What transpired that thirty-four verses later they could not have the results they had formerly seen?

WE NEED TO REALIZE THAT POWERLESSNESS IS THE BLIGHT OF THE MODERN WESTERN CHURCH

5. *I besought thy disciples to cast him out and they could not.* Here is an important point for you to be aware of. People are clearly aware when you have the power of God and people are equally aware when you don't have it. Our powerlessness is not a hidden secret: It is an open manifestation before others. You can fool some people sometimes but you cannot fool everybody all the time. People know when you have the power and people know when you don't. The lack of results is clear evidence. In effect the man said, 'I brought my son to your disciples to cast the devil out of him but your disciples failed and could not get the result that I was looking for.' The same is being said today by many people who bring their needs to the church. People come burdened and oppressed, looking for a way out but unfortunately they leave the same way they came: no miracle, no breakthrough and no touch.

Then came the disciples to Jesus apart, and said, Why could not we cast him out? And Jesus said unto them, Because of your unbelief: for verily I say unto you, If ye have faith as a grain of mustard seed, ye shall say

*unto this mountain, Remove hence to yonder place; and it shall remove;
and nothing shall be impossible unto you. Howbeit this kind goeth not
out but by prayer and fasting.*

MATTHEW 17: 19-21

*And when he was come into the house, his disciples asked him privately,
Why could not we cast him out?*

MARK 9:28

6. *His disciples asked him privately, Why could not we cast him out?* This
    means the disciples were privately concerned about their public act
    of powerlessness. Are you disturbed that your powerlessness is in
    public view? What takes place privately is what will show up publicly.
    What is not being displayed publicly is what was never cultivated
    privately. This is the reason why we must have a strong and healthy
    private life. If you are privately weak, it will publicly show up. If you
    are privately in much fastings, much prayers and much studies then
    it will manifest in much power in the public arena. We must learn
    to be like Jesus.

*But so much the more went there a fame abroad of him: and great
multitudes came together to hear, and to be healed by him of their
infirmities. And he withdrew himself into the wilderness, and prayed.*

LUKE 5:16

But Jesus often withdrew to the wilderness for prayer.

NEW LIVING TRANSLATION (©2007)

But he would withdraw to desolate places and pray.

ENGLISH STANDARD VERSION (©2001)

But Jesus Himself would often slip away to the wilderness and pray.

NEW AMERICAN STANDARD BIBLE (©1995)

However, he continued his habit of retiring to deserted places and praying.

INTERNATIONAL STANDARD VERSION (©2012)

I want you to notice that Jesus had a very strong private devotion to God. If this was most modern preachers, we would think that we had it made when the multitude came to the crusade ground. However Jesus was not moved by the crowd. He had an appointment with his Father that He would not miss. Nothing was permitted to come between Him and His Father. Nothing was permitted to separate him from private prayer time with God. Herein is the secret to having a powerful ministry upon the earth. His private connection with heaven is what determined the public success of his ministry. Adam Clarke's commentary tells us that the original version of this text means that this was a frequent habit of Jesus:

> *And he withdrew himself into the wilderness – or rather, He frequently withdrew into the desert. This I believe to be the import of the original words, ην ύποχωρων. He made it a frequent custom to withdraw from the multitudes for a time, and pray, teaching hereby the ministers of the Gospel that they are to receive fresh supplies of light and power from God by prayer, that they may be the more successful in their work; and that they ought to seek frequent opportunities of being in private with God and their books. A man can give nothing unless he first receive it; and no man can be successful in the ministry who does not constantly depend upon God, for the excellence of the power is all from him. Why is there so much preaching, and so little good done? Is it not because the preachers mix too much with the world, keep too long in the crowd, and are so seldom in private with God? Reader! Art thou a herald for the Lord of hosts? Make full proof of thy ministry! Let it never be said of thee, "He forsook all to follow Christ, and to preach his Gospel, but there was little or no fruit of his labor; for he ceased to be a man of prayer, and got into the spirit of the world." Alas! alas! is this luminous star, that was once held in the right hand of Jesus, fallen from the firmament of heaven, down to the Earth!*
> ADAM CLARKE'S COMMENTARY ON THE BIBLE

7. *Because of your unbelief... if you have faith... Howbeit this kind goeth not out but by prayer and fasting.*

Here we see the connection of faith, fasting and prayer to bring results. When the disciples asked the reason for not obtaining a result, Jesus exposed them to the truth:

Because of your unbelief: for verily I say unto you, If ye have faith as a grain of mustard seed, ye shall say unto this mountain, Remove hence to yonder place; and it shall remove; and nothing shall be impossible unto you. Howbeit this kind goeth not out but by prayer and fasting.
                                                           MATTHEW 17:20-21

Jesus made this threefold connection in order to obtain Bible results. The combination of faith, prayer and fasting is an offensive secret weapon to bring down the stronghold of Satan. I want you to combine these three forces to unleash supernatural depths and dimensions in your life. In the Sermon on the Mount, Jesus further revealed that whatever we do in secret, our Heavenly Father will reward openly. The three things that will undeniably be rewarded by the Father are **giving, praying** and **fasting**. I call these three the **unbeatable trinity**. I want you to come with me on a journey out of mundane and powerless Christianity to a life of power and results. After perusing and meditating upon the upcoming pages, you can expect your fasting life, faith life and prayer life to take on another dimension to remove you from the blight of powerlessness.

WHEN FASTING HAD A PROMINENT ROLE IN THE CHURCH, THE POWER OF GOD WAS PRE-EMINENT

CHAPTER 2
IS FASTING PASSED AWAY?

FROM the start we have to answer this critical question: Is fasting for the New Testament believers? Or is it something that only the prophets of old delved into and there is no need for us in the so-called enlightened world to partake of?

§ **What does the Bible have to say about fasting?**

§ **What was the position of Jesus and Paul when it comes to the subject of fasting?**

Many leaders in the modern church today will tell you that fasting is not necessary. In fact many will claim that you are being religious or legalistic if you fast, and since we are under grace there is no need for such an act. I find it astonishing that Spirit-filled people who claim to be Continuationist (meaning believing that the gifts of the Spirit are still operational today) have become Cessationist when it comes to fasting. In Christian theology, cessationism is the view that the miraculous gifts of the Holy Spirit – such as speaking in tongues, prophetic utterances and healings – ceased to be practiced early in Christian Church history.

It is to be noted that throughout the ages, when the church demonstrated great power, fasting played a major role. Fasting also played a major role in the life of Jesus. He did not enter full-time ministry until after He fasted. Miracles, healings and the casting out of devils occurred in His ministry after He came back from a fast. Since Jesus said that no servant and disciple can be above his master (Matthew 10:24), if Jesus fasted then we need to fast. Actually, any serious student of the Scriptures will observe that there is a great cloud of witnesses, of people who fasted and had a major impact upon the earth.

When God's people and the church demonstrated great power, fasting played a major role. In the Scriptures we have a record of the good, the bad and the ugly, fasting. Here are a few examples:

1. Moses the Deliverer fasted and came down the mountain with the Ten Commandments.
2. Esther the Queen fasted when her nation was facing extinction and God turned the situation around.
3. Nehemiah the cupbearer fasted over the broken walls of Jerusalem and rebuilt it in 52 days.
4. Ezra the Scribe fasted for protection.
5. David the sweet Psalmist of Israel and King was a man accustomed to fasting.
6. The people of Nineveh fasted to avert the judgment of God.
7. Jehoshaphat and Judah fasted to overcome an oncoming conglomerate of armies.
8. Daniel fasted for revelation and to end the Babylonian's captivity.
9. The apostles fasted for direction.
10. Anna the prophetess fasted to see the fulfillment of the Promised Seed.
11. Samuel the prophet fasted.
12. Cornelius the Centurion fasted to receive salvation for himself and his household.
13. Joshua the military leader fasted to expose the cause of failure.
14. Ahab the evil king fasted to be forgiven.
15. Jehoshaphat the king fasted when he was outnumbered in battle and he obtained a great victory.
16. Darius the king fasted to shut the mouths of the lions when Daniel was thrown into the den.
17. Daniel the prophet fasted to mourn over the sins of Israel and for revelations.

18. Paul the Apostle fasted and was delivered from a shipwreck.

19. Peter the fisherman fasted before he went to the house of Cornelius to bring the Gospel to the Gentile World.

20. The elders, prophets and teachers in the Antioch church fasted to receive direction.

21. Barnabas the encourager fasted.

22. John the Baptist, the forerunner of the Messiah, fasted.

23. The disciples of John fasted often.

24. The Pharisees fasted often.

25. Jesus fasted.

We also read from the Bible that women, children and animals fasted too.

Can you see this great cloud of witnesses who believed in fasting? You will be in great company when you learn to fast. You will not find a general decree or commandment in the Old or New Testament that says, 'Thou shall fast.' Fasting was a personal issue and you must learn to fast! I submit to you that fasting is imperative and not optional if you want depth in the spirit, supernatural dimensions and are tired of a life of no results. Now you do not have to fast if you do not want to because God will never force you but there are some things you will never see and taste until you learn to fast. There are people today who have taken the stance and declared that we do not need to fast since we are no longer under the Law. They contend that this practice was only for the Old Testament patriarchs and the early church. However when we scrutinize the Scriptures, we find that the Lord Jesus never did away with the principle of fasting, but man – flesh driven man – has attempted to do away with it. Let us look at what Jesus said about fasting.

THERE ARE SOME THINGS YOU WILL NEVER SEE AND TASTE UNTIL YOU LEARN TO FAST

§ What Jesus said about fasting

We can get no higher authority on the subject of fasting than Jesus the Messiah Himself. What did the Lord have to say about fasting?

Then came to him the disciples of John, saying, Why do we and the Pharisees fast oft, but thy disciples fast not? And Jesus said unto them, Can the children of the bridechamber mourn, as long as the bridegroom is with them? but the days will come, when the bridegroom shall be taken from them, and then shall they fast. No man putteth a piece of new cloth unto an old garment, for that which is put in to fill it up taketh from the garment, and the rent is made worse. Neither do men put new wine into old bottles: else the bottles break, and the wine runneth out, and the bottles perish: but they put new wine into new bottles, and both are preserved.
MATTHEW 9:14-17

*And they said unto him, Why do the disciples of John **fast often, and make prayers,** and **likewise the disciples of the Pharisees;** but thine eat and drink? And he said unto them, Can ye make the children of the bridechamber fast, while the bridegroom is with them? But the days will come, when the bridegroom shall be taken away from them, and then shall they fast in those days.*
LUKE 5:33-35

Once when John's disciples and the Pharisees were fasting, some people came to Jesus and asked, "Why don't your disciples fast like John's disciples and the Pharisees do?" Jesus replied, "Do wedding guests fast while celebrating with the groom? Of course not. They can't fast while the groom is with them. But someday the groom will be taken away from them, and then they will fast. "Besides, who would patch old clothing with new cloth? For the new patch would shrink and rip away from the old cloth, leaving an even bigger tear than before. "And no one puts new wine into old wineskins. For the wine would burst the wineskins, and the wine and the skins would both be lost. New wine calls for new wineskins.
MARK 2:18-22 NEW LIVING TRANSLATION

The two major things that John the Baptist imparted into the lives of his disciples were *much prayer* and *fasting*. One of the disciples of Jesus bore witness to this fact when they asked Him, '*Lord, teach us how to pray even as John taught his disciples*' (Luke 11:1). We also see from the above verses that the disciples of John were used to much fasting. The reason why they were men of much power was because they were men of much prayer and fasting. Now this sheds some light as to why the Bible specifically mentions the diet of John, '*...and his meat was locusts and wild honey*' (Matthew 3:4). This indicates the nutrition of a person who had a strong lifestyle of fasting. In order to keep his protein and sugar level in balance and be fully functional while fasting he would partake of locust and wild honey.

The disciples of John came to Jesus, somewhat perplexed why his disciples were not given to fasting like themselves and the Pharisees. We know that the Pharisees wore fasting as a badge of spiritual pride. However for John and his disciples, fasting was for spiritual equipping and deployment. So the question was inquisitively posed to Jesus, 'Why do we fast often as do the Pharisees but your disciples are oblivious to it?' The response of Jesus was very concise and revealing, '*Do wedding guests fast while celebrating with the groom? Of course not. They can't fast while the groom is with them. But someday the groom will be taken away from them, and then they will fast.*'

Notice these words, '*But someday the groom will be taken away from them, and then they will fast.*'

THE PHARISEES WORE FASTING AS A BADGE OF SPIRITUAL PRIDE BUT FOR JOHN AND HIS DISCIPLES IT WAS FOR SPIRITUAL EQUIPPING AND DEPLOYMENT

Jesus said there would be a day when it would be imperative for the disciples to fast. What is that day and more importantly what does it mean the groom will be taken away? The key words here are 'taken away' and 'day'.

'Taken away' in Greek is 'airo' meaning:

❖ To raise up, elevate, lift up.
❖ To raise from the ground, take up.
❖ To raise upwards, elevate, lift up.
❖ To go up in the air.

From the word 'airo' we get our English word 'air'.

Therefore Jesus said a day was coming when He, the groom would be taken from the ground and up into the air. When that day arrived then it would befit the bride – that is the disciples or the church – to fast. Did that day arrive? Luke, the Beloved Physician is very accurate in his treatise,

> *The former treatise have I made, O Theophilus, of all that Jesus began both to do and teach, **Until the day in which he was taken up**... But ye shall receive power, after that the Holy Ghost is come upon you: and ye shall be witnesses unto me both in Jerusalem, and in all Judaea, and in Samaria, and unto the uttermost part of the earth. And when he had spoken these things, **while they beheld, he was taken up**; and a cloud received him out of their sight. **And while they looked stedfastly toward heaven as he went up**, behold, two men stood by them in white apparel; Which also said, Ye men of Galilee, why stand ye gazing up into heaven? **this same Jesus, which is taken up from you into heaven**, shall so come in like manner as ye have seen him go into heaven.*
> ACTS 1:1, 2, 8-11

Notice these words:

❖ Until the day in which He was taken up.
❖ While they beheld, He was taken up.
❖ Looked stedfastly toward heaven as He went up.
❖ This same Jesus, which is taken up from you into heaven.

Anyone who has some concept of Christianity knows that this day is commonly known as the Day of Ascension. Notice in the ninth verse where it says, '...*while they beheld, **he was taken up**; and a cloud received him out of their sight.*' The Greek word for 'taken up' is 'apairo' from the root 'airo' and it means 'to lift off'. Jesus was lifted into the air and received up into heaven away from His disciples on the day of Ascension. That was the monumental day that Jesus had referred to when answering the questions of John's disciples. Therefore after this event Jesus was physically taken and removed from the disciples. This would be the time that necessitated the disciples to fast. Now that gives us an inkling of what the disciples were doing from the Ascension to the day of Pentecost while they were tarrying for the promise of the Father.

Some people think that when Jesus said to 'tarry', the disciples were just waiting and killing time in the Upper room until Pentecost. This is due to attempting to understand the Bible from an English or Western mindset. To 'tarry' in today's vernacular means to 'linger, loiter, procrastinate, delay, wait, dawdle and hang around.' I can guarantee you that the disciples were not dawdling or lingering around until the day of Pentecost. There are two main words for 'tarry' in the Greek New Testament. One word is 'meno' as when Jesus was asked by the Samaritans to '*tarry with them and he abode there two more days*' (John 4:40) and when Jesus asked Peter and the two sons of Zebedee to '*tarry and watch with him*' in the Garden of Gethsemane (Matthew 26:37-38). Meno means 'to stay and remain in a position' or 'to stay over'. However when Jesus said to the disciples, '*but tarry ye in the city of Jerusalem, until ye be endued with power from on high*' (Luke 24:49), it is the Greek word 'kathidzo'. This word is employed several times in the New Testament. Let's have a brief look at how it is brought into play.

In the Sermon on the Mount, we read, '*And seeing the multitudes, he went up into a mountain: and when he was set...*' (Matthew 5:1). The word 'set' or 'sat down' is 'kathidzo'. We also see this in Luke 5:3, '*...he sat down, and taught the people out of the ship....*'

In these two accounts, kathidzo gives the understanding of sitting for the transmission and reception of instructions: it is the downloading of information.

In the parable of building a tower, Jesus said, '*For which of you, intending to build a tower, sitteth not down first, and counteth the cost, whether he have sufficient to finish it?*' (Luke 14:28). So kathidzo here means 'to sit down and count the cost'.

Excerpts from my book,
Exposing and Overcoming the spirit of barrenness

So when Jesus said to 'tarry ye in Jerusalem' and the word employed was kathidzo, it meant to stay connected until something comes through. The early church stayed connected to the words of Jesus until that promise became a reality to them. **They fasted and prayed through** for the promise of God to them to become manifested. This is so important to grasp: they prayed and fasted through until the promise made to them became a reality.

FASTING HELPS TO EXPRESS, TO DEEPEN, AND TO CONFIRM THE RESOLUTION THAT WE ARE READY TO SACRIFICE ANYTHING – TO SACRIFICE OURSELVES – TO ATTAIN WHAT WE SEEK FOR THE KINGDOM OF GOD – ANDREW MURRAY

How can we know that they were fasting and praying prior to the Pentecost experience? Firstly, we know for a fact that they were all in one accord and praying in the upper room:

*And when they were come in, they went up into an upper room, where abode both Peter, and James, and John, and Andrew, Philip, and Thomas, Bartholomew, and Matthew, James the son of Alphaeus, and Simon Zelotes, and Judas the brother of James. **These all continued with one accord in prayer and supplication,** with the women, and Mary the mother of Jesus, and with his brethren.*

Acts 1:13, 14

And when the day of Pentecost was fully come, they were all with one accord in one place.

ACTS 2:1

With that established in our minds – that they were in prayer and supplication – how can we know for sure they were fasting prior to the great outpouring? The answer comes from Peter's answers when questioned about the phenomenon that was occurring on the day of Pentecost:

And they were all amazed, and were in doubt, saying one to another, What meaneth this? Others mocking said, These men are full of new wine. But Peter, standing up with the eleven, lifted up his voice, and said unto them, Ye men of Judaea, and all ye that dwell at Jerusalem, be this known unto you, and hearken to my words: For these are not drunken, as ye suppose, seeing it is but the third hour of the day. But this is that which was spoken by the prophet Joel:

And it shall come to pass in the last days, saith God, I will pour out of my Spirit upon all flesh: and your sons and your daughters shall prophesy, and your young men shall see visions, and your old men shall dream dreams: And on my servants and on my handmaidens I will pour out in those days of my Spirit; and they shall prophesy: And I will shew wonders in heaven above, and signs in the earth beneath...

ACTS 2:12-19

The key words are:

❖ New wine.
❖ These are not drunken, as ye suppose.
❖ This is that which was spoken by the prophet Joel.
❖ It shall come to pass in the last days.

Peter's defense of the event of the day of Pentecost was to confirm it as the fulfillment of the prophecy of Joel. Now I want you to look closely at the prophecies of Joel and the words of Peter and see if you can spot the differences.

THE EARLY CHURCH PRAYED AND FASTED THROUGH UNTIL THE PROMISE MADE TO THEM BECAME A REALITY

> Joel's words

And it shall come to pass afterward, that I will pour out my spirit upon all flesh; and your sons and your daughters shall prophesy, your old men shall dream dreams, your young men shall see visions: And also upon the servants and upon the handmaids in those days will I pour out my spirit. And I will shew wonders in the heavens...

JOEL 2:28-30

> Peter's words

And it shall come to pass in the last days...

ACTS 2:17

> The difference

Joel used the term 'afterward' and Peter employed 'in the last days'. Joel was referring to a favorable change that will take place after an initiative. What was the initiative or prerequisite before the great change and outpouring? Remember that Israel was going though national economic and spiritual disaster:

*Blow the trumpet in Zion, **sanctify a fast**, call a solemn assembly: Gather the people, sanctify the congregation, assemble the elders, gather the children, and those that suck the breasts: let the bridegroom go forth of his chamber, and the bride out of her closet. Let the priests, the ministers of the Lord, weep between the porch and the altar, and let them say,*

Spare thy people, O Lord, and give not thine heritage to reproach, that the heathen should rule over them: wherefore should they say among the people, Where is their God?

JOEL 2:15-17

The prerequisite was to blow a trumpet in Zion to gather the people for a time of corporate fast and then it will come to pass afterward. After what? After the sanctified fast! It was a cause and effect situation. Therefore for Peter to employ the words of Joel as fulfillment of prophecy, fasting had to be initiated and delved into. Secondly, Peter responded to the people being drunk on the wine by saying they are not drunk in the traditional sense of the word but they were drunk on something different. The Apostle Paul informed the Ephesian saints that they can be drunk on a different kind of wine other than alcohol and that is the new wine of the Spirit (Ephesians 5:18). Jesus, referring to fasting when probed said that *'no man puts new wine in old bottles'* (Mark 2:22). Here again we see the connection of new wine and fasting. Therefore the disciples in the upper room prior to Pentecost were in prayer and fasting to download the promise of the new wine of the Spirit.

> ### The Lord also declared

*Moreover **when ye fast**, be not, as the hypocrites, of a sad countenance: for they disfigure their faces, that they may appear unto men to fast. Verily I say unto you, They have their reward. But thou, when thou fastest, anoint thine head, and wash thy face; That thou appear not unto men to fast, but unto thy Father which is in secret: and thy Father, which seeth in secret, shall reward thee openly.*

MATTHEW 6:16-18

Jesus said *when* and not *if* you fast, implying we have to set a time to fast. The phrase here is 'Hotan de nesteioo', with the structure of the verbiage meaning *'whenever, inasmuch, as often as, every time that'* implying regularity of a usual and repeated act. The phrase implies that Jesus' disciples would fast with regularity and when they would, they would posture themselves differently to the Pharisee's hypocritical performance.

Furthermore Jesus told us that fasting is unto the Father and that there will be an open reward. That should be enough incentive for a believer to realize that there is recompense when we tap into the secret of fasting.

Therefore to conclude the matter, fasting is for today because:

Jesus stamped his seal of approval on it!

CHAPTER 3
PAUL'S PERSPECTIVE OF FASTING

L IKE Moses, Jesus and John the Baptist, Paul was a man given to much fasting. To begin with, before he was converted, Paul was a Pharisee. We know that when the disciples of John approached Jesus they enquired, *'Why do we and the Pharisees fast oft...'* (Matthew 9:14). The word 'oft' is 'poloos' meaning 'much, plenteous, abundantly, common and many times'. In essence they were saying that they, as well as the Pharisees, commonly fasted much and many times. Therefore Paul as a Pharisee would have been accustomed to a life of fasting. Jesus revealed to us that a Pharisee fasted a minimum of two days weekly (Luke 18:12) and Paul would have flawlessly observed this tradition. In his own words, he exposed his former lifestyle to the Galatians when he wrote:

> *For ye have heard of my conversation in time past in the Jews' religion, how that beyond measure I persecuted the church of God, and wasted it: And profited in the Jews' religion above many my equals in mine own nation, **being more exceedingly zealous of the traditions of my fathers.***
> GALATIANS 1:13-14

How about after his conversion to Christianity: did he give himself to fasting.? The very first thing he did after his encounter with the Lord on the road to Damascus was to go on a total fast.

> *And Saul arose from the earth; and when his eyes were opened, he saw no man: but they led him by the hand, and brought him into Damascus. **And he was three days without sight, and neither did eat nor drink.***
> ACTS 9:8-9

Paul began his Christian life with fasting and prayer. We know he was praying because God told Ananias, '*Arise, and go into the street which is called Straight, and enquire in the house of Judas for one called Saul, of Tarsus: for, behold, he prayeth*' (Acts 9:11). This tells us that fasting is to be coupled with prayer, otherwise we are just going on a hunger strike. As we go through the book of Acts and the Pauline epistles we will ascertain that Paul had much to say about fasting.

Why did Paul fast after his initial encounter with the Lord on the road to Damascus? Because when he saw the light and fell down he had a conversation with Jesus:

> *And he trembling and astonished said, Lord, what wilt thou have me to do? And the Lord said unto him, **Arise, and go into the city, and it shall be told thee what thou must do.***
>
> ACTS 9:6

Jesus, the General of the Church, charged Paul to go into the city and his commission would be revealed to him. Within the three days of fasting and prayer, Paul received his calling and commission to preach the Gospel to the Gentiles. We know this is so from Ananias' conversation with Jesus and Paul's own testimony. When Ananias was told to go and lay hands on Paul in order for him to receive his sight, he argued with the Lord but the Lord reassured him of the calling of Paul:

> *Go thy way: for he is a chosen vessel unto me, to bear my name before the Gentiles, and kings, and the children of Israel: For I will shew him how great things he must suffer for my name's sake.*
>
> ACTS 9:15-16

Now look at Paul's own testimony of the Damascus experience before King Agrippa. In it he revealed the fullness of the two conversations that he had with Jesus that only he was privy to. The first part of the conversation was, 'go to the city and you will be told what to do.' and the second is the following:

And when we were all fallen to the earth, I heard a voice speaking unto me, and saying in the Hebrew tongue... But rise, and stand upon thy feet: for I have appeared unto thee for this purpose, to make thee a minister and a witness both of these things which thou hast seen, and of those things in the which I will appear unto thee; Delivering thee from the people, and from the Gentiles, unto whom now I send thee, To open their eyes, and to turn them from darkness to light, and from the power of Satan unto God, that they may receive forgiveness of sins, and inheritance among them which are sanctified by faith that is in me...

ACTS 26:14, 16-18

Paul fasted because Jesus told him that the rest of his commission would be revealed after he obeyed and went to the city. Paul did not want to miss any pieces of the puzzle. He fasted to obtain the fulness of his assignment. Many are floundering aimlessly in the earth because they have never taken the time to discover their commission from their Master.

In Acts 13, we see Paul actively involved once again in fasting:

*Now there were in the church that was at Antioch certain prophets and teachers; as Barnabas, and Simeon that was called Niger, and Lucius of Cyrene, and Manaen, which had been brought up with Herod the tetrarch, **and Saul. As they ministered to the Lord, and fasted**, the Holy Ghost said, **Separate me Barnabas and Saul for the work whereunto I have called them.** And when they had **fasted and prayed**, and laid their hands on them, they sent them away. **So they, being sent forth by the Holy Ghost, departed unto Seleucia; and from thence they sailed to Cyprus.***

ACTS 13:1-4

In his first fast after his conversion, Paul had a generic idea of his assignment but as he gave of himself to further fasting in Acts 13, more of the puzzle was unveiled to him on a specific level. Now he knew who to go with and where exactly he was to go: he discovered the right association and the right direction. You see, fasting takes you from the generic to the specific.

FASTING TAKES YOU FROM THE GENERIC TO THE SPECIFIC. IT PUTS ALL THE PIECES OF THE PUZZLE TOGETHER

In Acts 27, an interesting situation occurred when Paul was being transported as a prisoner to Italy. Being sensitive to the Spirit, Paul perceived that the oncoming trip was not safe and danger awaited. However the centurion and the master of the ship turned a deaf ear to Paul's warning and set out to go nonetheless. The perception was, 'What would a preacher know about sailing, weather and danger? Leave it to the professional!' They overruled Paul's leading and set out! The professionals were wrong. The preacher, *led by the Spirit* was right. Sure enough they ran into a storm and things looked bleak. It is one thing for you to make a decision, go in a certain direction and get it wrong but it is a different matter altogether when someone else makes a wrong decision and your life is directly threatened to be cut short as a consequence. Because of a bad decision, all the cargo was thrown overboard and they lost control of the ship that was being beaten mercilessly by the storm of wind and waves while waiting for death. Sometimes in life someone will make a decision that directly affects your wellbeing or lack of it. What do you do? Well what did Paul do?

> *But after long **abstinence** Paul stood forth in the midst of them, and said, Sirs, ye should have hearkened unto me, and not have loosed from Crete, and to have gained this harm and loss.*
>
> ACTS 27:21

The word 'abstinence' is 'aseeteeah' meaning 'the state of fasting'. It is from the root word 'asitos' which literally means 'no food or corn'. Aseeteeah informs us that Paul had been in a long state of fasting to overcome this death-doomed decision. If it was left up to Paul, he would not have set out in the first place to obtain this harm but he was at the mercy of the decision of others. In order not to pay the consequences of other people's foolish decision he had to fast. This teaches us a very important lesson about fasting: you can fast to escape the foolish decision of others when it affects your life but you cannot fast away the consequences of your own decisions. David tried that when his baby son was sick unto death but he could not fast away the consequence of his foolish action. (2 Samuel 12:13-23).

Paul also told us that he approved himself as a minister of God through fasting. Note his words:

*We then, as workers together with him, beseech you also that ye **receive not the grace of God in vain**... Giving no offence in any thing, that the ministry be not blamed: But in all things **approving ourselves as the ministers of God**, in much patience, in afflictions, in necessities, in distresses, in stripes, in imprisonments, in tumults, in labours, **in watchings, in fastings**...*
2 CORINTHIANS 6:1, 3-5

YOU CAN FAST TO ESCAPE THE FOOLISH DECISION OF OTHERS WHEN IT AFFECTS YOUR LIFE BUT YOU CANNOT FAST AWAY THE CONSEQUENCES OF YOUR OWN FOOLISH DECISION

Note that Paul said he did not take the grace of God in vain but that he approved himself as a minister through watchings (prayers) and fastings. Notice it is 'fastings' meaning plural: this was not a one time event with him but a constant stretch of fasting sessions. There needs to come a time in your life as a minister of God that you prove yourself. Many are happy to go through the motions of a minister but without the exhibition of power. Paul told Timothy to make full proof of his ministry (2 Timothy 4:5). This means provide evidence to yourself, the world and the devil. How was Timothy going to do this? The same way his spiritual father did it: by much fasting! Now look again at the words of Paul, '*approving ourselves as the ministers of God*' and connect it with this verse, '*Jesus of Nazareth, a man approved of God among you by miracles and wonders and signs, which God did by him in the midst of you, as ye yourselves also know*' (Acts 2:22). Both Jesus and Paul were men of fasting and prayer. Fasting will prove to you the potency of your calling, giving evidences to the world and the devil of the validity of your commission.

Finally, as Paul was defending the credibility of life and ministry to the Corinthians because of some of the accusing, deceptive and false apostles, he says:

*Are they ministers of Christ? (I speak as a fool) I am more; in labours more abundant, in stripes above measure, in prisons more frequent, in deaths oft... In weariness and painfulness, in watchings often, in hunger and thirst, **in fastings often**, in cold and nakedness. Beside those things that are without, that which cometh upon me daily, the care of all the churches.*

2 CORINTHIANS 11:23, 27-28

Notice he said he was in 'fastings often'. This simply means he was adept at all different kinds, types and intensities of fasting. He exercised them frequently because of the great demands upon his life and ministry. He had to fast due to external and internal circumstances.

Therefore to conclude the matter, fasting is for today because:

Paul stamped his seal of approval on it!

FASTING WILL PROVE TO YOU THE POTENCY OF YOUR CALLING, GIVING EVIDENCES TO THE WORLD AND THE DEVIL OF THE VALIDITY OF YOUR COMMISSION

CHAPTER 4
DEFINING FASTING

I thought I knew what fasting was even before I was saved as I saw how people in other religions fasted but before I was saved, there was not one day of my life that I deliberately fasted; that notion was nowhere near my mind. If I ever fasted, it would have been a forced fast, caused by sickness which triggered a lost of appetite. As far back as I can remember I was eating three meals a day and a lot of snacks in between. Nonetheless, from my unsaved mind I understood that fasting meant to abstain from food; that was what I saw when the other religions fasted. It was only after I was born-again that I astonishingly discovered the modern church had redefined the meaning of fasting. The definitions of fasting had been stretched to mean a lot of other things that are beneficial but not necessarily biblical. Here is what we were being told: 'Fasting is not necessarily abstaining from food but also includes refraining from television and newspapers.' Of course today, we can stretch that to abstaining from using a cell phone, Facebook and the Internet.

As great and beneficial as it is for one to abstain from the things mentioned, that is not what the Scriptures define as fasting. Allow me to reiterate this one more time: it is highly praiseworthy for you to abstain from television, the Internet and the newspapers. For one thing that will stop the cares of this world and the lust of other things (Mark 4:19) – as Jesus would call it – to enter into your heart, thereby choking the Word. I congratulate and applaud your resolutions; however, biblical fasting really has to do with abstaining from food or from certain kinds of food.

The Synoptic Gospels aptly clear this concept for us:

Then was Jesus led up of the Spirit into the wilderness to be tempted of the devil. And when **he had fasted** *forty days and forty nights, he was* **afterward an hungered.**

MATTHEW 4:1-2

And Jesus being full of the Holy Ghost returned from Jordan, and was led by the Spirit into the wilderness, Being forty days tempted of the devil. **And in those days he did eat nothing:** *and when they were ended, he afterward hungered.*

LUKE 4:1-2

Please note: Matthew stated that Jesus fasted and Dr. Luke, expanding on the same scenario, stated that 'he did eat nothing'. Luke, as a doctor, gave us the understanding that fasting meant to cease from the consumption of food. Therefore fasting for the Lord Jesus implied not eating. I want you to note it said, 'He afterward hungered'. It did not say He was thirsty because the fast that Jesus did was to abstain from solids, not liquids. Jesus also reinforced the fact (that fasting meant to go without food) in His earthly ministry:

In those days the multitude being very great, and **having nothing to eat,** *Jesus called his disciples unto him, and saith unto them, I have compassion on the multitude, because they have now been with me three days, and* **have nothing to eat: And if I send them away fasting to their own houses, they will faint by the way:** *for divers of them came from far.*

MARK 8:1-3

From these verses above we glean that according to Jesus, fasting was abstaining from food, which made one aware of the pain of hunger. Notice that Jesus said there was a possibility of people fainting from fasting. In other words, fasting is not easy nor is it convenient. If it was, everybody would be doing it. Fasting is a road less traveled in this modern easy-convenience world.

IT IS HIGHLY PRAISEWORTHY FOR YOU TO ABSTAIN FROM
TELEVISION, THE INTERNET AND THE NEWSPAPERS.
HOWEVER, BIBLICAL FASTING REALLY HAS TO DO WITH
ABSTAINING FROM FOOD OR FROM CERTAIN KINDS OF FOOD

> Paul of Tarsus

The Apostle Paul – who was a man given to a life of much fasting
(2 Corinthians 11:27) – also gave us an example of fasting in the midst of a
sea storm:

*And while the day was coming on, Paul besought them all to take meat,
saying, This day is the fourteenth day that ye have tarried and continued
fasting, having taken nothing. Wherefore I pray you to take some meat:
for this is for your health: for there shall not an hair fall from the head
of any of you.*

ACTS 27:33, 34

Observe that Paul said they had been fasting for fourteen days and took
nothing to eat. He encouraged them to break their fast on the fourteenth
day by consuming some food. Therefore it is to be noted that in Paul's
estimation, fasting is abstaining from food and to break a fast is to partake
of food. Remember, after his conversion on the Road to Damascus, Paul went
on a three-day absolute fast where he did not eat or drink anything in that
time (Acts 9:9). It was crystal-clear to the saints in the Old Testament – as
well as the New Testament – that fasting involved some kind of abstinence
from food. Let us look at the Hebrew and Greek definitions of fasting from
the Scriptures.

In Hebrew the word for fasting is 'tsom', which means 'to cover or close
the mouth' meaning no food. It is used 26 times in 22 verses in the Hebrew
concordance of the Authorized Version. There is a logical reason why the
Hebrew renders the meaning as 'to cover the mouth': this is done in order
that you and I do not put a Big Mac or Double Whopper meal in there!

FASTING IS A ROAD LESS TRAVELED IN THIS MODERN EASY CONVENIENCE WORLD

Another word employed in the Old Testament for fasting is the Aramaic word *tĕvath* which means 'not having taken food'. It is used one time when the king fasted all night long for Daniel, who had been thrown in the lion's den (Daniel 6:18).

In the Greek New Testament, there are two major words for fasting and they are 'nesteia' and 'asito's which basically mean no food or no eating.

Nesteia means 'no eating' because of the etymology of the word. It is a combination of two words. The first being 'ne', a negative prefix, and the second word is 'esthio' meaning 'to ea'. There are other derivatives of nesteia in the New Testament and they are 'nestis' and 'nesteuo' and they have the same meaning. These words are used to indicate:

❖ Voluntary abstinence from food (Luke 2:37; Acts 14:23; also in Matthew 17:21; Mark 9:29); fasting had become a common practice among Jews, and was continued among Christians; in Acts 27:9 *the Fast* refers to the Day of Atonement (Leviticus 16:29); that time of the year would be one of dangerous sailing.

❖ Involuntary abstinence (perhaps voluntary is included), consequent upon trying circumstances, 2 Corinthians 6:5; 11:27.

Nestis is used in Matthew 15:32; Mark 8:3.

Nesteuo is used in Matthew 4:2; 6:16-18; 9:14-15; Mark 2:18-20; Luke 5:33-35; 18:12; Acts 13:2-3.

The second word employed is 'asitos' and it means 'to be without food'. Once again the 'a' is a negative and 'sitos' means 'corn' or 'food'. It is used in Acts 27:33.

(Vine's Expository of Greek New Testament Words).

Tenfold definitions of fasting

The word 'fast' literally means 'to shut the mouth so as to abstain from food'. When you 'breakfast' you partake of food and when you 'fast' you abstain from food. In its simplest definition, fasting means to abstain from food for spiritual purposes. However if you simply think that fasting is not partaking of food then you would be doing a great injustice to yourself, to God and to fasting. People do not partake of this great phenomenon because they do not know what fasting is, what it does and what it entails. Studying the Scriptures and from my own personal experiences in fasting, allow me to give you ten working definitions of fasting:

1. Fasting is humbling yourself before God and turning towards Him.
2. Fasting is engaging God for spiritual, mental, physical, financial, ministerial, familial, municipal and personal breakthrough.
3. Fasting is entreating God for divine intervention.
4. Fasting is connecting with God to force the impossible to become possible.
5. Fasting is making a demand upon the supply of the Spirit.
6. Fasting is telling God that we are not relying upon our own hands but upon His hand to remove the hand of Satan from our lives.
7. Fasting is your spirit making your body an altar to connect with God for spiritual and physical transactions.
8. Fasting is inducing labor in order to give birth to your destiny: it breaks delay and the spirit of opposition.
9. Fasting is the slowing of the flesh in order to fast forward your spirit and destiny.

When was the last time you truly engaged God in a particular situation? When was the last time you made a deliberate demand upon the supply of the Spirit? You will be provoking divine intervention when you fast. Equally important is the aspect of breaking the spirit of delays by inducing the birth of your dreams and destiny. We will delve deeper into this aspect later in this book. Too many believers live and die with their destiny sabotaged and their dreams stillborn. God does not approve of this phenomenon as his word clarifies:

> *To subvert a man in his cause, the Lord approveth not.*
>
> LAMENTATIONS 3:36

> ❯ Old Presbyterian Preacher politician

Many years ago, I heard an old preacher, who was also a renowned politician in the United Kingdom. He was Irish and his name was Ian Paisley. He was fiery, both in his politics and preaching of the Scriptures. He was talking about fasting and hunger strikes. The point he was making was the similarity between the two. He said the world uses hunger strikes – which is another form of fasting – *'to close the mouth in order to move the hand of the politicians or government on or off'* I like that! The closing of the mouth to either get the hand of the government off because of the sense of injustice, or to get the hand of the government on to see justice done. So for our tenth definition of fasting:

10. Fasting is the closing of the mouth to move the hand of Satan off and to move the hand of God on.

The hands of Satan bring injustice and failure in life but God's hand will bring you justice and victory.

> ❯ Just to mark your thinking

I'm sure, like me, you remember watching the movie 'The Karate Kid'. I am referring to the original film that came out in the 1980's. In one scene of the movie, as Mr Miagi was putting Daniel through his exercises, he brought him to a car and gave him two cloths telling him to 'wax on and wax off'. I am sure you remember that scene, 'wax on and wax off'. You see, that is what fasting does. It takes Satan's hand off you and puts God's hand on you.

Throughout the rest of the book, this is the tenfold theme that I want imprinted and impacted upon your mind and spirit. As you keep reading this book, you will see from the Scriptures how many times impossibilities were turned to glorious victories. You will see how people entreated God for divine intervention to what was set in motion against their lives. It is clear that some breakthroughs can only occur when you fast and seek God; there are some things that only God can do.

Now let's look at the nine occasions to fast.

CHAPTER 5
WHEN SHOULD YOU FAST?

A s you flip through the pages of the Scriptures, you'll see that there were always reasons why and when people went on a fast. Sometimes people today will say, 'I am waiting to be led into a fast'. This will only be valid for those who have a proclivity to being led by the Spirit but for most people, waiting to be led into a fast will be, just as the expression goes, *'when pigs fly'* meaning it is not going to happen! Don't fool yourself. Another reason why people do not fast is because they say, 'I don't feel the inspiration to fast'. I have not felt inspired to fast. I don't always feel inspired to read my Bible and pray but I do it anyway because it is the right thing to do. In the same vein I do not always feel motivated to fast but I do it anyway because it is the right thing to do. I fast because of situations that I need to see resolved or some things that need to be broken or some things that need to be fixed. Let us look at some instances when people fasted in the Bible. Allow me to give you nine instances when you should fast.

1 WHEN YOU ARE AFRAID, OVERWHELMED AND DON'T KNOW WHAT TO DO

King Jehoshaphat's tiny nation of Judah was outnumbered by a coalition of enemy nations bent on their destruction. Jehoshaphat quickly realized that his tiny army and armaments were no match for the oncoming army with their weapons of mass destruction. He felt afraid, overwhelmed and did not know what to do.

*And Jehoshaphat **feared**, and set himself to seek the Lord, and **proclaimed a fast** throughout all Judah. And Judah gathered themselves together, to ask help of the Lord: even out of all the cities of Judah they came to seek the Lord... O our God, wilt thou not judge them? for we have no might* *against this great company that cometh against us; **neither know we what to do:** but our eyes are upon thee.*

2 CHRONICLES 20:3-4, 12

Jehoshaphat was afraid, overwhelmed and did not know what to do; so he fasted. The fear, the approaching enemies and not knowing a plan to defeat his oppositions drove him to declare a fast. You should fast when you face terrifying situations and don't have the wherewithal to handle what is in front of you. From today, when you feel overwhelmed and don't know what do... you *know* what to do: **it is time to fast and seek help from the Lord.** Fasting is another weapon we use to resist the spirit of fear and obtain help from the Lord. Please note that it said, 'Jehoshaphat feared'. The spirit of fear was trying to envelop his life; in its final analysis, fear is geared to bring paralysis. What do I mean by that? Have you ever had a nightmare in which you were trying to say something but you were unable to open your mouth to speak because of the dread that you felt? This is what fear does: it paralyzes your movements and moves against you to destroy you. When fear encroaches, it stops your forward movement. Jehoshaphat did not let fear paralyze him but used it as a catalyst to drive him to seek the face of God in fasting.

FASTING IS TELLING GOD THAT WE ARE NOT RELYING UPON OUR OWN HANDS BUT UPON HIS HAND TO REMOVE THE HAND OF SATAN FROM OUR LIVES

---

2 WHEN WHAT YOU SEE YOU HAVE IN YOUR HANDS IS NOT SUFFICIENT TO BRING YOU YOUR DESIRED RESULTS

*O our God, wilt thou not judge them? **for we have no might against this great company** that cometh against us; neither know we what to do: **but our eyes are upon thee***

2 CHRONICLES 20:12

WHEN SHOULD YOU FAST?

Jehoshaphat and Judah knew their resources were not sufficient to deal with the evil conglomerate coming against them. He surveyed his arsenal and said to himself and God, 'we *have no might against this great army.*' Have you ever felt helpless when you look at what you have and what is coming against you? Have you felt that no matter how much you stretch it or shift things around you cannot get the desired result, that what is in your hands cannot meet your needs? Through fasting, you are saying to God that you are taking your eyes off *your* hands and that you are looking to His hands. In fasting, your eyes will quit looking down and will look up to Him. As the Psalmist declared many years ago:

> *I will lift up mine eyes unto the hills, from whence cometh my help. My help cometh from the Lord, which made heaven and earth. He will not suffer thy foot to be moved: he that keepeth thee will not slumber. Behold, he that keepeth Israel shall neither slumber nor sleep. The Lord is thy keeper: the Lord is thy shade upon thy right hand. The sun shall not smite thee by day, nor the moon by night. The Lord shall preserve thee from all evil: he shall preserve thy soul. The Lord shall preserve thy going out and thy coming in from this time forth, and even for evermore.*
> PSALM 121

3 WHEN A DEATH DECREE HAS BEEN PRONOUNCED AGAINST YOUR EXISTENCE

Haman the Agagite had hoodwinked King Ahasuerus to sign an executive order to kill all the Jews in his 120 provinces from India to Ethiopia. This was because of his deep hatred for Mordecai, who would never bow before him. So a death sentence was in motion against all Jews. Understand today that Satan has a deep desire to kill you. Jesus said, '*The thief comes to steal, kill and destroy*' (John 10:10). How did Mordecai and Esther respond to this death sentence? They went on a fast and not only reversed the decree of death but in the process, sealed the demise of the wicked Haman who would never be able to threaten them again. If Satan cannot destroy you physically, he will endeavor to destroy you in other ways. If he cannot kill you physically, he will try to kill your career, your business, your finances and other aspects of your life. Like Esther and Mordecai, you can fast and reverse the decrees of death against any part of your life.

FASTING IS ENTREATING AND CONNECTING WITH GOD FOR DIVINE INTERVENTION AND FORCING THE IMPOSSIBLE TO BECOME POSSIBLE

---

4 WHEN STAGNANCY AND BARRENNESS HAVE SET IN YOUR LIFE

Hannah was married to Elkanah an Ephrathite; he loved her and gave her double portions every year. However Hannah's problem was that she was barren; although she was married to an Ephrathite – which means fruitfulness – she was experiencing fruitlessness and stagnation in her life. As the church, you are the bride of Christ and He is the fruitful one. Although we are in Christ, many are tasting the bitter fruit of barrenness and fruitlessness. For many, their lives, ministries and businesses are at a standstill or on a downward spiral. How did Hannah destroy barrenness? She went on a fast after Peninnah her adversary provoked her with reproaches and mockery (1 Samuel 1:6-8). The result was the birth of Samuel and five more children born after him. Are you going to let stagnation get the better of you? Are you going to allow barrenness in your church, finances, career or ministry? No! Like Hannah, it is time to fast; it is time to give birth to your Samuel and break the hold of stagnation over your destiny.

FASTING IS MAKING DEMANDS UPON THE SUPPLY OF THE SPIRIT

---

5 WHEN THE BROKEN WALLS OF LIVES AND CITIES NEED TO BE REBUILT

Nehemiah was a cupbearer in the king's palace. Upon the return of some men who went on a trip to Jerusalem – his native city – Nehemiah enquired of them after the welfare of the people and the city:

*That Hanani, one of my brethren, came, he and certain men of Judah; and I asked them concerning the Jews that had escaped, which were left of the captivity, and concerning Jerusalem. And they said unto me, **The remnant that are left of the captivity there in the province are in great affliction and reproach**: the wall of Jerusalem also is broken down, and the gates thereof are burned with fire. And it came to pass, **when I heard these words**, that I sat down and wept, and mourned certain days, and fasted, and prayed before the God of heaven.*

NEHEMIAH 1:2-4

The report of the condition of the people – and the city – did not please Nehemiah. The walls of the city and the walls of the people's lives were broken: they were an open target for their enemies. This drove Nehemiah to fast. There may come a time in your life when you look at your city and the people in it, or your own family members and you realize that the walls are broken down. If you look at the cities of America and the world, you can see that walls are broken down: people's lives are broken. Drugs, violence, corruption and immorality are on our streets. Nehemiah did not stay in the comfort of the palace, sipping wine while the city and people's lives lay in ruins. Today we have people who are happy to be sipping the King's wine in the church, with little concern for their city and will not go to rebuild the broken walls and lives. Nehemiah went on a fast and the king released him and provided the wood and equipment to rebuild the walls thus removing shame from Jerusalem. When you go on a fast, your King will release you and give you the Word and necessary equipment to rebuild your broken city and the broken lives. It is time to fast for the broken walls to be repaired.

This is why in Isaiah 58, one of the blessing of fasting is:

*And they that shall be of thee shall **build the old waste places**: thou shalt **raise up the foundations of many generations; and thou shalt be called, The repairer of the breach,** The restorer of paths to dwell in.*

ISAIAH 58:12

FASTING IS ENGAGING GOD FOR SPIRITUAL, MENTAL, PHYSICAL, FINANCIAL, MINISTERIAL, FAMILIAL, MUNICIPAL AND PERSONAL BREAKTHROUGH

---

6 WHEN YOU NEED TO SEE THE FULFILLMENT OF A PROPHETIC PROMISE

Some people have the idea that just because something was promised in the Scriptures or from a prophecy that it will automatically come to pass. There's a rude awakening when they find it is not happening. Why is this so? Because there is a devil and spiritual opposition that will hinder your easy access to God's promised land. God told Jeremiah that Israel would be in captivity for seventy years and that after the seventy years were over, the people would return from exile:

For thus saith the Lord, That after seventy years be accomplished at Babylon I will visit you, and perform my good word toward you, in causing you to return to this place.

JEREMIAH 29:10

Daniel happened to be reading the book of Jeremiah and discovered this promise and realized that seventy years had transpired since the promise was made. Daniel could have nonchalantly say, 'Well, here's God's promise. So it is just going to happen' but he didn't do that. Look at what he did:

In the first year of his reign I Daniel understood by books the number of the years, whereof the word of the Lord came to Jeremiah the prophet,

that he would accomplish seventy years in the desolations of Jerusalem.
And I set my face unto the Lord God, to seek by prayer and supplications,
with fasting, and sackcloth, and ashes.

DANIEL 9:2-3

When he saw the promise of a better prophetic future, he pursued it with
fasting and it was no lackadaisical approach to the promise but rather a
dogged determination – through fasting – to see it through. The important
thing to realize is that although promises are in the Bible, many are denied
or are being delayed because of the assumption that they will automatically
happen instead of being pulled from the pages of the Scriptures into reality
by our prayers, confessions and fastings. The prophecies of the coming
Messiah were all over the Old Testament yet Anna the prophetess, *'an old*
widow of eighty four years, did not depart from the temple, but served God
with fastings and prayers night and day. And she coming in that instant gave
thanks likewise unto the Lord, and spake of him to all them that looked for
redemption in Jerusalem.' (Luke 2:37-38). She prayed and fasted for the safe
delivery of prophetic destiny. The people were looking for redemption and
it came as Anna prayed and fasted through. Both Daniel and Anna teach
us that it is time to fast to see what we are looking for in the Word.

FASTING IS INDUCING LABOR IN ORDER TO GIVE BIRTH TO YOUR DESTINY. IT BREAKS DELAY AND THE SPIRIT OF OPPOSITION

---

7 WHEN YOU NEED TO HEAR THE INSTRUCTIONS AND DIRECTION OF
THE HOLY SPIRIT

There are times in our lives when we do not know what the next move
is. Even though we love God and are faithfully going to church it can feel
like we are stuck in a maze, forever moving yet getting nowhere. Many
are floundering aimlessly on the earth because they have never taken the
time to discover their commission from their Master. At these times we
can become agitated, irritated and feel a sense of inward restlessness.

Unfortunately when many go through these times of restlessness, instead of seeking God's direction they get up and leave abruptly, only to regret these decisions later. Restlessness is never a time to make rash decisions or sudden moves but a time to seek the leading and direction of the Spirit. When facing these difficult times it's crucial that you fast and seek the Lord for direction and instruction. Citing two examples in the life of Paul from the previous chapter, we can deduce that Paul was in a period of fasting when he discovered his call to the Gentiles. Later while he – along with others – were ministering to the Lord in fasting, he received further instructions from the Holy Spirit concerning his assignment (Acts 13:1-4). Fasting opens us up to the voice and the leading of the Holy Spirit and it is only as He guides that we do not suffer thirst (Isaiah 48:21).

RESTLESSNESS IS NEVER A TIME TO MAKE RASH DECISIONS OR SUDDEN MOVES BUT A TIME TO SEEK THE LEADING AND DIRECTION OF THE SPIRIT

You need to fast when you need further information and direction. Paul was not like most of us – who receive the first initial instruction and then go out, all guns blazing, figuring out how to make it happen. No, he kept looking for more instruction from the Holy Spirit. This is why he was successful in ministry: Paul was constantly seeking the leading of the Spirit. This is humility: seeking God's ways rather than the ways of the world. Solomon said, '*There is a way that seems right unto a man but the end thereof are the ways of death*' (Proverbs 14:12). Don't go your way, go His way, which leads to life and victory.

FASTING IS HUMBLING YOURSELF BEFORE THE HOLY SPIRIT, TURNING TOWARDS HIM FOR INSTRUCTIONS AND DIRECTIONS

8 WHEN SICKNESS IS ATTACKING YOUR LOVED ONES

Many times when your loved ones are going through a trial of sickness they cannot fast for themselves. It is at this time that you need to fast for them. There are two examples in the Scriptures of fasting on behalf of those who are sick and both came from the life of David (2 Samuel 12:15-23; Psalm 35:13). David recorded these words, *'But as for me, when they were sick, my clothing was sackcloth: I humbled my soul with fasting; and my prayer returned into mine own bosom'* (Psalm 35:13). David saw fasting as an avenue for physical healing in the lives of other people. Jesus amplified this thought when He said to the disciples, who had a futile encounter with a man who brought his lunatic son to be delivered, *'This kind can come forth by nothing, but by prayer and fasting'* (Mark 9:29).

9 WHEN YOU NEED A BREAKTHROUGH AND PROTECTION

Be ever conscious that attached to fasting is breakthrough: physical, spiritual and financial breakthrough. After Jehoshaphat fasted, it took three days to carry all the spoil away. After Nehemiah fasted, the finances and all necessary tools to rebuild the wall were released. Ezra had so much money, silver and gold to rebuild the temple that he fasted for the protection of their goods and the lives of their little ones. They fasted for the protection of their children:

> *Then I proclaimed a fast there, at the river of Ahava, that we might afflict ourselves before our God, to seek of him a right way for us, and for our little ones, and for all our substance. For I was ashamed to require of the king a band of soldiers and horsemen to help us against the enemy in the way: because we had spoken unto the king, saying, The hand of our God is upon all them for good that seek him; but his power and his wrath is against all them that forsake him. So we fasted and besought our God for this: and he was intreated of us."*
>
> EZRA 8:21-22

Ezra and the rest of the people were on a journey to rebuild the temple. The journey was dangerous with the risk of hijacking, killing and terrorizing from armed robbers. Sounds familiar in today's age! He did not want to ask the king for armed protection as he had bragged on the power of God. Nevertheless the terrorist threat was real! So they set themselves to fast for traveling mercies, the protection of their children and their money. You need to fast that your life will not be hijacked by the enemy. You need to fast for your children so that they will not be the victim of life's journeys. The lives of your children cannot be hijacked by the terrors of life. You can no longer allow the enemy to rob you of your assets, inheritances and monies.

It is time to fast!

FAST TO PROTECT THE FUTURE GENERATIONS FROM THE TERROR AND HANDS OF THE ENEMY

CHAPTER 6
GENRE, TYPES AND INTENSITY OF FASTING

LET me reiterate and make it clear to you: fasting is not easy! If it was, everybody would be doing it. It can be difficult and a lot of work. To deny oneself is not something we want to hear in this age of self-gratification. Fasting is painful and inconvenient, but very productive. The Bible shows us that people fasted publicly as well as privately. Going through the Scriptures, you will see there were a variety of fasting types; God is gracious to us and allows us to choose from a myriad of ways to fast. There are types of fasts to accommodate everybody. When it comes to fasting you have got to know your own level of ability and build from there. So let's get some light on fasting.

FASTING IS DIFFICULT, PAINFUL, HARD WORK AND INCONVENIENT – BUT VERY PRODUCTIVE

Levels of fasting

There are two levels at which a believer can and should fast: on a personal level and a corporate level.

§ Personal level

We see this vividly in the lives of Jesus, Paul, Daniel, Moses and Elijah to cite a few. Although there is no decree or commandment that we must fast, it will behoove you to fast regularly on a personal basis. If you are committed to seeing results in your life then you will want to fast. Here are a few examples of personal fasts in the Bible.

THERE ARE TYPES OF FASTS TO ACCOMMODATE EVERYBODY

> King David

2 Samuel 12:16; '*... and David fasted, and went in, and lay all night upon the earth.*'

Psalms 35:13; '*But as for me, when they were sick, my clothing was sackcloth: I humbled my soul with fasting...*'

> King Ahab

1 Kings 21:27; '*And it came to pass, when Ahab heard those words, that he rent his clothes, and put sackcloth upon his flesh, and fasted, and lay in sackcloth, and went softly.*'

> King Darius

Daniel 6:18; '*Then the king went to his palace, and passed the night fasting: neither were instruments of musick brought before him: and his sleep went from him.*'

> Daniel

Daniel 9:3; '*And I set my face unto the Lord God, to seek by prayer and supplications, with fasting, and sackcloth, and ashes.*'

> Anna

Luke 2:36-37; '*And there was one Anna, a prophetess, the daughter of Phanuel, of the tribe of Aser: she was of a great age, and had lived with an husband seven years from her virginity; And she was a widow of about fourscore and four years, which departed not from the temple, but served God with fastings and prayers night and day.*'

> Jesus

Luke 4:14; *'And Jesus returned in the power of the Spirit into Galilee: and there went out a fame of him through all the region round about.'*

> Paul

Acts 9:8-9; *'And Saul arose from the earth; and when his eyes were opened, he saw no man: but they led him by the hand, and brought him into Damascus. And he was three days without sight, and neither did eat nor drink.'*

> Cornelius

Acts 10:30; *'And Cornelius said, Four days ago I was fasting until this hour; and at the ninth hour I prayed in my house, and, behold, a man stood before me in bright clothing.'*

As you can see from the above list, anyone can fast on a personal level. In fact from this list we see the good, the bad and the ugly, fasted. Jesus, Anna, Paul and Cornelius are examples of the good fasting. The Pharisees exemplified the bad and King Ahab exemplified the ugly.

IF YOU ARE COMMITTED TO SEE RESULTS IN YOUR LIFE THEN YOU WILL WANT TO FAST

---

§ **Corporate level**

We see some examples of corporate fasts in:

❖ Daniel and his three friends in order not to defile themselves.
❖ Mordecai, Esther and Israel for national survival.
❖ King Jehoshaphat and Judah for deliverance.
❖ Ezra and the exiles of Judah for a safe trip.
❖ Ninevites to escape judgment.

❖ Church in Antioch for direction.

❖ Paul and Barnabas to ordain and establish elders.

❖ Samuel and Israel who fasted for the ark of His presence.

❖ The disciples of John the Baptist.

As you can see, corporate fasting can be done by a group of friends, a church or as few as two people together. Corporate fasting is appropriate for a church, business, city or national breakthrough. In fact a lot of churches worldwide have a corporate fast for twenty one days at the beginning of the year. When we fast corporately, it is another added element to the prayer of agreement.

Types of fast

Going through the Scriptures, you will discover that there were three major types of fasting that were practiced in the Old as well as the New Testament. However there was another special category of fast that was not common but demonstrated by a few individuals in the Scripture. I will list it after the three major fasts.

1. **Normal** or **Regular Fast.** Traditionally, a regular fast means refraining from eating all food. Most people still drink water or juice during a regular fast: it is advisable to take plenty of fluids. When Jesus fasted in the desert, the Bible says, '*After fasting forty days and forty nights, He was hungry*' (Matthew. 4:2 NIV). This verse does not mention Jesus being thirsty.

2. **Partial Fast.** This fast is also commonly known as the 'Daniel Fast'. This type of fast generally asks that you omit a specific meal from your diet or refrain from certain types of foods. This is suitable for those who are new to fasting, those with health issues, and the elderly. Some people have been foolish in fasting at the cost of their health, and a few have even died. Use wisdom when you fast! Remember that you are doing your fast unto the Lord and not for the eyes of people.

3. **Absolute Fast.** Also known as a 'Full Fast' or 'Dry Fast', these fasts are complete – no food and no drink. This kind of fast can be done for one day, and the maximum would be only three days. Going longer can cause serious damage to your body. It is imperative for you to understand that your body can go for days without food but not without water. You need water! An absolute fast was an exceptional and unusual measure for an exceptional and unusual purpose.

4. **Special Dedicated Fast.** Also known as a 'Fasted lifestyle'. We see it in the lives of Samson and John the Baptist. Samson's incredible strength, or anointing was directly linked to his level of consecration to the Lord; he was under the Nazarite vow from his birth. The word Nazarite comes from the Hebrew word 'nazir', meaning 'consecrated' or 'separated'. This vow was voluntarily made by those who desired 'to separate themselves unto the Lord' for a determined season as described in the book of Numbers:

The Lord said to Moses, speak to the Israelites and say to them: If a man or woman wants to make a special vow, a vow of separation to the Lord as a Nazirite, he must abstain from wine and other fermented drink and must not drink vinegar made from wine or from other fermented drink. He must not drink grape juice or eat grapes or raisins. As long as he is a Nazirite, he must not eat anything that comes from the grapevine, not even the seeds or skins. During the entire period of his vow of separation no razor may be used on his head. He must be holy until the period of his separation to the Lord is over; he must let the hair of his head grow long. Throughout the period of his separation to the Lord he must not go near a dead body. Even if his own father or mother or brother or sister dies, he must not make himself ceremonially unclean on account of them, because the symbol of his separation to God is on his head. Throughout the period of his separation he is consecrated to the Lord.

NUMBERS 6:1-8 NIV

Samson's Nazarite vow bound him to three absolute demands:

1. He had to abstain from drinking wine or fermented drink. The Nazarite was not allowed to drink wine or grape juice or eat anything that came from the vine.
2. He was forbidden to cut his hair. It was a sign of submission. Samson's strength was not in his hair. Instead, it was an outward symbol of the vow he had taken.
3. He was not allowed to touch a dead body including his own family members since death depicted sin and the fall of man and the Nazarite was to typify life: '*Wherefore come out from among them, and be ye separate, saith the Lord, and touch not the unclean thing; and I will receive you*' (2 Corinthians. 6:17).

John the Baptist also operated under the Nazarite vow. The angel that announced the birth of John declared, '*he shall be great in the sight of the Lord, and shall drink neither wine nor strong drink; and he shall be filled with the Holy Ghost, even from his mother's womb*'. This is why his diet was not as regular folks: we read that he ate wild locust and honey. These two who lived *fasted lives* were very effective in their ministry. The normal, partial or absolute fast is simply denying yourself food or certain types of food for a particular length of time. After the result is obtained one goes back to regular eating. A fasted life, however is a continuous fast at all times, no matter the season. Living a fasted life means separation for a season or permanently. Evidently, you can't separate yourself from food forever and live. As in Samson's and John's lives, they were to separate themselves from fruit of the vine and certain food all their lives. These two men wielded great power in their ministry.

SOME HAVE EXALTED RELIGIOUS FASTING BEYOND ALL SCRIPTURE AND REASON, AND OTHERS HAVE UTTERLY DISREGARDED IT - JOHN WESLEY

Before we delve into the types of fasting intensity I want you to know there were several *called fasts* in the Scriptures. Allow me to briefly list the different genres to amplify your study.

> **God Called Fast**

This is when God Himself called His people on a fast.

Blow the trumpet in Zion, sanctify a fast, call a solemn assembly: Gather the people, sanctify the congregation, assemble the elders, gather the children, and those that suck the breasts: let the bridegroom go forth of his chamber, and the bride out of her closet. Let the priests, the ministers of the Lord, weep between the porch and the altar, and let them say, Spare thy people, O Lord, and give not thine heritage to reproach, that the heathen should rule over them: wherefore should they say among the people, Where is their God?

JOEL 2:15-17

> **King Called Fast**

This is when the king of the nation called for a national fast.

And Jehoshaphat feared, and set himself to seek the Lord, and proclaimed a fast throughout all Judah.

2 CHRONICLES 20:3

> **Prophet Called Fast**

This is when the prophet of God summoned the people to fast.

Then I proclaimed a fast there, at the river of Ahava, that we might afflict ourselves before our God, to seek of him a right way for us, and for our little ones, and for all our substance. For I was ashamed to require of the king a band of soldiers and horsemen to help us against the enemy in the way: because we had spoken unto the king, saying, The hand of our God is upon all them for good that seek him; but his power and his wrath is against all them that forsake him. So we fasted and besought our God for this: and he was intreated of us.

EZRA 8:21-23

> **Spirit Called Fast**

This is when the Holy Spirit himself leads a person on a fast for a specific task. We see this in the lives of Jesus, Moses and Elijah:

Then was Jesus led up of the Spirit into the wilderness to be tempted of the devil. And when he had fasted forty days and forty nights, he was afterward an hungred.

MATTHEW 4:1-2

And Moses went up into the mount, and a cloud covered the mount. And the glory of the Lord abode upon mount Sinai, and the cloud covered it six days: and the seventh day he called unto Moses out of the midst of the cloud. And the sight of the glory of the Lord was like devouring fire on the top of the mount in the eyes of the children of Israel. And Moses went into the midst of the cloud, and gat him up into the mount: and Moses was in the mount forty days and forty nights.

EXODUS 24:15-18

And the angel of the Lord came again the second time, and touched him, and said, Arise and eat; because the journey is too great for thee. And he arose, and did eat and drink, and went in the strength of that meat forty days and forty nights unto Horeb the mount of God.

1 KINGS 19:7-8

> **Observed Called Fast**

These types of fast are observed in Israel such as the one on the day of atonement and as the Pharisee did, who observed a twice weekly fast:

And the Lord spake unto Moses, saying, Also on the tenth day of this seventh month there shall be a day of atonement: it shall be an holy convocation unto you; and ye shall afflict your souls, and offer an offering made by fire unto the Lord.

LEVITICUS 23:26-27

The Pharisee stood and prayed thus with himself, God, I thank thee, that I am not as other men are, extortioners, unjust, adulterers, or even as this publican. I fast twice in the week, I give tithes of all that I possess.

LUKE 18:11-12

Intensity of fasting

By intensity, I mean the length and the type of fast employed by a person. Throughout the Bible you will discover that people fasted for different lengths of time and employed different types of fast. When it comes to fasting you have to know yourself and your capacity; if you have never fasted before, then it would be foolish of you to say, "I am going on a forty day fast with no food". You won't last forty minutes. When it comes to fasting, you have got to know your level and then start building on it. If you've never fasted before, you need to start slow. **Begin with short fasts and gradually move to longer periods of time as you grow**. Often, people fasted from sun up to sun down but there are also records where people fasted for an extended time. Here are a few examples and levels of intensity.

WHEN IT COMES TO FASTING YOU HAVE TO KNOW YOURSELF AND YOUR CAPACITY

---

1 day – normal fast

There are numerous accounts of God's people fasting for one day on many occasions in the Scriptures but allow me to list two examples:

Then all the children of Israel, and all the people, went up, and came unto the house of God, and wept, and sat there before the Lord, and fasted that day until even, and offered burnt offerings and peace offerings before the Lord.

JUDGES 20:26

Therefore go thou, and read in the roll, which thou hast written from my mouth, the words of the Lord in the ears of the people in the Lord's house upon the fasting day: and also thou shalt read them in the ears of all Judah that come out of their cities. It may be they will present their supplication before the Lord, and will return every one from his evil way: for great is the anger and the fury that the Lord hath pronounced against this people.

JEREMIAH 36:6-7

1 night – normal fast

King Darius spent the night in a fast on behalf of Daniel who was thrown in the lion's den:

Then the king went to his palace, and passed the night fasting: neither were instruments of musick brought before him: and his sleep went from him.

DANIEL 6:18

3 day – absolute fast

Esther, Mordecai and the Jewish people employed the absolute fast when Israel was threatened with extinction:

Go, gather together all the Jews that are present in Shushan, and fast ye for me, and neither eat nor drink three days, night or day: I also and my maidens will fast likewise; and so will I go in unto the king, which is not according to the law: and if I perish, I perish.

ESTHER 4:16

Ezra the scribe and priest also went without food and water for three days:

*Then Ezra rose up from before the house of God, and went into the chamber of Johanan the son of Eliashib: and when he came thither, **he did eat no bread, nor drink water**: for he mourned because of the transgression of them that had been carried away. And they made proclamation throughout*

Judah and Jerusalem unto all the children of the captivity, that they should gather themselves together unto Jerusalem; And that whosoever would not come within three days, according to the counsel of the princes and the elders, all his substance should be forfeited, and himself separated from the congregation of those that had been carried away. Then all the men of Judah and Benjamin gathered themselves together unto Jerusalem within three days. It was the ninth month, on the twentieth day of the month; and all the people sat in the street of the house of God, trembling because of this matter, and for the great rain. EZRA 10:6-9

Paul went on a three-day absolute fast after his Damascus' road experience:

And Saul arose from the earth; and when his eyes were opened, he saw no man: but they led him by the hand, and brought him into Damascus. And he was three days without sight, and neither did eat nor drink. ACTS 9:8-9

4 days – normal fast

Cornelius fasted for four days before Peter came to his house and presented the Gospel to the gentile world:

And Cornelius said, Four days ago I was fasting until this hour; and at the ninth hour I prayed in my house, and, behold, a man stood before me in bright clothing. ACTS 10:30

7 days – Normal fast

Israel, because of the death of Saul and Jonathan:

And they took their bones, and buried them under a tree at Jabesh, and fasted seven days. 1 SAMUEL 31:13

David, for the sickly baby (who eventually died) conceived after David committing adultery with Bathsheba and had Urriah her husband executed:

And David said unto Nathan, I have sinned against the Lord. And Nathan said unto David, The Lord also hath put away thy sin; thou shalt not die. Howbeit, because by this deed thou hast given great occasion to the enemies of the Lord to blaspheme, the child also that is born unto thee shall surely die. And Nathan departed unto his house. And the Lord struck the child that Uriah's wife bare unto David, and it was very sick. David therefore besought God for the child; and David fasted, and went in, and lay all night upon the earth. And the elders of his house arose, and went to him, to raise him up from the earth: but he would not, neither did he eat bread with them. And it came to pass on the seventh day, that the child died...

2 SAMUEL 12:13-18

10 days – partial fast

Daniel and his three friends, for not defiling themselves with the king's meat:

But Daniel purposed in his heart that he would not defile himself with the portion of the king's meat, nor with the wine which he drank: therefore he requested of the prince of the eunuchs that he might not defile himself. Now God had brought Daniel into favour and tender love with the prince of the eunuchs. And the prince of the eunuchs said unto Daniel, I fear my lord the king, who hath appointed your meat and your drink: for why should he see your faces worse liking than the children which are of your sort? then shall ye make me endanger my head to the king. Then said Daniel to Melzar, whom the prince of the eunuchs had set over Daniel, Hananiah, Mishael, and Azariah, Prove thy servants, I beseech thee, ten days; and let them give us pulse to eat, and water to drink. Then let our countenances be looked upon before thee, and the countenance of the children that eat of the portion of the king's meat: and as thou seest, deal with thy servants. So he consented to them in this matter, and proved them ten days. And at the end of ten days their countenances appeared fairer and fatter in flesh than all the children which did eat the portion of the king's meat.

DANIEL 1:8-15

14 days – normal fast

Paul, Luke and the boat crew during the shipwreck:

And while the day was coming on, Paul besought them all to take meat, saying, This day is the fourteenth day that ye have tarried and continued fasting, having taken nothing. Wherefore I pray you to take some meat: for this is for your health: for there shall not an hair fall from the head of any of you. And when he had thus spoken, he took bread, and gave thanks to God in presence of them all: and when he had broken it, he began to eat. Then were they all of good cheer, and they also took some meat. And we were in all in the ship two hundred threescore and sixteen souls.

ACTS 27:33-37

21 days – partial fast

Daniel, for revelation and breaking the delay of his desired answer:

In the third year of Cyrus king of Persia a thing was revealed unto Daniel, whose name was called Belteshazzar; and the thing was true, but the time appointed was long: and he understood the thing, and had understanding of the vision. In those days I Daniel was mourning three full weeks. I ate no pleasant bread, neither came flesh nor wine in my mouth, neither did I anoint myself at all, till three whole weeks were fulfilled.

DANIEL 10:1-3

40 days – absolute

Moses fasted for forty days twice, supernaturally, without food and water:

Moses was up the mountain with the Lord forty days and forty nights; he ate no bread and drank no water

EXODUS 34:28

Elijah fasted forty days:

And he arose, and did eat and drink, and went in the strength of that meat forty days and forty nights unto Horeb the mount of God.

1 KINGS 19:8

Jesus fasted forty days:

Then was Jesus led up of the Spirit into the wilderness to be tempted of the devil. And when he had fasted forty days and forty nights, he was afterward an hungred.

MATTHEW 4:1-2

4 months – normal and partial fast

Nehemiah fasted for four months for the Jews and the city of Jerusalem's plight and broken walls between the Jewish months of Kislev and Nisan:

*The words of Nehemiah the son of Hachaliah. And it came to pass **in the month Chisleu**, in the twentieth year, as I was in Shushan the palace... And it came to pass, when I heard these words, that I sat down and wept, and mourned certain days, and **fasted, and prayed** before the God of heaven...*

NEHEMIAH 1:1, 4

*And it came to pass **in the month Nisan**, in the twentieth year of Artaxerxes the king, that wine was before him: and I took up the wine, and gave it unto the king. Now I had not been beforetime sad in his presence.*

NEHEMIAH 2:1

120 days – Miraculous fast

If you read the Deuteronomy account, it would seem that Moses fasted for three periods of forty days, bringing the total to 120 days:

*When I was gone up into the mount to receive the tables of stone, even the tables of the covenant which the Lord made with you, **then I abode in the mount forty days and forty nights, I neither did eat bread nor drink water.***

DEUTERONOMY 9:9

And I fell down before the Lord, as at the first, forty days and forty nights: I did neither eat bread, nor drink water, because of all your sins which ye sinned, in doing wickedly in the sight of the Lord, to provoke him to anger.

Deuteronomy 9:18

*And I stayed in the mount, **according to the first time, forty days and forty nights;** and the Lord hearkened unto me at that time also, and the Lord would not destroy thee.*

Deuteronomy 10:10

3 years – partial fast

Daniel and his three friends before standing before King Nebuchadnezzar:

And the king appointed them a daily provision of the king's meat, and of the wine which he drank: so nourishing them three years, that at the end thereof they might stand before the king...But Daniel purposed in his heart that he would not defile himself with the portion of the king's meat, nor with the wine which he drank: therefore he requested of the prince of the eunuchs that he might not defile himself... Now God had brought Daniel into favour and tender love with the prince of the eunuchs. And the prince of the eunuchs said unto Daniel, I fear my lord the king, who hath appointed your meat and your drink: for why should he see your faces worse liking than the children which are of your sort? then shall ye make me endanger my head to the king. Then said Daniel to Melzar, whom the prince of the eunuchs had set over Daniel, Hananiah, Mishael, and Azariah, Prove thy servants, I beseech thee, ten days; and let them give us pulse to eat, and water to drink. Then let our countenances be looked upon before thee, and the countenance of the children that eat of the portion of the king's meat: and as thou seest, deal with thy servants. So he consented to them in this matter, and proved them ten days. And at the end of ten days their countenances appeared fairer and fatter in flesh than all the children which did eat the portion of the king's meat. Thus Melzar took away the portion of their meat, and the wine that they should drink; and gave them pulse. As for these four children, God gave them knowledge and skill in all learning and wisdom: and Daniel had understanding in all visions and dreams. Now at the end of the days that the king had said he should bring them in, then the prince of the eunuchs brought them in before Nebuchadnezzar. And the king communed with them; and among them all was found none like Daniel, Hananiah, Mishael, and Azariah: therefore stood they before the king. And in all matters of wisdom and understanding, that the king enquired of them, he found them ten times better than all the magicians and astrologers that were in all his realm.

DANIEL 1:5-20

Daniel and his three compatriots stretched their fast to three years and would not defile themselves with the king's meat and wine. After three years of such a fast and dedication to God, at their presentation before King Nebuchadnezzar, it was discovered they had ten times more wisdom than their competitors.

Fasted lifestyle – partial fast

In the Old Testament, this is epitomized by Samson:

Now see to it that you drink no wine or other fermented drink and that you do not eat anything unclean, because you will conceive and give birth to a son. No razor may be used on his head, because the boy is to be a Nazirite, set apart to God from birth, and he will begin the deliverance of Israel from the hands of the Philistines.

JUDGES 13:4-5

In the new Testament, this is epitomized by John the Baptist:

For he shall be great in the sight of the Lord, and shall drink neither wine nor strong drink; and he shall be filled with the Holy Spirit, even from his mother's womb.

LUKE 1:15

For John the Baptist came neither eating bread nor drinking wine...

LUKE 7:33

As you can see from the examples above, different characters in the Bible fasted for different reasons and at different levels of intensity. I recommend that you start with a partial fast and move on to a normal fast. We must use wisdom when we fast. If you have never fasted before, there is no point in saying that you will go on a forty-day fast. As I already mentioned – and it bears repeating – many have not used wisdom in regard to fasting and have damaged their health; for some it has even been fatal. So please don't be foolish. **Think through your plan to fast thoroughly, and talk to your doctor about it, especially if you have medical issues, are on medication or are elderly.** Fasting is good for your spiritual empowerment, but fast according to your ability. You give according to your ability and you minister according to your ability, so the same rule should apply to fasting.

BEGIN WITH SHORT FASTS AND GRADUALLY MOVE TO LONGER PERIODS OF TIME AS YOU GROW

My start up

Here is a little guide of how I started my life of fasting:

9AM – 3PM   no food, but plenty of fluid; *or* no food and no liquid.

9AM – 6PM   no food, but plenty of fluid; *or* no food and no liquid.

12AM – 3PM no food, but plenty of fluid.

6AM – 6PM   no food, but plenty of fluid; *or* no food no fluid.

6AM – 6AM (24 hrs) no food, but plenty of liquid.

6PM – 6PM (24 hrs) no food but plenty of liquid

Then from there I built to where I could do 3 days normal fast, 4 days, 7 days, 21 days and the longest I have been was one year of Daniel's fast. There are times where I would fast 110 days to 150 days yearly alternating between normal fast and the Daniel fast when I am traveling. I did not get there overnight: it was a process.

You can customize your fast! When you fast, you are getting away from food to be with God; this is the main purpose! When you read the Word and you discover that you are not experiencing that which is written then it is time to fast. The Prophet Daniel is our great example. Stop making excuses today. Learn to fast. Take baby steps if you have to. Don't say "I can't do it". When it comes to fasting it is not a case of whether you can or cannot, it is more of whether you want or don't want to. So learn to fast.

FASTING IS GOOD FOR YOUR SPIRITUAL EMPOWERMENT, BUT FAST ACCORDING TO YOUR ABILITY. YOU GIVE ACCORDING TO YOUR ABILITY AND YOU MINISTER ACCORDING TO YOUR ABILITY, SO THE SAME RULE SHOULD APPLY TO FASTING

If your fast does not mean anything to you, it won't mean anything to God; if it doesn't move you it won't move heaven. Make it count! The primary reason people do not partake of this great blessing is because the belly has enthroned itself as a god over their lives. Like Esau, many are losing their blessings because of uncontrolled appetite. The author of Hebrews tells us that Esau begged for his blessing after he lost it and sought it with tears but never got it back. What are you losing due to the uncontrolled belly-god? Many of us, as soon as the belly-god cries, we run to the altar of the kitchen and feed him three meal-offerings and drink-offerings and we wonder why there is no power in our lives. Many in the Bible rewrote their story and created history through fasting. Esther and Mordecai did so; Israel is still in existence today because of Queen Esther's fasting. How about you? Are you shaping your destiny and creating a wonderful history through fasting?

IF YOUR FAST DOES NOT MEAN ANYTHING TO YOU, IT WON'T MEAN ANYTHING TO GOD. IF IT DOESN'T MOVE YOU IT WON'T MOVE HEAVEN. SO MAKE IT COUNT!

Yes fasting is uncomfortable! For the majority, our bodies have never gone without food for longer than a few hours. The constant snacking on sweets, chocolates and potato chips have been part of our daily lifestyle. Therefore be prepared for some headaches, bad breath, hunger pains, a smelly body and nausea in the early stage. Most people give up because of these symptoms, not realizing that all these symptoms indicate that the fast is actually working as the body is clearing itself of all the toxins consumed over time. You may well find yourself highly irritable or easily angered. This is so because the belly-god is demanding to be fed.

If you do lose your temper, repent and stick with your fast: do not let the devil or you yourself use it as an excuse to break your fast. Simply notify your loved ones that you are going on a fast and that the first few days might be a bit rough; inform them that if you are a bit ratty with them not to take it personally. Of course, do not use this as an excuse to bite off everyone's head! Learn to control your flesh and temper.

This is all part of the teething process when you begin to fast. As you break through these walls, you will find there is great pleasure to derive from fasting. It will bring you closer to your God and unleash tremendous breakthroughs in your life.

CHAPTER 7
THE THREEFOLD CORD OF PRAYER, GIVING AND FASTING

I want to bring to your attention a powerful key in the Scriptures that is so often overlooked but is crucial in order for major breakthroughs in all realms of life. In the Bible, you will discover that people faced unsurmountable problems and many times it looked like they were not going to make it. Yet somehow they did! What did these people do? What switch did they flip to provoke the miraculous? What master key did they use to get their breakthrough? How did Hannah overcome years of barrenness and shame to bear the prophet Samuel? How did Cornelius, an Italian centurion, become the catalyst that released revival among the gentile world? God has clearly hidden wisdom for the righteous. All it takes is a little study and you will see this powerful nugget of truth in both the Old and New Testament. In part of the sermon on the Mount, Jesus gave us a powerful threefold disclosure that I want to inject into your mind.

§ Giving

Take heed that ye do not your alms before men, to be seen of them: otherwise ye have no reward of your Father which is in heaven. Therefore when thou doest thine alms, do not sound a trumpet before thee, as the hypocrites do in the synagogues and in the streets, that they may have glory of men. Verily I say unto you, They have their reward. But when thou doest alms, let not thy left hand know what thy right hand doeth: That thine alms may be in secret: and thy Father which seeth in secret himself shall reward thee openly.

MATTHEW 6:1-4

Prayer

And when thou prayest, thou shalt not be as the hypocrites are: for they love to pray standing in the synagogues and in the corners of the streets, that they may be seen of men. Verily I say unto you, They have their reward. But thou, when thou prayest, enter into thy closet, and when thou hast shut thy door, pray to thy Father which is in secret; and thy Father which seeth in secret shall reward thee openly.

MATTHEW 6:5-6

Fasting

Moreover when ye fast, be not, as the hypocrites, of a sad countenance: for they disfigure their faces, that they may appear unto men to fast. Verily I say unto you, They have their reward. But thou, when thou fastest, anoint thine head, and wash thy face; That thou appear not unto men to fast, but unto thy Father which is in secret: and thy Father, which seeth in secret, shall reward thee openly. Lay not up for yourselves treasures upon earth, where moth and rust doth corrupt, and where thieves break through and steal: But lay up for yourselves treasures in heaven, where neither moth nor rust doth corrupt, and where thieves do not break through nor steal: For where your treasure is, there will your heart be also. The light of the body is the eye: if therefore thine eye be single, thy whole body shall be full of light. But if thine eye be evil, thy whole body shall be full of darkness.

MATTHEW 6:16-20

Here is the threefold cord that Jesus revealed to us:

1. When you do your alms... Your Heavenly Father who sees in secret will reward you openly.
2. When you pray... Your Heavenly Father who sees in secret will reward you openly.
3. When you fast... Your Heavenly Father who sees in secret will reward you openly.

Here is the deal! Jesus deliberately implied that when we give, pray and fast, the Heavenly Father Himself will be directly involved in our affairs. The word 'reward' in Greek is 'apodidomi' and the meanings are:

❖ To deliver, to give away for one's own profit what is one's own.

❖ To pay off, discharge what is due.

❖ Things promised under oath.

❖ To give back, restore.

❖ To requite, recompense in a good or a bad sense.

Apodidomi is a combination of two words. 'Apo' meaning 'to take back to the origin' and 'didomi' meaning 'to give'. The combination of these two words means 'to give and take back to the origin'. I also want you to notice the significations given above. The meaning I want to drive into your mind is 'to discharge what is due and things promised under oath'. This is giving you an account of a court case where the judge will see to it that whatever has been stolen is returned. The author of Hebrews revealed God as a *'rewarder of those who diligently seek him'* (Hebrews 11:6). Rewarder is 'misthapodotes', from the root word 'misthos' which means:

❖ Dues paid for work; wages, hire.

❖ Reward: used of the fruit naturally resulting from toils and endeavors, in both senses, rewards and punishments.

❖ Of the rewards which God bestows, or will bestow, upon good deeds and endeavors.

❖ Of punishments (Strong's Concordance).

❖ Payment of price due.

Here is a vital point, the combinations of all these meanings imply that justice has to be done. Revenge will be meted out by the Righteous judge, the Heavenly Father, enforcing the rule that whatever was taken from you will be handed back to you. This is very good news if you feel a sense of injustice when it comes to your situation. I want you to pay attention to this threefold cord of *prayer, giving* and *fasting* that will see to it that justice is done on your behalf.

Examples of this threefold cord in action

The Word declares, '*In the mouth of two or three witnesses shall every word be established.*' (2 Corinthians 13:1) In this segment of the book, I want to show you examples of people who activated the threefold cord of prayer, fasting and giving to change their history and destiny.

Israel

In Judges 19 and 20, we see an atrocious crime that took place against the concubine of a Levite. After picking up his concubine, a Levite chose to spend the night in Gibeah rather than being in a non-Israeli city. The Scriptures reveal the thinking behind this move:

> *The servant said to his master, "Why don't we stop and spend the night here in this Jebusite city?" But his master said, "We're not going to stop in a city where the people are not Israelites. We'll pass on by and go a little farther and spend the night at Gibeah or Ramah."*
> JUDGES 19:11-13 GOOD NEWS BIBLE

The logical deduction of the Levite – that it would be safer to dwell among Israelis than among heathens – proved to be flawed; the event that transpired was shocking and unbelievable. The Levite and his companions were graciously given abode in the house of a hospitable old man where:

> *They were enjoying themselves when all of a sudden some sexual perverts from the town surrounded the house and started beating on the door. They said to the old man, "Bring out that man that came home with you! We want to have sex with him!" But the old man went outside and said to them, "No, my friends! Please! Don't do such an evil, immoral thing! This man is my guest. Look! Here is his concubine and my own virgin*

daughter. I'll bring them out now, and you can have them. Do whatever you want to with them. But don't do such an awful thing to this man!" But the men would not listen to him. So the Levite took his concubine and put her outside with them. They raped her and abused her all night long and didn't stop until morning. At dawn the woman came and fell down at the door of the old man's house, where her husband was. She was still there when daylight came. Her husband got up that morning, and when he opened the door to go on his way, he found his concubine lying in front of the house with her hands reaching for the door. He said, "Get up. Let's go." But there was no answer. So he put her body across the donkey and started on his way home. When he arrived, he went in the house and got a knife. He took his concubine's body, cut it into twelve pieces, and sent one piece to each of the twelve tribes of Israel. Everyone who saw it said, "We have never heard of such a thing! Nothing like this has ever happened since the Israelites left Egypt! We have to do something about this! What will it be?"

JUDGES 19:22-30 – GOOD NEWS BIBLE

I am sure you will agree with me that this is both weird and grotesque. The eleven tribes congregated and demanded that the Benjamites hand over the sons of Belial who committed this atrocity but the latter refused. Israel was now in a predicament where brothers would have to fight brothers. They went about their task in the right way in that they sought for the wisdom of God before they moved against the tribe of Benjamin:

They set out and went to Bethel to inquire of God. The People of Israel said, "Who of us shall be first to go into battle with the Benjaminites?" God said, "Judah goes first." The People of Israel got up the next morning and camped before Gibeah. The army of Israel marched out against Benjamin and took up their positions, ready to attack Gibeah. But the Benjaminites poured out of Gibeah and devastated twenty-two Israelite divisions on the ground. The army took heart. The men of Israel took up the positions they had deployed on the first day. The Israelites went back to the sanctuary and wept before God until evening. They again inquired of God, "Shall we again go into battle against the Benjaminites, our brothers?" God said, "Yes. Attack." On the second day, the Israelites again advanced against Benjamin. This time as the Benjaminites came out of the city, on this second day, they devastated another eighteen Israelite divisions, all swordsmen.

JUDGES 20:18-23 – GOOD NEWS BIBLE

What do you do when you believe that you have heard from God but you still taste defeat? This is where a lot of people find themselves, which has totally confused them: they cannot fathom or wrap their head around what is happening to them when they have sought the mind of God and expected victory but instead saw devastation. Israel sought for the voice of God; they heard from Him and proceeded with confidence to deal with their problem and the first day had 22,000 of their men cut to the ground. This is not just a light defeat but a heavy one. This is not what they anticipated. Like all of us – who have believed we have heard from God – we move with great confidence, with total expectation of victory. To the Israelite's dismay, they had 22,000 fatal casualties. Yet like the modern day Spirit-filled believer, they shook it off and went again after the enemy. After all the reasoning is, "I heard from God; I may have taken a licking but I keep on ticking."

They encouraged themselves. Why?

Because they believed they had already heard from God.

What happened next?

They lost another 18,000 men. So in 48 hours they lost 40,000 men. That is a serious defeat to experience when you have heard from the Lord. What do you do when you have prayed and still see no victory ahead? This may be where you are today: like Israel, disillusionment has set in; you have tasted a loss when you thought you prayed and heard from God. What do you do when you have a word from God and still taste defeat? What did Israel do?

Then all the children of Israel, and all the people, went up, and came unto the house of God, and wept, and sat there before the LORD, and fasted that day until even, and offered burnt offerings and peace offerings before the LORD. And the children of Israel enquired of the LORD, (for the ark of the covenant of God was there in those days, And Phinehas, the son of Eleazar, the son of Aaron, stood before it in those days) saying, Shall I yet again go out to battle against the children of Benjamin my brother, or shall I cease? And the LORD said, Go up; for to morrow I will deliver them into thine hand.

JUDGES 20:26-28

When all else failed, Israel employed the threefold cord of prayer, fasting and giving:

❖ They fasted that day until evening.
❖ They offered burnt offerings and peace offerings. That's giving.
❖ They enquired of the Lord. That's praying.

The end result was they received *the right time* to move for their victory and destroyed that which had been destroying them. Through employing the threefold cord of prayer, fasting and giving, Israel synchronized their actions with the timing of God; they discovered their 'kairos' moment, meaning 'divine timing'. The problem with them was that they heard from God but they moved 72 hours too soon and experienced heavy loss. You may very well have heard from God but have you sought Him for divine timing? If not, you may have God's plan and still experience heavy loss. Learn to activate these three powerful forces in your life.

⟩ Hannah

Looking at the life of Hannah, one could easily employ the expressions she had a 'raw deal' or was 'dealt a bad hand'. Her husband, Elkanah had two wives, Hannah and Peninnah (who provoked Hannah constantly).

To make matters worse, Peninnah had children but Hannah was barren (1 Samuel 1:1-8) and consequently endured years of vicious mockery, disgrace and taunting from Peninnah. She was childless in a society that considered not having a child the ultimate failure. How did Hannah break the shame and curse of barrenness?

*And as he did so year by year, when she went up to the house of the LORD, so she provoked her; therefore she wept, **and did not eat.** Then said Elkanah her husband to her, Hannah, why weepest thou? and **why eatest thou not?** and why is thy heart grieved? am not I better to thee than ten sons?.. And she was in bitterness of soul, and **prayed unto the LORD,** and wept sore. And she vowed a vow, and said, O LORD of hosts, if thou wilt indeed look on the affliction of thine handmaid, and remember me, and not forget thine handmaid, but wilt give unto thine handmaid a man child, then **I will give him unto the LORD all the days of his life,** and there shall no rasor come upon his head. And it came to pass, as she **continued praying** before the LORD, that Eli marked her mouth. Now Hannah, she spake in her heart; only her lips moved, but her voice was not heard: therefore Eli thought she had been drunken. And Eli said unto her, How long wilt thou be drunken? put away thy wine from thee. And Hannah answered and said, No, my lord, I am a woman of a sorrowful spirit: I have drunk neither wine nor strong drink, but have **poured out my soul before the LORD.** Count not thine handmaid for a daughter of Belial: for out of the abundance of my complaint and grief have I spoken hitherto. Then Eli answered and said, Go in peace: and the God of Israel grant thee thy petition that thou hast asked of him. And she said, Let thine handmaid find grace in thy sight. So the woman went her way, and did eat, and her countenance was no more sad. And they rose up in the morning early, and worshipped before the LORD, and returned, and came to their house to Ramah: and Elkanah knew Hannah his wife; and the LORD remembered her. Wherefore it came to pass, when the time was come about after Hannah had conceived, that she bare a son, and called his name Samuel, saying, Because I have asked him of the LORD.*

1 Samuel 1:7-8, 10-20

Hannah was in a dire situation! After years of abuse and shame, with constant effort being made physically with no results, she decided to activate the threefold cord of prayer, fasting and giving:

❖ She wept and did not eat. That's fasting.

❖ She poured her soul unto the Lord. That's prayer.

❖ She vowed to give him unto the Lord. That's giving.

What was the end result? The divine visitation of God, the birth of Samuel and the birth of more children.

And the Lord visited Hannah, so that she conceived, and bare three sons and two daughters. And the child Samuel grew before the Lord.
                                                              1 SAMUEL 2:21

What she had hoped for and had not experienced for many years was speedily granted as she activated the threefold cord, the unbeatable trinity of prayer, fasting and giving. You too can provoke a divine visitation in your life as you engage in prayer, fasting and giving.

⟩ The Ark of the Covenant, the Philistines and Samuel

The two sons of Eli, Hophni and Phinehas, had led Israel into national apostasy. Although Eli was none too pleased with the actions of his sons, he was a coward and never really dealt with their profligate debauchery. These two were stealing the offerings of the Lord and having sex with women in the temple in Shiloh, to name just two of their reckless acts. The end result was that Israel suffered heavily at the hands of the Philistines:

And the Philistines fought, and Israel was smitten, and they fled every man into his tent: and there was a very great slaughter; for there fell of Israel thirty thousand footmen. And the ark of God was taken; and the two sons of Eli, Hophni and Phinehas, were slain.
                                                              1 SAMUEL 4:10-11

Israel assumed that in their state of apostasy they could simply bring the Ark of the Covenant into battle and the victory would be secured. Alas, they were mistaken!

❖ Israel lost thirty thousand men.

❖ The two wicked sons of Eli were slain.

❖ The Ark was taken by the Philistines into their camp.

❖ After hearing the news, Eli fell backwards broke his neck and died.

❖ Phinehas' wife – who was pregnant – died in childbirth her son was named Ichabod, meaning *the glory has departed Israel*.

❖ The Ark was away from Shiloh for twenty years.

❖ The people lived in fear of the Philistines.

What a sad state of affairs for the children of Israel! To be without the Ark is to be without the presence of God:

> *And it came to pass, while the ark abode in Kirjath–jearim, **that the time was long; for it was twenty years: and all the house of Israel lamented after the Lord.***
>
> 1 SAMUEL 7:2

They were tired of being without the Ark of God. They wanted it back in Shiloh where it belonged. How was Israel going to retrieve the most precious thing that they lost?

> *And Samuel spake unto all the house of Israel, saying, If ye do return unto the Lord with all your hearts, then put away the strange gods and Ashtaroth from among you, and prepare your hearts unto the Lord, and serve him only: and he will deliver you out of the hand of the Philistines. Then the children of Israel did put away Baalim and Ashtaroth, and served the Lord only. And Samuel said, Gather all Israel to Mizpeh, and **I will pray for you unto the Lord.** And they gathered together to Mizpeh,*

*and **drew water, and poured it out before the Lord, and fasted on that day,** and said there, We have sinned against the Lord. And Samuel judged the children of Israel in Mizpeh. And when the Philistines heard that the children of Israel were gathered together to Mizpeh, the lords of the Philistines went up against Israel. And when the children of Israel heard it, they were afraid of the Philistines. And the children of Israel said to Samuel, **Cease not to cry unto the Lord our God for us,** that he will save us out of the hand of the Philistines. **And Samuel took a sucking lamb, and offered it for a burnt offering wholly unto the Lord:** and Samuel cried unto the Lord for Israel; and the Lord heard him. And as Samuel was offering up the burnt offering, the Philistines drew near to battle against Israel: but the Lord thundered with a great thunder on that day upon the Philistines, and discomfited them; and they were smitten before Israel.*

1 SAMUEL 7:3-10

They were tired of being disgraced by the Philistines. So how did they change the situation?

❖ I will pray for you unto the Lord / cease not to cry unto the Lord. That's prayer.

❖ Fasted on that day. That's fasting.

❖ Offered a sucking lamb wholly unto the Lord. That's giving.

What was the end result? While Israel was in a trinity period of fasting, prayer and giving, the Philistines launched their attack; but God thundered from heaven upon the Philistines confusing and immobilizing them. Israel marched out against them, destroying them and taking back the cities that the Philistines had previously occupied. The Scripture records:

So the Philistines were subdued, and they came no more into the coast of Israel: and the hand of the Lord was against the Philistines all the days of Samuel.

1 SAMUEL 7:13

As you employ the trinity of prayer, fasting and giving, may God thunder upon your enemies. You will retrieve what the enemy has stolen from you. Notice these words, '*they came no more into the coast of Israel and the hand of the Lord was against the Philistines.*' May this become a reality in your life where what used to intrude and overtake your life will come no more as the hand of the Lord prevents them. Are you ready for a 'Never again, devil' moment? Then apply this trinity of power!

〉 Anna The Prophetess

Dr. Luke gives us great insight into the life of a widow prophetess that aptly describes the value of praying, fasting and giving:

*And there was one Anna, a prophetess, the daughter of Phanuel, of the tribe of Aser: she was of a great age, and had lived with an husband seven years from her virginity; And she was a widow of about fourscore and four years, **which departed not from the temple, but served God with fastings and prayers night and day**. And she coming in that instant gave thanks likewise unto the Lord, and spake of him to all them that looked for redemption in Jerusalem.*

LUKE 2:36-38

We can learn a lot from this great woman of God. Her name means 'Grace' and she was the offspring of 'Phanuel' meaning 'face of God' and she was from the tribe of 'Asher' meaning 'happy and blessed'. The lesson is when we are happy to seek the face of God, grace will flow into our lives. What else was special about this lady who had the unfortunate situation of losing her husband at a young age? She was a prophetess and an intercessor who, although she never had any children of her own was pivotal in the birth of the Lord Jesus Christ. She also employed the threefold cord of prayer, fasting and giving, to give birth to a new dispensation in the earth:

❖ She served God with fastings.

❖ She prayed night and day.

❖ She departed not from temple. That's giving of herself.

The end result was seeing the birth of the Messiah. Sometimes when we think of giving, all that comes to our minds is in terms of finance, but Hannah gave of herself; her giving, praying and fasting brought in a new era upon the earth. Are you ready to bring a new dispensation into your life? Then deploy the powers of prayer, fasting and giving!

> Cornelius

Once again Dr Luke is pivotal in revealing to us the trinity of praying, fasting and giving in the life of the Italian centurion Cornelius. He would be responsible for bringing a new era where 'the gospel of salvation' is not limited to the Jews only but made its grand entry into the Gentile world:

There was a certain man in Caesarea called Cornelius, a centurion of the band called the Italian band, A devout man, and one that feared God with all his house, which gave much alms to the people, and prayed to God alway. He saw in a vision evidently about the ninth hour of the day an angel of God coming in to him, and saying unto him, Cornelius. And when he looked on him, he was afraid, and said, What is it, Lord? And he said unto him, Thy prayers and thine alms are come up for a memorial before God... And on the morrow Peter went away with them, and certain brethren from Joppa accompanied him. And the morrow after they entered into Caesarea. And Cornelius waited for them, and had called together his kinsmen and near friends. And as Peter was coming in... I ask therefore for what intent ye have sent for me? And Cornelius said, Four days ago I was fasting until this hour; and at the ninth hour I prayed in my house, and, behold, a man stood before me in bright clothing, And said, Cornelius, thy prayer is heard, and thine alms are had in remembrance in the sight of God.

ACTS 10:1-4, 23-24, 29-31

❖ Cornelius gave much alms to the people. That's giving.

❖ Cornelius prayed to God always. That's praying.

❖ Cornelius was fasting for four days. That's fasting.

While Peter yet spake these words, the Holy Ghost fell on all them which heard the word. And they of the circumcision which believed were astonished, as many as came with Peter, because that on the Gentiles also was poured out the gift of the Holy Ghost. For they heard them speak with tongues, and magnify God. Then answered Peter, Can any man forbid water, that these should not be baptized, which have received the Holy Ghost as well as we? And he commanded them to be baptized in the name of the Lord.

ACTS 10: 44-48

The end result was that a new day dawned upon the Gentile world: salvation and the baptism of the Holy Spirit fell on those gathered as Peter was preaching. Today, you and I are a product of this great move of God. It all came through the threefold cord of prayer, fasting and giving. What new door will you open and what new thing will you unleash in the earth that no one ever heard of as you delve into prayer, fasting and giving?

〉 Pharisees

As obnoxious as the Pharisees were in their dealings with Christ and the religious community, they also believed in the trinity of prayer, fasting and giving. The New Testament accounts of the Pharisees portrayed the worst of the group but generally, they were good and God-fearing, seeking to honor the Lord, as were Nicodemus, Joseph of Arimathea and Gamaliel.

Two men went up into the temple to pray; the one a Pharisee, and the other a publican. The Pharisee stood and prayed thus with himself, God, I thank thee, that I am not as other men are, extortioners, unjust, adulterers, or even as this publican. I fast twice in the week, I give tithes of all that I possess.

LUKE 18:10-12

* ❖ The Pharisee prayed.
* ❖ The Pharisee fasted twice weekly.
* ❖ The Pharisee gave tithes of all he possessed.

The end result was that The Pharisees were the most influential religious leaders in the time of Christ. According to Josephus, the Jewish historian, the Pharisees were the group most influential with the people, were noted for their accurate – and therefore authoritative – interpretations of Jewish law, and had their own traditions and way of life to which they were faithful. In the verse above, Jesus himself attested that the Pharisee engaged himself in praying, fasting and giving. Clearly the influence grew as they partook of the indomitable trio of prayer, fasting and giving.

> ### The ministry of Jesus in the feeding of 4,000

We see another example of the threefold cord in the ministry of Jesus in the wilderness. The habit of Jesus was to go to the mountain to seek the face of God through prayer and fasting. On one occasion a great multitude followed him for three days:

*And Jesus departed from thence, and came nigh unto the sea of Galilee; and **went up into a mountain,** and sat down there. And great multitudes came unto him, having with them those that were lame, blind, dumb, maimed, and many others, and cast them down at Jesus' feet; and he healed them: Insomuch that the multitude wondered, when they saw the dumb to speak, the maimed to be whole, the lame to walk, and the blind to see: and they glorified the God of Israel. Then Jesus called his disciples unto him, and said, **I have compassion on the multitude, because they continue with me now three days, and have nothing to eat: and I will not send them away fasting, lest they faint in the way.** And his disciples say unto him, **Whence should we have so much bread in the wilderness, as to fill so great a multitude?** And Jesus saith unto them, How many loaves have ye? And they said, Seven, and a few little fishes. And he commanded the multitude to sit down on the ground. And he took the seven loaves and the fishes, and gave thanks, and brake them, and gave to his disciples, and the disciples to the multitude. **And they did all eat, and were filled:** and they took up of the broken meat that was left seven baskets full. **And they that did eat were four thousand men, beside women and children.***

MATTHEW 15:29-38

- ❖ Jesus departed and went to the mountain. That's prayer.
- ❖ Continued three days with nothing to eat. That's fasting.
- ❖ Gave the seven loaves and few fish. That's giving.

The end result was a miracle of abundant supply in the wilderness. The unbeatable trinity of praying, fasting and giving unleashed a miracle of provision unparalleled in that day. The ministry of Jesus experienced abundant supply as these three powerful forces were put into motion. We also see the miraculous breakthrough of healings; there were creative healings that took place also. You must realize that there is a connection between the miraculous and fasting; that is the trigger for the healing ministry. We can learn much from the ministry of Jesus. Sometimes we find ourselves on the mountain and there does not seem to be provision around but as we press through with our praying, giving and fasting we shall see rivers in the desert.

> ## The ministry of Paul

Apart from the ministry of the Lord Jesus, there is no doubt that the ministry of Paul has had more impact on the earth than any other ministry. I say this not to undermine the ministries of the other foundational apostles but the fact of the matter is that the apostle Paul wrote about two thirds of the New Testament. He was a phenomenal author and scholar as well as a prolific minister of the Gospel, who walked in signs and wonders. Did the apostle Paul employ the indomitable trio? Absolutely! Of course you know that before he became the great apostle, he was Saul of Tarsus, a Pharisee and as such he would have been accustomed to the weekly practice of two days of fasting. Therefore it was not an isolated experience that he began his ministry on a three days absolute fast after his Damascus' road experience. Fasting was a normal way of life for Paul. Like the prophetess Anna who gave herself to much fastings, Paul likewise practiced this great discipline. On two occasions, Paul made references to the Corinthian saints; his words were very distinctive and informative:

But in all things approving ourselves as the ministers of God, in much patience, in afflictions, in necessities, in distresses, In stripes, in imprisonments, in tumults, in labours, in watchings, in fastings.

2 CORINTHIANS 6:4-5

In weariness and painfulness, in watchings often, in hunger and thirst, in fastings often, in cold and nakedness.

2 CORINTHIANS 11:27

Please note Paul deliberately used the words, '*approving ourselves as ministers of God*'. What does that mean? Newer translations of the Bible use the word, 'commending'. The Greek word is 'sunistao' a combination of two words, 'sun' and 'histemi'. 'Sun' means 'with or accompany'. 'Histemi' means:

❖ To cause or make to stand, to place, put, set.

❖ To make firm, fix establish.

❖ To cause a person or a thing to keep his or its place.

❖ To establish a thing, cause it to stand.

❖ To uphold or sustain the authority or force of anything.

The combination of these two words means:

❖ To set and place a person with.

❖ To establish a person with.

❖ To uphold and sustain the authority and force of a person with.

Paul was saying the authority and force of his ministry was sustained by fasting often. Paul understood the vitality and dynamics behind fasting. Mark your mind with the fact that to the apostle Paul, fasting was part and parcel of the life of a minister. Notice he also mentioned hunger before mentioning fasting. Why? Because hunger is what he suffered from when going through trials, testings, persecutions and afflictions, from circumstances beyond his control, whereas 'fasting often' is when Paul deliberately withdrew from food for spiritual empowerment.

We also know that Paul was a man of prayer; there are numerous verses in the Bible that reveal the prayer life of Paul. We also have the wordings of his prayers in the epistles such as Galatians and Ephesians. Paul was also a man who was a great giver; in his life and ministry, Paul engaged the indomitable trio of fasting, prayer and giving. Here are some verses to prove these facts.

> Paul's Fasting

And he was three days without sight, and neither did eat nor drink.

ACTS 9:9

But after long abstinence Paul stood forth in the midst of them...

ACTS 27:2

And while the day was coming on, Paul besought them all to take meat, saying, This day is the fourteenth day that ye have tarried and continued fasting, having taken nothing. Wherefore I pray you to take some meat: for this is for your health: for there shall not an hair fall from the head of any of you. And when he had thus spoken, he took bread, and gave thanks to God in presence of them all: and when he had broken it, he began to eat. Then were they all of good cheer, and they also took some meat. And we were in all in the ship two hundred threescore and sixteen souls.

ACTS 27:33-37

But in all things approving ourselves as the ministers of God, in much patience, in afflictions, in necessities, in distresses, In stripes, in imprisonments, in tumults, in labours, in watchings, in fastings.

2 CORINTHIANS 6:4-5

In weariness and painfulness, in watchings often, in hunger and thirst, in fastings often, in cold and nakedness.

2 CORINTHIANS 11:27

> Paul's Praying

And the Lord said unto him, Arise, and go into the street which is called Straight, and enquire in the house of Judas for one called Saul, of Tarsus: for, behold, he prayeth.

ACTS 9:11

For if I pray in an unknown tongue, my spirit prayeth, but my understanding is unfruitful. What is it then? I will pray with the spirit, and I will pray with the understanding also.

1 CORINTHIANS 14:14-15

I thank my God, I speak with tongues more than ye all.

1 CORINTHIANS 14:18

For this cause we also, since the day we heard it, do not cease to pray for you, and to desire that ye might be filled with the knowledge of his will in all wisdom and spiritual understanding.

COLOSSIANS 1:9

Now I beseech you, brethren, for the Lord Jesus Christ's sake, and for the love of the Spirit, that ye strive together with me in your prayers to God for me.

ROMANS 15:30

Cease not to give thanks for you, making mention of you in my prayers.

EPHESIANS 1:16

> Paul's Giving

I have coveted no man's silver, or gold, or apparel. Yea, ye yourselves know, that these hands have ministered unto my necessities, and to them that were with me. I have shewed you all things, how that so labouring ye ought to support the weak, and to remember the words of the Lord Jesus, how he said, It is more blessed to give than to receive.

ACTS 20:33-35

Now after many years I came to bring alms to my nation, and offerings.
ACTS 24:17

Only they would that we should remember the poor; the same which I also was forward to do.
GALATIANS 2:10

❖ In fastings often. That's Paul's fasting.
❖ I pray for you without ceasing. That's Paul's praying.
❖ I came to bring alms and offerings. That's Paul's giving.

The end result was a supernatural and international ministry that is shaking the world up till today. I am sure you will not disagree with me when I tell you that this man had unusual, special and extraordinary miracles in his life and ministry. In his own words, Paul said:

And my speech and my preaching was not with enticing words of man's wisdom, but in demonstration of the Spirit and of power. That your faith should not stand in the wisdom of men, but in the power of God.
1 CORINTHIANS 2:4-5

As we come to the end of this chapter, I want to encourage you to give yourself to these threefold strands of praying, fasting and giving. While Paul encouraged the Corinthian saints in their marriage, he injected a powerful thought for couples, *'Defraud ye not one the other, except it be with consent for a time, that ye may give yourselves to fasting and prayer; and come together again, that Satan tempt you not for your incontinence'* (1 Corinthians 7:5). Therefore a believer, a minister, a couple, a family and a church should:

❖ Give themselves to prayer. That's *your* praying.
❖ Give themselves to fasting. That's *your* fasting.
❖ Give themselves to giving. That's *your* giving.

The end result will be a life endued with power and miracles. The words, 'give yourselves' is 'scholazo' from which we get our English words, 'school' and 'schooling'. Learn to school yourself in praying, giving and fasting and your life and ministry will become an adventure. Learn to give your tithes and offerings; learn to give to the poor; learn to give of yourselves to your church and in the service of God. The giving of yourself to God and His service will bring great blessings to you. Commit to your church and ministry and become an asset by investing in prayers, fastings and givings.

> *The same God who gave people unusual and outrageous breakthroughs, is no respecter of persons, and will give you unusual breakthroughs.*

CHAPTER 8
101 BENEFITS OF FASTING

Section 1: Benefits 1-25

OVER the next four sections, I want to give you 101 benefits of fasting. I want to show you – from the Scriptures – the advantages and supernatural upper-hand that fasting gives you. As you learn to school yourself in fasting, you can begin to make demands for these benefits to be living realities in your life. Everything that you find on a subject in the Bible is yours. You have a right to partake of the promises and their benefits. Never allow the devil to deceive you and tell you that it's for others and not for you: that is a lie! As you embark on a journey of little steps into fasting, may all these benefits and good things come to you. As you shut down the bodily system in order to open the spiritual system, may you be enlarged in your life, business and ministry.

These 101 benefits are not an exhaustive look at the physical health rewards that come from fasting (although it might be mentioned briefly) but at the biblical rewards. There have been many books written on the subject of the health benefits of fasting and you would do well to read them.

I have not put these benefits in any particular order as they are all equally important. Meditate upon them and call for them to manifest in your life. You will find some that speak to your specific need right at this moment in time; claim, confess and call for their manifestation, for your betterment. You will also discover that within these 101 benefits there are nuggets, pull-outs and power principles that, if applied, become many more in number than the 101. However for the sake of keeping it shorter, I have called it 101 benefits.

In some of the benefits I have provided further information to substantiate the thought; with others I have cited just the benefits – with Scripture references – as the meaning should be self explanatory. This is applied particularly to the benefits of Isaiah 58.

1 FASTING IS THE MASTER KEY TO OPERATING IN THE SUPERNATURAL. IT BRINGS A SUPERNATURAL EDGE TO YOUR LIFE AND MINISTRY

One thing is for sure, you cannot have a sustained and supernatural ministry without learning the art and secret of fasting. Study the lives of people who have walked on a high-level of the supernatural and you will discover that they knew the secret of fasting.

The ministry of Moses was one characterized by fasting and the supernatural:

> *And there arose not a prophet since in Israel like unto Moses, whom the Lord knew face to face, In all **the signs and the wonders**, which the Lord sent him to do in the land of Egypt to Pharaoh, and to all his servants, and to all his land, And in all that mighty hand, and in all the great terror which Moses shewed in the sight of all Israel.*
>
> DEUTERONOMY 34:10-12

The ministry of Jesus was also characterized by fasting and miracles:

> *And Jesus being full of the Holy Ghost returned from Jordan, and was led by the Spirit into the wilderness, Being forty days tempted of the devil. And in those days he did eat nothing: and when they were ended, he afterward hungered.*
>
> LUKE 4:1-2

> *And a great multitude followed him, because **they saw his miracles** which he did on them that were diseased.*
>
> JOHN 6:2

*Ye men of Israel, hear these words; **Jesus of Nazareth, a man approved of God among you by miracles and wonders and signs, which God did by him in the midst of you,** as ye yourselves also know.*

ACTS 2:22

The ministry of the apostle Paul was also characterized by fasting and miracles:

*But in all things approving ourselves as the ministers of God, in much patience, in afflictions, in necessities, in distresses, In stripes, in imprisonments, in tumults, in labours, **in watchings, in fastings.***

2 CORINTHIANS 6:4-5

*...in watchings often, in hunger and thirst, **in fastings** often, in cold and nakedness.*

2 CORINTHIANS 11:27

*For I will not dare to speak of any of those things which Christ hath not wrought by me, to make the Gentiles obedient, by word and deed, Through **mighty signs and wonders**, by the power of the Spirit of God; so that from Jerusalem, and round about unto Illyricum, I have fully preached the gospel of Christ.*

ROMANS 15:18-19

The bridge between the supernatural and signs and wonders is fasting; you must add fasting to your repertoire if you want to have the supernatural edge that you crave for. Look at ministers who walk in the supernatural with creative miracles and you will deduce that they are committed to fasting. There must come a time in your life where you become tired of powerlessness, a lack of signs and feeling helpless before ailing people as you pray for them. The day you get tired with these sentiments is the day that you will take fasting seriously. When you do, get ready for the supernatural.

FASTING IS THE SECRET TO A LIFE OF POWER IN YOUR GOSPEL

2   FASTING TRIGGERS AN OPEN PHYSICAL REWARD AND MANIFESTATION

But thou, when thou fastest, anoint thine head, and wash thy face; That thou appear not unto men to fast, but unto thy Father which is in secret: and thy Father, which seeth in secret, shall reward thee openly.

MATTHEW 6:17-18

'*Your Father who sees in secret, shall reward you openly.*' The word 'openly' (which is also used by the Lord in verses 4 and 7 of that chapter in reference to alms and prayer) literally means 'in the apparent'. This means 'clearly visible' and 'in public'. Therefore fasting is a private devotion that triggers an open manifestation and reward. Your Father sees what you do in secret. This means your fasting catches His eyes! Jesus also said that, '*there is nothing hid, which shall not be manifested; neither was any thing kept secret, but that it should come abroad.*' (Mark 4:22; Luke 8:17).

3   FASTING MOVES GOD THE FATHER ON THE SCENE AS THE RIGHTEOUS JUDGE TO BRING JUSTICE

That thou appear not unto men to fast, but unto thy Father which is in secret: and thy Father, which seeth in secret, shall reward thee openly.

MATTHEW 6:18

These words came from the mouth of Jesus. He said that when you fast, your Heavenly Father, God Almighty Himself will come on the scene and see to it that you are recompensed and your enemy retributed. As mentioned earlier in this book, the word 'reward' is' apodidomi', a combination of two words: 'apo' meaning 'to take back to the origin' and 'didomi' meaning 'to give'. Once again, I will insert the full meanings of the word.

Apodidomi means:

❖ To deliver, to give away for one's own profit what is one's own.

❖ To pay off, discharge what is due.

❖ Things promised under oath.

❖ To give back, restore; *and*

❖ To requite, recompense in a good or a bad sense.

Apodidomi is a combination of two words. Apo meaning 'to take back to the origin' and didomi meaning 'to give'. The combination of these two words means 'to give and take back to the origin'. I also want you to notice the significations given above. The meaning I want to drive into your mind is 'to discharge what is due and things promised under oath'. This is giving you an account of a court case where the judge will see to it that whatever has been stolen is given back to its owner. The author of Hebrews revealed God as a *'rewarder of those who diligently seek him'* (Hebrews 11:6). Rewarder is 'misthapodotes', from the root word 'misthos' which means:

❖ Dues paid for work; wages, hire.

❖ Reward: used of the fruit naturally resulting from toils and endeavors, in both senses, rewards and punishments.

❖ Of the rewards which God bestows, or will bestow, upon good deeds and endeavors.

❖ Of punishments (Strongs Concordance); *and*

❖ Payment of price due.

The culmination of all these meanings implies that justice has to be done; a revenge will be meted out by the Righteous judge, the Heavenly Father, ensuring that whatever was taken from you will be handed back to you. This is very good news if you feel a sense of injustice when it comes to your situation. In essence, fasting is judicial prayer at its optimum level. Fasting brings God onto the scene as the judge who will see to it that justice is done for you and whatever judgment needs to be meted out will be done. See the words of Abraham:

> *That be far from thee to do after this manner, to slay the righteous with the wicked: and that the righteous should be as the wicked, that be far from thee: Shall not the Judge of all the earth do right?*
>
> GENESIS 18:25

FASTING IS JUDICIAL PRAYER AT ITS OPTIMUM LEVEL.
FASTING BRINGS GOD ON THE SCENE AS THE JUDGE
WHO WILL SEE TO IT THAT JUSTICE IS DONE FOR YOU

---

4 FASTING IS THE PATH OF HUMILITY, TURNING YOU TOWARDS THE LORD AND ACCESSING THE GRACE OF GOD

When you fast you are humbling yourself before the Lord. Fasting and humility are synonymous terms. You see, one of the meanings of 'humble' is fasting. I have discovered that there is just as much pride in the lives of believers as there is in unbelievers. The Apostle James said in his epistle, *'God resists the proud but he gives grace to the humble'* (James 4;7). This was written to the believers of the day; they were walking in pride then and many believers are walking in pride today. Now you may say to yourself, "I don't walk in pride!" It is prideful to assume that you are not walking in pride! Human nature tends to be prideful. God knows that the heart of man is desperately wicked – meaning twisted. Some of the signs of pride are:

* When we want to do things our own way and get our own way.
* When we move ahead with a decision without consulting God.
* When we try to solve our problems by our own hands.
* When we cannot say sorry for wrongdoing.
* When we value our opinion above the Scriptures.
* When we always want to be right.
* When we feel a sense of self-importance.
* When we feel easily offended for a lack of recognition.
* When we look down on others who are different from us.
* When we feel that some people are beneath us.

Now you might think that these situations are seen in the world but surely not in the church. The truth is, this is in the church, *among believers* and most certainly among preachers. When you are walking in pride, God Himself will resist you. Why? Because pride is the expression of the devil. We must always check ourselves to see whether pride has crept in; we will know when it happens because the Holy Spirit will frown upon certain acts that we do.

We know that when we submit ourselves to the commands of the Word and act upon them, this is humility in action. In the Scriptures, fasting is always attached to humility and the chastising of the soul. When you connect these two words together, you will unlock the meaning of many verses. In the Old testament, fasting was employed to enable a person to humble himself before God. As the scribe Ezra said, '*I proclaimed a fast… that we might humble ourselves before our God*' (Ezra 8:21). David echoed the same sentiment as he penned the Psalms, '*I humbled my soul with fasting*' (Psalms 35:13). The response of evil King Ahab to fast because of the judgment pronounced from the prophet's mouth provoked God to say, '*Seest thou how Ahab humbleth himself before Me?*' (1 Kings 21:29).

Fasting is the deliberate act of humbling yourself before the Lord and acknowledging your total dependency upon Him as your source of strength, which positions you to receive the grace and favor [preferential treatment] of God. So when the Scripture tells you to humble yourself before God, now you know what to do: you fast!

When you read Scriptures such as:

*If my people, which are called by my name, **shall humble themselves**, and pray, and seek my face, and turn from their wicked ways; **then will I hear from heaven, and will forgive their sin, and will heal their land.***
         2 CHRONICLES 7:14

*But he giveth more grace. Wherefore he saith, God resisteth the proud, but **giveth grace unto the humble.***

JAMES 4:6

Humble** yourselves in the sight of the Lord, and **he shall lift you up.

JAMES 4:10

Humble yourself** therefore under the mighty hand of God, that **he may exalt you in due time.

1 PETER 5:6

Now insert the word 'fast' and these verses come alive. Fasting gives you access to the grace of God. What does that mean? It means help in a time of need (Hebrews 4:16); it means sufficient power to deal with your problems (2 Corinthians 12:9).

But as for me, when they were sick, my clothing was sackcloth: I humbled my soul with fasting...

PSALM 35:13

While pride is the expression of Satan, humility is the expression and nature of Jesus. If you want to receive grace to help in time of need then humble yourself before God.

FASTING IS THE DELIBERATE ACT OF HUMBLING YOURSELF BEFORE THE LORD

---

5   FASTING WILL FUSE EXOUSIA AND DUNAMIS THUS RELEASING KRATOS. IT PUTS YOU IN A COMMANDING POSITION OF DOMINION

'*Jesus returned in the power of the Spirit... and His fame went throughout all the regions round about*' (Luke 4:14). You have to remember that although Jesus was and is God, He did not operate and heal people in the earth as God, but as a man, anointed with the Holy Spirit. He walked by faith and was led by the Holy Spirit to give us an example of how we are to live as a new creation in Him, on the earth. He was a man of the Word, a man of prayer and a man of fasting. As He combined these three he tapped into 'exousia' and 'dunamis' and released 'kratos' on the earth. Let's define these three Greek words:

- Exousia is authority or right to exert.
- Dunamis is ability or power.
- Kratos is eruptive, exhibited and demonstrative power.

When these three are combined, you will walk in dominion. There are people who have been *authorized* and even have the *ability*, but never *erupt* with their authorized ability and thus relinquish their dominion. In Greek mythology, Kratos was the personification of strength and power. Jesus manifested kratos as He fused the forces of dunamis and exousia and He walked in dominion as an anointed man over sin, sickness, diseases and demons. Fasting creates a crater inside of you that allows an eruption of power, from the exertion of authority within.

FASTING MAKES YOU A CRATER THROUGH WHICH THE VOLCANIC POWER OF THE ANOINTING CAN ERUPT

6 FASTING TURNS YOUR HEART BACK TO GOD, REKINDLING YOUR FIRST LOVE

Therefore also now, saith the Lord, turn ye even to me with all your heart, and with fasting, and with weeping, and with mourning

JOEL 2:12

Many times in our Christian life, we find ourselves going in our own direction and not following the path that God has set before us. Fasting will recalibrate our movement and put us on the right track as we seek God. Fasting points us in the right direction and that is towards God. It rekindles our love and passion for Him.

7   FASTING ACTS AS A WEAPON OF MASS DESTRUCTION FOR THE PULLING DOWN OF STRONGHOLDS

This is a crucial point to grasp: fasting is not just about going hungry or dieting, it's a powerful weapon to create havoc in the camp of the enemy; it's a weapon of mass destruction that Satan fears and hates; it pulls down his strongholds that may have been erected and established for many years. Paul, in his second epistle to the Corinthian believers, stated, '*For the weapons of our warfare are not carnal but mighty through God to the pulling down of strongholds*' (2 Corinthians 10:4). Men and women who have obtained major victories in the Scriptures and throughout history have been those who have employed, engaged and unleashed this mighty weapon. The modern believer needs to understand this truth: Jesus our Lord, employed this great weapon before He entered into full time ministry:

> *And Jesus being full of the Holy Ghost returned from Jordan, and was led by the Spirit into the wilderness. Being forty days tempted of the devil. And in those days he did eat nothing: and when they were ended, he afterward hungered.*
>
> LUKE 4:1, 2

> *Then was Jesus led up of the Spirit into the wilderness to be tempted of the devil. And when he had fasted forty days and forty nights, he was afterward an hungred. And when the tempter came to him...*
>
> MATTHEW 4:1-3

There is something I want to draw your attention to. Many times we think we know what a verse means or we think we have understood the chapter simply because we have read it. However, many times we are reading through traditional or educational 'lenses' and not by the revelation of the Spirit. If you were to ask the average believer, 'Why did Jesus go or was led into the wilderness?' The automatic response would be, 'To fast'. Actually this is only partially true! According to Matthew, the reason Jesus went into the wilderness was '*to be tempted of the devil.*' This is a very important distinction. After the decree that came from the Father saying, '*This is my beloved Son in whom I am well pleased*', He was due to have an encounter with His enemy, Satan. This was going to be His first heavyweight battle with the enemy – on the enemies turf – who would hurl at Him his most powerful and trusted weapons. Satan already encountered and defeated the first Adam with these weapons and no doubt planned to use the same tactics against the last Adam. Would Jesus succeed where Adam failed? Jesus knew to employ the mighty weapon of fasting. When the enemy arrived, Jesus was already loaded up with the Word, prayed up and fasted up: He was more than ready for the enemy and He did not fail. Notice the words, '*when the tempter came to him*'. This attack did not take Jesus by surprise, causing Him to scramble and try to get His act together before He faced the enemy. No! Jesus, knowing that He would face this encounter, had great perception to engage the weapon of fasting to destroy the three strongholds of Satan:

And when the tempter came to him, he said, If thou be the Son of God, command that these stones be made bread. But he answered and said, It is written, Man shall not live by bread alone, but by every word that proceedeth out of the mouth of God. Then the devil taketh him up into the holy city, and setteth him on a pinnacle of the temple, And saith unto him, If thou be the Son of God, cast thyself down: for it is written, He shall give his angels charge concerning thee: and in their hands they shall bear thee up, lest at any time thou dash thy foot against a stone. Jesus said unto him, It is written again, Thou shalt not tempt the Lord thy God. Again, the devil taketh him up into an exceeding high mountain, and sheweth him all the kingdoms of the world, and the glory of them; And saith unto him, All these things will I give thee, if thou wilt fall down and worship me. Then saith Jesus unto him, Get thee hence, Satan: for it is written, Thou shalt worship the Lord thy God, and him only shalt thou serve.

MATTHEW 4:3-10

There are three major strongholds that a person will encounter in their life. You need to understand that the word 'stronghold' started out as a good, positive word but by the time the apostle Paul used that word, it had no positivity to it but became a word that would describe a prison fortress or a death cage. As Paul was from Cilicia, he knew of the history of the Cilician pirates. You may have seen the movie, 'Pirates of the Caribbean'. Paul's experience was with the original, 'Pirates of the Mediterranean' which had Rome almost on its knees as they kept hijacking and abducting the cargo boats that would be bringing victuals to and from Rome. Although Rome – with a great military – was the superpower of the time, its navy was not as prolific a war winning machine as its land counterpart. Consequently, they were regularly subject to terrorist attacks from the Mediterranean pirates. The Cilicians pirates, would later become known as one of the most ruthless and barbarous pirate groups in the ancient Greco-Roman world, especially to Rome. To make matters worse the pirates used the stronghold of Cilicia to locate their cargo ships and would then launch their attacks from this stronghold. Rome had no answer until Pompei the Great devised mighty weapons to deal with and destroy the stronghold of the Cilician pirates (For more info on this subject, please order my book – Tetelestai).

Here is one important lesson we must bear in mind. When it comes to the subject of *strongholds*, people in different Christian camps differ and don't seem to reconcile their beliefs but use it as a point of separation. We see this phenomenon when it comes to *Tongues (glossalalia)* and *The Second Coming (eschatology)*. This is also true when it comes to the subject of strongholds. While we can find many types of strongholds they can all be summed up in three categories: *mental, spiritual* and *physical*. One camp will tell you that all strongholds refer to the mind, another camp will tell you it is spiritual, while another will tell you it is physical. Which one is right? They are all right.

Strongholds can manifest in any of these ways:

❖ Mental strongholds – false reasonings that resist the truth of God's Word.

❖ Spiritual strongholds – demonic influences over cities and regions resisting and hindering the Gospel.

❖ Physical strongholds – diseases (which can be generational), traits, temptations or proclivities which seem to be very stubborn to shake.

These three strongholds can be so intertwined that it would be difficult to put a clear distinction between them: a spiritual stronghold can create a mental stronghold and physical stronghold for example. We see this in certain parts of the world (territorial) where a spiritual stronghold, has become a way of thinking (mental) and way of living for the people (physical) in the region. To the people in that region, their beliefs, lifestyle and actions are perfectly normal because that's all they know.

A quick definition of a stronghold is *that which prohibits a person from walking in the fullness of what God has intended for his or her life.* A stronghold is the master key that Satan uses to keep the believer in defeat and frustration; it is Satan's death cage, or death trap, to keep people from walking in and experiencing the fullness of the redemption that Jesus already paid for.

One camp will tell you that all you have to do to get rid of strongholds is to renew your mind, another camp will tell you that you need to fast and pray to get rid of strongholds, while another will tell you that you have to pull down the principalities over the atmosphere, thus destroying their strongholds. The point I am endeavoring to make is that there are different weapons to deal with different strongholds. There are some strongholds that only renewing of the mind can destroy, such as mental strongholds. In this aspect, no matter how much you fast and pray, it will not remove false reasonings or mental strongholds. On the other hand, if it is a demonic or spiritual stronghold, you will need prayer and fasting; it will not matter how much you renew your mind to pull these strongholds down, prayer and fasting are the required weapons. The point is there are different weapons to deal with different strongholds.

Strongholds can be brought down in these ways:

- ❖ Mental strongholds – renewing of the mind to resist and overthrow false beliefs or false reasonings.
- ❖ Spiritual strongholds – removal by resisting in prayer and fasting.
- ❖ Physical strongholds – rejecting by resisting with the Covenantal Word and positional truth.

Jesus faced all three and won:

Physical stronghold – *command that these stones be made bread.* Jesus did not permit his flesh to have the ascendancy over Him. Jesus responded, *'Man shall not live by bread alone but by every word that proceedeth out of the mouth of God'* (Matthew 4:4). Adam failed here as he lived by bread rather than by the word that proceeded from God's mouth. Jesus, the last Adam, succeeded because He chose to live by the word that proceeded from God's mouth rather than eating bread. It is interesting that the first temptation was to break the fast that Jesus was on. Satan tempted Adam to break the partial fast he was on but could not do so with Jesus.

Mental stronghold – *cast thyself down: for it is written, He shall give his angels charge concerning thee: and in their hands they shall bear thee up, lest at any time thou dash thy foot against a stone.* Satan tried to play mind games with Jesus; he will also play mind games with you. This is where the renewing of the mind is very important, to pull down the psychological walls that Satan erects in your mind. Renewing of the mind is simply making the *logos* of God's Word your logic. Like Jesus did, it is allowing the Word to be the final authority in your life.

Spiritual stronghold – *sheweth him all the kingdoms of the world, and the glory of them; And saith unto him, All these things will I give thee, if thou wilt fall down and worship me.* Although that is what Jesus came to claim back, He would do it God's way.

Knowing that He would have a face-to-face encounter with Satan, who would be using his master tactics of strongholds, Jesus launched the preemptive strike of fasting to nullify the devil's course of actions. You would be wise to employ the weapon of fasting as a weapon of mass destruction, to destroy the strongholds of the devil in your own life.

8   FASTING GIVES YOU DOMINION IN THE SPIRIT

Dominion in the spirit is crucial to bringing revival to a church, city and country. Being a great orator does not give you power in the spirit; it does not give you power over the atmosphere. Luke emphasized a specific thought after Jesus returned from his fast:

And Jesus returned in the power of the Spirit into Galilee: and there went out a fame of him through all the region round about.

LUKE 4:14

Looking at this verse from a traditional standpoint would have us thinking that Jesus became famous. How could that be so when he had not even preached his first sermon, healed the sick or cast a devil out? Therefore this is not referring to his notoriety, popularity and fame but to another issue entirely. The news that spread throughout the region was done so in the realm of the spirit. The moment fasting takes place, there is an announcement in the spirit realm: every devil and every demon takes notice when you begin to fast. It gives you power over the atmosphere. We can prove that by looking at the reign and decree of King Ahasuerus in the book of Esther, which begins with the stretch of authority, power and dominion of the King. He was head over 120 provinces that stretched from India to Ethiopia (Esther 1:1). That is from Asia, through the Middle East and into Africa. After being duped by evil Haman, a decree was signed into effect by King Ahasuerus to have all the Jews killed in all 120 provinces.

Bulletins were sent out by couriers to all the king's provinces with orders to massacre, kill, and eliminate all the Jews—youngsters and old men, women and babies—on a single day, the thirteenth day of the twelfth month, the month Adar, and to plunder their goods. Copies of the bulletin were to be posted in each province, publicly available to all peoples, to get them ready for that day.

ESTHER 3:13-14 THE MESSAGE

However, Esther and Mordecai went on a total fast for three days and the decree was reversed in all the provinces. The evil motion set against the Jews was canceled as God's people fasted. The day that you fast, there will be an announcement in the spirit realm concerning your arrival. You see, you announce your arrival in the spirit when you fast: alarm bells start to go off in hell and the heavenlies when you begin to fast. Today the distance between New Delhi and Addis Ababa is 2,845 miles. So their fasting affected an area of more that 3,500 miles across. It turned a dire situation into a glorious miracle. Imagine that! When you fast, the atmosphere over your home, church, city and nation will be affected for the better. This is the key to taking a city for Christ. We need power in the spirit.

9 FASTING WEAKENS AND REMOVES SPIRITUAL OPPOSITION AND WICKEDNESS

The apostle Paul unveiled to the Ephesian believers that the battle is not against flesh and blood but against principalities, powers, rulers of the darkness of this age and wicked spirits in high places (Ephesians 6:12). Therefore we don't use physical weapons to deal with these unseen adversaries. These four classes of demonic opposition are adversarial to our destiny and progress. The way to weaken the present opposition over your life, church, city and nation is through fasting and the Word. Each generation has strongholds that need to be weakened and removed in order to make rapid progress. A simple way to understand what a principality means is a 'prince in a palace'. Therefore a principality is a prince ruling in a palace for a long time.

Different cities display different oppositions, principalities or strongholds. The same can be said about different nations. For example, we can see that generally Europeans are not as open to the Gospel as Africans. We also know there are more Christian persecutions in the 10/40 Window countries than anywhere else in the world. This window forms a band encompassing Saharan and Northern Africa, as well as almost all of Asia (West Asia, Central Asia, South Asia, East Asia and much of Southeast Asia). Roughly two-thirds of the world population lives in the 10/40 Window. The 10/40 Window is populated by people who are predominantly Muslim, Hindu, Buddhist, Jewish or Atheist. Many governments in the 10/40 Window are formally or informally opposed to Christian work of any kind within their borders.

With this in mind, how do we break the opposition? This is where fasting should play a prominent role. In many of these places, even having a Bible is prohibited. Therefore one of the most powerful weapons employed by believers is fasting. Daniel shows us a great example of how to weaken spiritual opposition when he fasted for twenty one days. He needed some answers but the principality over Persia was opposing his prayers. The applied consistency of his fasting and prayers weakened the resistance of the prince of Persia. Whatever opposition or wickedness is in your family or city that is resisting you can come down as you tap into this incredible gift of fasting. If Daniel could dethrone and unseat the Persian principality then you can unseat and dethrone any spiritual wickedness withholding your passage to your promised land.

10 FASTING WILL PRECIPITATE THE ANSWER WHICH HAS BEEN DELAYED AND OBSTRUCTED. IT IS A BLOW TO THE SPIRIT OF DELAY

If anyone was a living example of breaking the spirit of delay, it was Daniel. The spirit of delay is one of the major problems for the believer today. Attached to delay is frustration and discontent. When you have constantly been delayed, time has passed you by and a sense of despair and loss overwhelms your spirit, you will become frustrated. One of the most striking verses in the Bible is found in the book of Joshua, as God talked openly to the old general of war:

> *Now Joshua was old and stricken in years; and the Lord said unto him, Thou art old and stricken in years, and there remaineth yet very much land to be possessed.*
>
> JOSHUA 13:1

The Ancient of days, Elohim, who lives outside of time looked at Joshua and told him, 'Thou art old'. If God looks at you and tells you that you are old then you really have a problem. Joshua was ready to move forty years prior but the children of Israel's unbelief delayed him. Now God looked at him forty years later and said, '*You are old and there remains much land to possess.*' Joshua did not run out of land but he ran out of time. How frustrating! Daniel knew God had some stuff for Israel and yet there was a blockage concerning God's will. This may also be your problem: you will never run out of promises, you will simply run out of time. We must realize that God's will is not automatic, it has to be *downloaded*. When we refuse to fast, pray and stand on the Word we delay our destiny. In chapters 9 and 10 of the book of Daniel he shows us the expediency of fasting to break the delay tactics of Satan.

11   FASTING RELEASES ANGELS: IT SUMMONS WARRING ANGELS ON A WARRING ASSIGNMENT

This is powerful! What a thought! When you fast, angels who excel in strength are released. The first thing to understand is that angels are not little fat babies with a bow and arrow: angels are supreme beings created by God. Essentially there are three kinds of angels:

1. Worshiping angels. These are the ones who worship God before the throne, night and day.
2. Warring angels, such as Michael who fights for Israel and the angels who surrounded Elisha when the Syrians came to assassinate him.
3. Working angels. Every believer has guardian angels.

Angels are agents of deliverance: they have been sent forth to minister for those who are heirs of salvation (Hebrews 1:14). How are angels activated? They are activated when we fast. Allow me to list four examples for you.

> Daniel

*In those days I Daniel was **mourning three full weeks. I ate no pleasant bread, neither came flesh nor wine in my mouth,** neither did I anoint myself at all, till three whole weeks were fulfilled... **And he said unto me,** O Daniel, a man greatly beloved, understand the words that I speak unto thee, and stand upright: for unto thee am I now sent. And when he had spoken this word unto me, I stood trembling. **Then said he unto me,** Fear not, Daniel: **for from the first day that thou didst set thine heart to understand, and to chasten thyself before thy God, thy words were heard, and I am come for thy words. But the prince of the kingdom of Persia withstood me one and twenty days: but, lo, Michael, one of the chief princes, came to help me;** and I remained there with the kings of Persia.*

DANIEL 10:2-3,11-13

> Jesus

*Then was Jesus led up of the Spirit into the wilderness to be tempted of the devil. And when **he had fasted** forty days and forty nights, he was afterward an hungered... Then the devil leaveth him, and, **behold, angels came and ministered unto him.***

MATTHEW 4:1-2, 11

> Cornelius

There was a certain man in Caesarea called Cornelius, a centurion of the band called the Italian band, A devout man, and one that feared God with all his house, which gave much alms to the people, and prayed to God alway. **He saw in a vision evidently about the ninth hour of the day an angel of God coming in to him,** *and saying unto him, Cornelius....* **And Cornelius said, Four days ago I was fasting until this hour;** *and at the ninth hour I prayed in my house, and, behold, a man stood before me in bright clothing, And said, Cornelius, thy prayer is heard, and thine alms are had in remembrance in the sight of God.*

ACTS 10:1-3, 30-31

> Paul

But after long abstinence *Paul stood forth in the midst of them, and said, Sirs, ye should have hearkened unto me, and not have loosed from Crete, and to have gained this harm and loss. And now I exhort you to be of good cheer: for there shall be no loss of any man's life among you, but of the ship.* **For there stood by me this night the angel of God,** *whose I am, and whom I serve, Saying, Fear not, Paul; thou must be brought before Caesar: and, lo, God hath given thee all them that sail with thee... And while the day was coming on, Paul besought them all to take meat, saying, This day is the fourteenth day that ye have tarried and* **continued fasting,** *having taken nothing. Wherefore I pray you to take some meat: for this is for your health: for there shall not an hair fall from the head of any of you.*

ACTS 27:21-24, 33-34

Here are four classic examples of angels activated through the power of fasting. Whenever the angels were activated they always brought in a message of victory and aided in obtaining victory. You can see that Paul faced a dire situation, but through fasting the Lord made a way out of an impossible situation. In fact Dr. Luke, who was also in the boat, could not see a way out. That is why he said, '*And the third day we cast out with our own hands the tackling of the ship. And when neither sun nor stars in many days appeared, and no small tempest lay on us, all hope that we should be saved was then taken away.*' (Acts 27:19-20). Luke could only see death but Paul saw life. As you begin to fast and pray, summon warring angels to come to your aid. This is part of your rightful inheritance.

I want to drive this into your spirit: angels are agents of deliverance and agents of vengeance; they will not only deliver you, they will also avenge you. Herod the King found this out the hard way after he had decapitated James, the brother of John and went after Peter: as the church prayed incessantly, an angel of the Lord was released and delivered Peter from jail. At the opportune time he then slew Herod, whose body was eaten up by worms (See Acts 12). Remember also, when Daniel was cast into the lion's den, the king fasted the whole night and went earnestly to see Daniel in the morning to inquire if he was still alive. Daniel replied, '*My God hath sent his angel, and hath shut the lions' mouths, that they have not hurt me...*' (Daniel 6:22). Your angels will deliver and avenge you as you fast and pray!

12   FASTING WILL INDUCE THE BIRTH AND SAFE DELIVERY OF YOUR DESTINY

One of the worst things that can ever happen to a woman in life is to be pregnant and not be able to deliver the child, or the baby dies in the womb. Hezekiah aptly said it, '*This day is a day of trouble, and of rebuke, and of blasphemy: for the children are come to the birth, and there is not strength to bring forth.*' (Isaiah 37:3). It is a terrible thing to be pregnant and never be able to give birth.

> A woman in Morocco

I once watched a fascinating program on television about a Moroccan woman who carried a child *for 46 years*. In 1955 in a small village just outside of Casablanca, Zahra Aboutalib became pregnant with her first child. Naturally she was excited and looking forward to giving birth. When the time drew near and after 48 hours of painful labor, without the delivery of the baby, she was rushed to her local hospital. The doctors explained to her that in order for this child to be born, she would need to go through Cesarean Section. However in the hospital ward, Zahra witnessed a woman dying in agonizing and excruciating pain through child birth. Feeling horrified, she fled the hospital fearing the same fate would befall her if she were to stay. During the following days, Zahra suffered excruciating labor pains but the baby remained fastened to her womb. However after a few more days the excruciating pains relented, the baby stopped moving but was never delivered. There is a belief in the Moroccan culture and among the wider Maghrebian people, where it is said that a baby can sleep inside the mother to protect her honor. Believing this myth and putting this experience behind her, Zarah went on with her life adopting three children who later made her a grandmother.

Forty six years later when Zahra was 75 years old, all of a sudden the pains suddenly returned. Her adopted son, caring for her mother's welfare, desired her to see a specialist and they traveled to Rabat where they saw Professor Taibi Ouazzani. After seeing her protruding belly, his first prognosis was an ovarian tumor but he arranged for her to have an ultra-sound scan which revealed a large mass that he could not identify. He then referred Zahra to a specialist radiographer for a second opinion. He realized it was a calcified structure of some sort, but it took a detailed MRI scan to reveal that it was the baby that Zahra was pregnant with forty six years earlier.

Now they were faced with the difficult decision whether it would be safe to try and remove the fetus which weighed 7 pounds and measured 42 centimeters in length. During the surgery they discovered that the fetus had calcified and was a hard, solid lump which is know as a stone-baby.

The surgery was successful and Zarah lived but her baby had died and calcified within her. She had carried him for forty six years and never gave birth to this child.

This is what is happening to so many millions of believers: they have been pregnant with a vision or dream for a number of years and have never been able to give birth to this dream and it has calcified in them. Isaiah tells us, *'As soon as Zion travailed, she brought forth her children.'* (Isaiah 66:8). God further asked the question:

> *Shall I bring to the birth, and not cause to bring forth? saith the Lord: shall I cause to bring forth, and shut the womb? saith thy God.*
>
> ISAIAH 66:9

Why would God give you a vision for you never to give birth to it? That would be cruel! God's will is always for us to be fruitful and multiply. That's one of the fundamental laws of Genesis!

› Jodie's birth

I remember when my wife, Rosanna was pregnant with our daughter Jodie. We were living in England at the time and after examination and check up we were told that the baby would be born in Mid-October. I believe the due date was October 19th. As usual I had an extensive itinerary but I decided to take the whole month of October off to welcome the arrival of my third little-one. My first trip out after October would be to Cape Town on November 4th. I thought to myself that one month off was enough and that would give us plenty of time for the baby. I also had my Mom to come over on a six-month visit to help us take care of our new arrival. By October 17th, I was ready for that baby to come but nothing happened. October 17th, 18th, 19th and 20th came and went and still nothing was happening, except that the baby was happily kicking inside. I told Rosanna, 'This baby better hurry up, I got to go to work in November.'

Her reply to me was, 'Well, the baby will come when she is ready.'

That didn't help me at all; I was getting frustrated; I had to wait until the baby was ready. By October 27th still nothing had happened. Even Rosanna was getting tired of waiting; she was big, uncomfortable and had some back pains. Sleep was not easy as she could not get comfortable. By October 30th *still* nothing had happened and I was getting frantic as I knew I would have to leave the country on November 4th. On the evening of the 30th, the phone rang and it was the hospital staff calling. My wife picked up the phone and in the conversation that transpired, she was told, 'Mrs Arekion, you are two weeks overdue.' I was in the background mumbling to myself, 'Really, you don't say! She's late, the baby is late. All these women are blooming late.'

She was told to come to the hospital the next day. Because of her overdue situation, the doctor gave her an injection to induce her in order to precipitate the safe delivery of Jodie.

This is what fasting does. It gives an *injection* and *induces* the delivery of your destiny and miracle. Many are irritated and uncomfortable because although they are pregnant they are yet to give birth; there is delay and frustration! Many are frustrated because they are in an overdue mode. However just as a woman is induced to give birth, through fasting you can be induced to give birth and forget all the discomfort and pain you endured.

(Isaiah 66:7-9, Mark 9:29, Galatians 4:19, Genesis 25:21-26)

FASTING WILL BE THE INJECTION TO INDUCE THE DELIVERY OF YOUR MIRACLE AND DESTINY

---

13 FASTING GIVES BIRTH TO THE PROPHETIC AND THE MIRACULOUS

Both Samuel and Samson were born to barren women. Hannah and Hazelelponi (according to the Jewish Midrash, this was the name of Samson's mother) were desirous of children but suffered greatly for many years because of sterility. What was the force that was employed to obliterates fruitlessness? It was fasting.

> Samson's mother

And the angel of the Lord appeared unto the woman, and said unto her, Behold now, thou art barren, and bearest not: but thou shalt conceive, and bear a son. Now therefore beware, I pray thee, and drink not wine nor strong drink, and eat not any unclean thing: For, lo, thou shalt conceive, and bear a son; and no razor shall come on his head: for the child shall be a Nazarite unto God from the womb: and he shall begin to deliver Israel out of the hand of the Philistines.

JUDGES 13:3-5

> Samuel's mother

And as he did so year by year, when she went up to the house of the Lord, so she provoked her; therefore she wept, and did not eat. Then said Elkanah her husband to her, Hannah, why weepest thou? and why eatest thou not?

1 SAMUEL 1:7-8

Hazelelponi was under specific instruction to engage in a partial fast before she gave birth therefore Samson was already fasting from her mother's womb. The results from these two mothers were the births of two of the greatest men who ever graced God's green earth. However they were not just men: they had special ministries.

> Samson

*And the woman bare a son, and called his name Samson: and the child grew, and the Lord blessed him. And **the Spirit of the Lord began to move** him at times in the camp of Dan between Zorah and Eshtaol.*

JUDGES 13:24-25

*Then his brethren and all the house of his father came down, and took him, and brought him up, and buried him between Zorah and Eshtaol in the buryingplace of Manoah his father. **And he judged** Israel twenty years.*

JUDGES 16:31

❯ **Samuel**

> *The boy Samuel served the LORD in Eli's presence. In those days the word of the LORD was rare and prophetic visions were not widespread.*
>
> 1 SAMUEL 3:1 HOLMAN CHRISTIAN STANDARD BIBLE

> *And the word of the LORD was precious in those days; there was no open vision... And Samuel grew, and the Lord was with him, and did **let none of his words fall to the ground**. And all Israel from Dan even to Beer–sheba knew that Samuel was established to be **a prophet of the Lord**.*
>
> 1 SAMUEL 3:1, 19-20

Hannah and Hazelelponi gave birth to the prophetic and the miraculous. In a time where the Word of the Lord was rare, Hannah gave birth to the prophetic and the Word of the Lord was no longer rare. It was also the trigger point of open vision.

At a time when Israel was subject to the Philistines, Hazelelponi gave birth to the miraculous and the moving of the Spirit, just like the early church fasted and provoked the moving of the Spirit on the day of Pentecost.

FASTING GIVES BIRTH TO THE PROPHETIC AND THE MIRACULOUS

---

14   FASTING WILL CAUSE A DIVINE SHIFT IN THE REALM OF THE SPIRIT

After Daniel fasted there was a shift in the realm of the spirit; the principality over Persia had to bow to the pressure of fasting and the answer manifested to Daniel. When Nehemiah fasted, the walls of Jerusalem – which were in a state of ruin – were rebuilt in fifty-two days; there was a divine shift in the heavenlies. Nothing will shift in the natural if there is no shifting in the spirit. The sooner you realize this, the sooner you will tap into victory.

One of the greatest lessons in the Old Testament – that depicts how battles are won in the realm of the spirit – is Jael and the evil commander of the Canaanite army, Sisera. His death in the Bible is an unforgettable act from the hands of a woman. Jael waited for Sisera to sleep then hammered a nail through his temple. The blow was so forceful that the peg pinned his head to the ground (Judges 4:21). When reading this story, most people do not realize that the battle was first won in the realm of the spirit; it was not just Jael's hammer and nail that did the job, look at what Deborah reveals in her song: '*The stars fought from heaven. They fought against Sisera from their heavenly paths*' (Judges 5:20 God's Word Translation). It was from the heavenlies that Sisera was first defeated. The stars refer to the angels of God.

In the book of Job, angels are referred to as morning stars (Job 38:7) and of course we know of the seven stars of the book of Revelation (Revelation 1:20). Paul fittingly told us that, '*we wrestle not against flesh and blood, but against principalities, against powers, against the rulers of the darkness of this world, against spiritual wickedness in high places*' (Ephesians 6:12). Newer translations of the Bible employ the word 'heavenlies' for high places. Our battles are won and lost in the spirit.

Paul also revealed Satan as the prince of the power of the air:

Wherein in time past ye walked according to the course of this world, according to the prince of the power of the air, the spirit that now worketh in the children of disobedience.

EPHESIANS 2:2

The word air is the Greek word, 'aer' meaning 'the lower, denser atmosphere'. The atmosphere is dominated by the prince of the power of the air, meaning Satan. Paul is telling us that the trend of the physical world is a result of the puppet master, who is forcefully pulling the strings in the atmosphere above us. If you want to shift the course of the environment in which you live, it is imperative that the heaven over you is open. That is why the great cry in the book of Isaiah was, '*Oh that thou wouldest rend the heavens, that thou wouldest come down, that the mountains might flow down at thy presence*' (Isaiah 64:1). The Hebrew word for 'rend' is 'qara' meaning 'to split asunder'. Paul also explained to us that everything that happened in the Old Testament served as an example, figure, a type and a shadow of things to come for us in the New Testament. So it is important that we have a shift in the spirit and operate under an open heaven. When the shift takes place, the outpouring follows. Elijah prayed, the heaven opened, and the rain came down. Moses in his writings (see Leviticus 26:19-20; Deuteronomy 11:16-17; 28:23-26) also talks about a closed and brass heaven above, which results in:

❖ Strength spent in vain, meaning working very hard and having nothing to show for it.
❖ Land shall not yield increase, meaning no harvest.
❖ Perish quickly, meaning premature death.
❖ Smitten before thine enemies, meaning abject defeat.

This is a crucial point for you to understand! If there is no shift in the atmosphere above you then the heaven is closed or shut up and consequently, hardship and calamity follow. Many believers live their lives without ever thinking about this truth. As mentioned earlier, Esther and Mordecai triggered a shift in the atmosphere by fasting and Israel escaped the evil intentions of Haman. Jesus fasted and there was a shift in the spirit as He returned with power and great healings and miracles followed. On the day of Pentecost, there was a divine shift as the Holy Ghost came in as a rushing mighty wind. What triggered this shift? Peter's answer is very revealing:

'*For these are not drunken, as ye suppose, seeing it is but the third hour of the day. But this is that which was spoken by the prophet Joel; And it shall come to pass in the last days, saith God, I will pour out of my Spirit upon all flesh...*'

ACTS 2:15-17

Notice the words, '*It shall come to pass in the last days*'. Peter was echoing the prophecy of Joel, stating that what was happening on the day of Pentecost was what Joel prophesied years before. However when you look at the prophecy of Joel, you will notice a small difference between what he said and Peter said:

> *And it shall come to pass afterward, that I will pour out my spirit upon all flesh...*
>
> JOEL 2:28

Peter said, 'in the last days' and Joel said, 'afterwards'. So the question to ask of Joel is, *after what?* The answer is *after* the calling of a solemn fast, as you can read in Joel; the shift that happened on the day of Pentecost was due to the disciples being in one accord and in one place, that of prayer and fasting.

15 FASTING WILL REVERSE ASSIGNMENTS AND DECREES OF DEATH AGAINST YOUR LIFE

King Ahasuerus had promoted Haman and whenever he passed through the gate, all the servants of the king were supposed to bow down before him with their faces in the dust. All of them did, except Mordecai the Jew, who would not bow down before any man, nor give Haman the honor that had been ascribed to God. This prompted disapproval from others who informed Haman of the predicament. Haman's pride was dented when he heard Mordecai refuse to honor him in this way. Aroused with anger, he set his goal to punish Mordecai. Thinking that punishing him alone was insufficient, he took his motivation even further and planned to kill all the Jews. However he was unaware that Esther was also Jewish.

As a high ranking member in the cabinet of the King, Haman assisted in the administrative rule of the kingdom of Persia and was frequently in the presence of the King. He devised a plan to get the King's consent to have all the Jews killed without letting on that it was a personal vendetta but rather that the Jewish people were a nuisance and an object of rebellion for the King's kingdom. He cunningly approached King Ahasuerus stating:

There is an odd set of people scattered through the provinces of your kingdom who don't fit in. Their customs and ways are different from those of everybody else. Worse, they disregard the king's laws. They're an affront; the king shouldn't put up with them. If it please the king, let orders be given that they be destroyed. I'll pay for it myself. I'll deposit 375 tons of silver in the royal bank to finance the operation." The king slipped his signet ring from his hand and gave it to Haman son of Hammedatha the Agagite, archenemy of the Jews. "Go ahead," the king said to Haman. "It's your money—do whatever you want with those people." The king's secretaries were brought in on the thirteenth day of the first month. The orders were written out word for word as Haman had addressed them to the king's satraps, the governors of every province, and the officials of every people. They were written in the script of each province and the language of each people in the name of King Xerxes and sealed with the royal signet ring. Bulletins were sent out by couriers to all the king's provinces with orders to massacre, kill, and eliminate all the Jews— youngsters and old men, women and babies—on a single day, the thirteenth day of the twelfth month, the month Adar, and to plunder their goods. Copies of the bulletin were to be posted in each province, publicly available to all peoples, to get them ready for that day. At the king's command, the couriers took off; the order was also posted in the palace complex of Susa. The king and Haman sat back and had a drink while the city of Susa reeled from the news'

ESTHER 3:8-15

The Jewish people reeled from the news they heard: they were all under a death sentence while Haman drank and was gleeful that his plan had worked. The thirteenth day of the month of Adar was the day chosen on which all the Jews would be executed; it created complete pandemonium as the people wept with loud cries, tearing their clothes, dressing themselves in sackcloth – many of them sitting in ashes – mourning and fasting. Mordecai also heard the despicable news concerning the Jews and he knew the culprit behind it. Tearing his clothes, he wrapped himself in sackcloth, throwing ashes upon his body, and went out into the streets, lamenting and sent a message to Esther. They decided that they would fast in unison against this death assignment that threatened the very existence of Israel. Esther, Mordecai and others went on a three-day total fast. The end result was that the death sentence was broken; Israel was not wiped out and is still here today because God's people fasted and reversed the death assignment that was signed into motion against them.

When King Jehoshaphat and Judah fasted, the deathly plans against them were overthrown. Daniel, under an irreversible death decree, was spared by the fasting of the King. You can also overthrow and reverse death assignments of the devil and witchcraft against your life through fasting.

16   FASTING WILL BRING TOTAL CONFUSION IN THE CAMP OF THE ENEMY AND FORCE THE IMPOSSIBLE TO BECOME POSSIBLE

It came to pass after this also, that the children of Moab, and the children of Ammon, and with them other beside the Ammonites, came against Jehoshaphat to battle. Then there came some that told Jehoshaphat, saying, There cometh a great multitude against thee from beyond the sea on this side Syria; and, behold, they be in Hazazontamar, which is Engedi. And Jehoshaphat feared, and set himself to seek the Lord, and proclaimed a fast throughout all Judah. And Judah gathered themselves together, to ask help of the Lord: even out of all the cities of Judah they came to seek the Lord.

2 CHRONICLES 20:1-3

King Jehoshaphat was outnumbered and faced an insurmountable situation: there was an evil conglomerate who conspired to bring destruction to the nation of Judah. News came to him that there was evil intent against his kingdom and what he heard provoked fear in him. However he did not allow the fear from the news to paralyze him; rather he used that fear to drive him to fast and seek the Lord. In life, many times we will face overwhelming circumstances that trigger fear in our lives. We have a choice! Do we allow fear to paralyze us or do we neutralize it with faith? Jehoshaphat neutralized fear by seeking God in fasting. It looked like death and doom were there to take them out. In the natural, victory looked impossible; they were outnumbered by the number of soldiers; they would not have enough weapons and ammunition in their arsenal to deal with their adversaries; it did not look good for Judah and Jehoshaphat. In his mind Satan planted seeds of defeat, and in the minds of his confederate adversaries, victory was inevitable.

Thank God, Jehoshaphat had enough sense to employ the mighty weapon of fasting when all looked bleak. Fasting forced the impossible to become possible.

Do you understand that? Jesus told the father who brought his son to be healed, '*All things are possible to him that believes*' (Mark 9:23).

When the disciples enquired why they could not cast that devil out, Jesus replied:

Because of your unbelief: for verily I say unto you, If ye have faith as a grain of mustard seed, ye shall say unto this mountain, Remove hence to yonder place; and it shall remove; and nothing shall be impossible unto you. Howbeit this kind goeth not out but by prayer and fasting.
                                                    MATTHEW 17:20-21

Please note that the impossible becomes possible with the injection of fasting. We hear that straight from the mouth of Jesus. Here are two important points:

❖ Unbelief makes that which is impossible to remain impossible;
❖ Faith forces the impossible to become possible.

Belief in the promises, coupled with prayer and fasting, forces impossible situations to bow the knee and let you go. Esther, Jehoshaphat and Paul forced impossible situations to change for the better. Please note that we are not saying that fasting forces God to do something: you can't force God to do anything when it comes to His children, God is more than willing to bless them. However fasting forces the impossible to become possible! Are you ready to force your circumstance to bow and yield before you? Then it is time to fast!

17   FASTING BREAKS BARRENNESS AND RELEASES A SEASON OF FRUITFULNESS

The book of Samuel opens with a very sad predicament for a godly woman:

Now there was a certain man of Ramathaimzophim, of mount Ephraim, and his name was Elkanah, the son of Jeroham, the son of Elihu, the son of Tohu, the son of Zuph, an Ephrathite: And he had two wives; the name of the one was Hannah, and the name of the other Peninnah: and Peninnah had children, but Hannah had no children. And her adversary also provoked her sore, for to make her fret, because the LORD had shut up her womb. And as he did so year by year, when she went up to the house of the LORD, so she provoked her; therefore she wept, and did not eat.

1 SAMUEL 1:1-2, 6-7

Hannah, who was married was unable to give birth to children. Peninnah, on the other hand had children and took it upon herself to make the life of Hannah bitter with her constant mockery and disdain. Her husband, Elkanah, who was a godly man loved God and loved her but could not do anything for Hannah; she was barren! Although the meaning of her name means 'grace', she found herself in a hard place rather than a place of favor. Although she was a godly woman, she was not fruitful. This is where so many people find themselves today: godly but unfruitful! How did Hannah break the spirit of barrenness and move into a season of fruitfulness? Note these words:

'therefore she wept, and did not eat.' When all else failed, she fasted and prayed. We know she prayed because the prophet Eli thought that she was drunk and was muttering nonsense to herself. 'And it came to pass, as she continued praying before the LORD, that Eli marked her mouth.

Now Hannah, she spake in her heart; only her lips moved, but her voice was not heard: therefore Eli thought she had been drunken. And Eli said unto her, How long wilt thou be drunken? put away thy wine from thee.'

1 SAMUEL 1:12-14

She replied that she was not drunk but making petition and pouring out her soul before the Lord. What was the end result?

...And the LORD remembered her. Wherefore it came to pass, when the time was come about after Hannah had conceived, that she bare a son, and called his name Samuel, saying, Because I have asked him of the LORD.

1 SAMUEL 1:19-20

Through fasting and prayer, the spirit of barrenness and fruitlessness was destroyed. She entered a new season of fruitfulness and kissed goodbye to fruitlessness. The same will be your portion. In fact I love how Hannah testified:

And Hannah prayed, and said, My heart rejoiceth in the LORD, mine horn is exalted in the LORD: my mouth is enlarged over mine enemies; because I rejoice in thy salvation. There is none holy as the LORD: for there is none beside thee: neither is there any rock like our God.

1 SAMUEL 2:1-2

Let's look at those verses more closely:

My heart rejoices in the Lord – This means the same heart that was aching yesterday is now rejoicing. God knows how to turn your captivity and put laughter in your heart and mouth. No longer will your enemy rejoice over you but your heart will rejoice in God. The enemy will not have the last word; God will give you the last word.

My horn is exalted in the Lord – This means her position and status were elevated. Peninnah could no longer look down upon her. Society could no longer treat her as a reject. She is exalted and promoted to her rightful position. No more shame! No more mockery!

My mouth is enlarged over mine enemies – This means that the enemy will not have the last word. God will give you the last word. As she fasted and prayed, God shut the mouth of her adversaries. Their words could no longer swallow up her hope. God enlarged her mouth over her enemies so that the only thing they could do was look at her, gobsmacked.

There is none holy as the LORD: for there is none beside thee, neither is there any rock like our God – Through fasting she discovered the power of God. She saw God for who He is. She saw the reality of God manifested in her life. Barrenness was broken over her life. Do you realize the very first prayer mentioned in the Bible, where a person prayed for another individual, was when Abraham prayed for King Abimelech:

> *So Abraham prayed unto God: and God healed Abimelech, and his wife, and his maidservants; and they bare children. For the LORD had fast closed up all the wombs of the house of Abimelech, because of Sarah Abraham's wife.*
> GENESIS 20:17-18

You will see the same thing too, as you fast and pray; you will move away from barrenness into a season of fruitfulness.

18   FASTING WILL OPEN YOU UP TO THE GIFTS OF THE SPIRIT

We see this fact manifested in the lives of Jehoshaphat, Cornelius, Peter and Paul. It is amazing to me how many believers – even Charismatic and Pentecostal ministers – are not tapping into the gifts of the Spirit. There are nine gifts, as revealed by Paul to the Corinthian believers. **These gifts are for us today!** They are not passed away. Even those in the circles that believe in the charismata gifts are not seeing them in greater manifestations: we have mentally assented to the existence of the gifts without seeing their manifestations; we believe but do not live them. Paul specifically told us to '*covet the best gifts*' (1 Corinthians 12:31).

The word 'covet' in Greek is 'zeloo' meaning:

- ❖ To desire one earnestly, to strive after.
- ❖ To exert one's self for one.
- ❖ To be the object of the zeal of others.
- ❖ To zealously seek after.

How does one do that? This is where fasting takes prominence. Did you notice in the Bible that Jesus operated in the gifts of the Spirit, especially those of healings and miracles, after He fasted? Jesus did not have an easy pass because He was the Son of God. No! He operated in the earth as the Son of man, anointed with the Spirit, just like you and I are supposed to. That's why He prayed! That's why He fasted! That's why He was constantly seeking the face of His Father in a solitary place on the mountain! Desiring these gifts will not mean they come simply by mere wishing; nothing falls into your lap. You strive for them by fasting. Call and make demands for them in your prayer and fasting time. Your fasting is a clue to what you really value. Now let's look at some of the real life stories in the Bible to validate our point.

❭ Jehoshaphat

As we have already seen, Jehoshaphat was in an impossible situation but he decided to seek the Lord by fasting. Look at what occurred:

> *Then upon Jahaziel the son of Zechariah, the son of Benaiah, the son of Jeiel, the son of Mattaniah, a Levite of the sons of Asaph, came the Spirit of the Lord in the midst of the congregation; And he said, Hearken ye, all Judah, and ye inhabitants of Jerusalem, and thou king Jehoshaphat, Thus saith the Lord unto you, Be not afraid nor dismayed by reason of this great multitude; for the battle is not yours, but God's. To morrow go ye down against them: behold, they come up by the cliff of Ziz; and ye shall find them at the end of the brook, before the wilderness of Jeruel.*
> 2 CHRONICLES 20:14-16

Once the Holy Spirit of God came upon Jahaziel, we see that Jehoshaphat and Judah received their answer in the combination of a word of knowledge and a word of wisdom. The word of wisdom was manifested in the revelation of **when** the enemy would attack. The Holy Spirit said, '*Tomorrow you go down*'. The word of knowledge manifested in the revealing of the **exact location**, '*behold, they come up by the cliff of Ziz; and ye shall find them at the end of the brook, before the wilderness of Jeruel.*'

> Cornelius

Cornelius was an Italian centurion who went on a fast, seeking God. He was not even saved; he himself needed salvation! After going on a fast, an angel of the Lord appeared to him stating that his prayers and givings had gone up before God as a memorial. He then proceeded to tell him who to find and where to find him:

And now send men to Joppa, and call for one Simon, whose surname is Peter: He lodgeth with one Simon a tanner, whose house is by the sea side: he shall tell thee what thou oughtest to do.

ACTS 10:5-6

The angel guided him to Joppa, to Simon the Tanner's house on the beach to find Simon Peter. This was a word of wisdom given to Cornelius. In those days, there was no Yellow Pages or directories to find where people resided. A word of wisdom, which was activated by fasting, settled the issue: salvation came not only to the house of Cornelius but to the Gentile world. At the same time, Peter was also fasting as well as praying, and before he broke his fast he had a vision, saw heaven opened and something coming down that looked like a large sheet being lowered by its four corners to the earth. In it were all kinds of animals, reptiles and wild birds:

The voice said to him, "Get up, Peter; kill and eat!" But Peter said, "Certainly not, Lord! I have never eaten anything ritually unclean or defiled." The voice spoke to him again, "Do not consider anything unclean that God has declared clean." This happened three times, and then the thing was taken back up into heaven. While Peter was wondering about the meaning of this vision, the men sent by Cornelius had learned where Simon's house was, and they were now standing in front of the gate. They called out and asked, "Is there a guest here by the name of Simon Peter?" Peter was still trying to understand what the vision meant, when the Spirit said, "Listen! Three men are here looking for you. So get ready and go down, and do not hesitate to go with them, for I have sent them." So Peter went down and said to the men, "I am the man you are looking for. Why have you come?

ACTS 10:10-21

Again, we see through fasting and prayer that Peter was opened to the realm of visions and the gifts of the Spirit. We need to make demands upon these nine wonderful gifts which are available for us today. Just like these men in the Scriptures opened themselves up to these gifts by fasting and prayer we also need to follow their example. It was after Paul was fasting on the boat that the angel told him how he was going to escape alive – both he and the passengers on board – from what looked like a doomed situation.

Are you ready to tap into these wonderful gifts? I know I am. This is why I fast and pray. When I am fasting I have made it a habit to go for long walks in my neighborhood, and there are certain points and places in my walk where I will call upon God for specific gifts to manifest in my life. I do not want to go to heaven and discover that I could have had the working of miracles operating in my ministry but did not have them because I was too busy eating and not desiring them. The world needs these gifts operating in you. As the gifts operate in you then you will become the hand of God to a sick and dying world.

19   FASTING OPENS YOU UP TO THE VOICE OF GOD

❖ Jehoshaphat fasted and he heard from God.

❖ Cornelius fasted and he heard from God.

❖ Paul fasted and he heard from God.

God wants to speak to you! He is not a silent God but a speaking God. Some people have the idea that God does not speak today and if He ever was to speak He would only speak to pastors and people in leadership. That is far from the truth. The problem that we have today is not that God does not speak, it is that we cannot hear him nor discern his voice. Our problem is a hearing, noticing, perceiving or discerning problem. Some people have the idea, 'I will fast to get God to hear me.' In reality it is the other way around. A person fasts to hear from God:

...he cried, He that hath ears to hear, let him hear.

LUKE 8:8

He who has an ear, let him hear what the Spirit says to the churches.

REVELATION 2:7

For God speaketh once, yea twice, yet man perceiveth it not. In a dream, in a vision of the night, when deep sleep falleth upon men, in slumberings upon the bed; Then he openeth the ears of men, and sealeth their instruction, That he may withdraw man from his purpose, and hide pride from man. He keepeth back his soul from the pit, and his life from perishing by the sword.

JOB 33:14-19

We all have physical ears on the sides of our head but it is our spiritual ears that need to be opened. In the above Scripture, Job said, '*God speaks but we do not perceive...*' He has been speaking to you all along and it has been your lack of perception that has gotten you in trouble and keeps you in trouble. If Jehoshaphat did not hear from God when trouble arose then he would have died in his troubles. Many are dying in their troubles today because they do not know how to hear from God. Paul – who was in the boat along with Dr Luke that was sailing to Italy – would have died if he had not heard from God (Acts 27:1-44). The reason why he heard from God and had an angelic visitation was because he was on a fast. On the third day of the journey he heard from God. The stormy trial lasted for fourteen days but the word that he received on the third day lasted and saw him through to victory. We all need to hear God's voice, especially when we face situations like Paul, who had not seen the sun nor moon for many days. Sometimes we find ourselves in situations where we do not see any light anywhere. You cannot survive off will-power! There comes a time where will-power will be broken but His voice will sustain you. Fast and tap into the voice of God.

(Scripture References: Acts 27:1-44)

20   FASTING CAUSES GOD TO SEE AND NOTICE YOU

How do you get the attention of God? There are many who will say that you cannot get the attention of God, but that's because they do not know how to do so. When you read the Gospels you will find there were some people who knew how to get the attention of Jesus. It was no haphazard act but a deliberate act that commanded the full attention of Jesus.

> Bartimaeus

He is a great example. As Jesus was passing by on His way out of Jericho, there was a huge crowd who no doubt needed His attention, but only Bartimaeus received what many were wishing for; he shouted and shouted until Jesus stopped and summoned for him.

> The woman with the issue of blood

Another great example of someone who knew how to get the attention of Jesus was the woman in Mark 5, that received healing from an ailment of twelve years. A great multitude was there but only her and Jairus received their miracles.

> Jairus

He is amazingly awesome because he got Jesus to follow him to his house. There were many people who would have loved to get Jesus to come to their homes but it was only Jairus among that crowd that day who got Jesus to do so.

> The widow with two mites

She certainly got the attention of Jesus as she threw the two mites into the treasury. The rich and religious were throwing all kinds of money in but only the little widow got the attention of Jesus.

> The centurion

This soldier unequivocally commanded the attention of Jesus. The Lord went as far as to say He has never seen such great faith in Israel. The man was a Gentile, yet Jesus marveled at his faith.

It was their audacity of faith that commanded the attention of Jesus the Healer and Provider. How can we gain the attention of God today? Through our faith. Your fast is an expression of your faith in God that will command His attention. Do we have Scriptures for this? Yes we do!

> Israel of Isaiah 58

To the Jews, fasting was equated with getting the attention of God, to get Him to notice them. This is clearly seen in the questions that were asked in Isaiah's great chapter on fasting:

Wherefore have we fasted, say they, and thou seest not? wherefore have we afflicted our soul, and thou takest no knowledge?
ISAIAH 58:3

They lament, 'Why don't you notice when we fast? Why don't you pay attention when we humble ourselves.
ISAIAH 58:3 NET

Fasting is aggressive faith in action and faith always gets the attention of God. He loves to be cornered by your faith. When you corner Him with your faith He will always come out swinging with power shots.

21   FASTING ATTRACTS GOD

As we read in the previous benefit, fasting causes God to see or notice you; it is another facet of faith at work totally relying upon the hands of God. God is attracted by our fasting for He knows we are looking to Him as the only source of supply, knowing that all other sources have been exhausted. In attracting God you attack Satan and his procedures in motion against your life. If a believer knows how to attract God there is nothing that he cannot have.

22   FASTING GIVES YOU THE EXACT STRATEGY TO TAKE THE LAND AND MOVE INTO YOUR DESTINY

When Jehoshaphat fasted, the Spirit of the Lord – through a prophecy – unfolded the strategy to obtain victory over the outnumbered Judah. When Esther and Mordecai fasted they had the strategy to get before the king in order to reverse the decree of death over all the Jews. As Saul and Barnabas were fasting they obtained the strategy for their ministry. When Paul fasted for three days after his conversion on the road to Damascus, he obtained the exact strategy of his calling from Jesus. Fasting is the triggering of the divine strategies that you need in order to fulfill the vision that God has given you. Vision without strategy leads to frustration. Therefore when you are fasting, it causes you to tap into divine wisdom. Many are languishing with their dreams because they do not have the strategies to get to their Promised Land. Solomon said, '*The labour of the foolish wearieth every one of them, because he knoweth not how to go to the city*' (Ecclesiastes 10:15). It is one thing to know that your destination is the city but it is another thing to know *how* to get there. Because many do not know how to get to their destination they are wearying themselves, and others with them. So, fast to obtain the right strategy. Cornelius was fasting and the angel of the

Lord appeared to him, giving him the right strategy to get Peter to his house. In fact the instruction that the angel gave was so specific to the place where and the person who Peter was staying with. You need to get instructions and strategies, then spend some time fasting before the Lord and open your ears.

23 FASTING OPENS YOU UP TO THE REALM OF VISIONS

Cornelius went on a four day fast and during his fast an angel appeared to him in a vision and gave him instruction to whom he must connect with in order for salvation to come to his household. When Peter asked him the reason why he was summoned, Cornelius explained:

> *Therefore came I unto you without gainsaying, as soon as I was sent for: I ask therefore for what intent ye have sent for me? And Cornelius said, Four days ago I was fasting until this hour; and at the ninth hour I prayed in my house, and, behold, a man stood before me in bright clothing, And said, Cornelius, thy prayer is heard, and thine alms are had in remembrance in the sight of God. Send therefore to Joppa, and call hither Simon, whose surname is Peter; he is lodged in the house of one Simon a tanner by the sea side: who, when he cometh, shall speak unto thee.*
>
> ACTS 10:29-32

Notice that Cornelius was on a fast when he broke into the realm of visions. The same thing happened to Daniel:

> *In the third year of Cyrus king of Persia a thing was revealed unto Daniel, whose name was called Belteshazzar; and the thing was true, but the time appointed was long: and he understood the thing, and had understanding of the vision.* **In those days I Daniel was mourning three full weeks. I ate no pleasant bread, neither came flesh nor wine in my mouth, neither did I anoint myself at all, till three whole weeks were fulfilled.** *And in the four and twentieth day of the first month, as I was by the side of the great river, which is Hiddekel. Then I lifted up mine eyes, and looked, and behold a certain man clothed in linen, whose loins were girded with*

*fine gold of Uphaz: His body also was like the beryl, and his face as the appearance of lightning, and his eyes as lamps of fire, and his arms and his feet like in colour to polished brass, and the voice of his words like the voice of a multitude. **And I Daniel alone saw the vision: for the men that were with me saw not the vision;** but a great quaking fell upon them, so that they fled to hide themselves.*

DANIEL 10:1-7

Daniel sought to understand a revelation that was given to him. In seeking God through twenty-one days of fasting and prayer, he broke into the heavenly sphere and had visions of the unseen realm. All this happened because he gave himself to a stretch of time in fasting. This is why you need to understand when you start to have a regular time of fasting in your life it will open you up to the unseen realms of God where visions and dreams become realities.

24   FASTING WILL RELEASE PROSPERITY INTO YOUR LIFE

Fasting provokes and releases the Spirit of prosperity in your life; it shuts the door on poverty and lack. We see this over and over again in the Scriptures. When Jehoshaphat and Judah were outnumbered and it looked like death and destruction were imminent, the king feared but quickly called for a national fast to avert annihilation. After calling the fast the Spirit of God moved and told them that God would fight for them. God did and it took them three days to gather all the loot:

And when Jehoshaphat and his people came to take away the spoil of them, they found among them in abundance both riches with the dead bodies, and precious jewels, which they stripped off for themselves, more than they could carry away: and they were three days in gathering of the spoil, it was so much. And on the fourth day they assembled themselves in the valley of Berachah; for there they blessed the Lord: therefore the name of the same place was called, The valley of Berachah, unto this day.'

2 CHRONICLES 20:25-26

We see the same thing in the book of Joel. God challenged his people to fast:

*Therefore also **now, saith the Lord, turn ye even to me with all your heart, and with fasting,** and with weeping, and with mourning... Blow the trumpet in Zion, **sanctify a fast,** call a solemn assembly: Gather the people, sanctify the congregation, assemble the elders, gather the children, and those that suck the breasts: let the bridegroom go forth of his chamber, and the bride out of her closet. Let the priests, the ministers of the Lord, weep between the porch and the altar, and let them say, Spare thy people, O Lord, and give not thine heritage to reproach, that the heathen should rule over them: wherefore should they say among the people, Where is their God? **Then will the Lord be jealous for his land, and pity his people. Yea, the Lord will answer and say unto his people, Behold, I will send you corn, and wine, and oil, and ye shall be satisfied therewith: and I will no more make you a reproach among the heathen.***

JOEL 2:12, 15-19

*And the floors shall be full of wheat, and the fats shall overflow with wine and oil. And I will restore to you the years that the locust hath eaten, the cankerworm, and the caterpiller, and the palmerworm, my great army which I sent among you. **And ye shall eat in plenty, and be satisfied, and praise the name of the Lord your God, that hath dealt wondrously with you: and my people shall never be ashamed.***

JOEL 2:24-26

After fasting, God promised that He would send corn and wine, which are symbolic of prosperity and satisfaction. You can break the curse of poverty and trigger abundance in your life through fasting.

- ❖ If Jehoshaphat did it, you can do it.
- ❖ If Judah and Israel can do it, you can do it.
- ❖ If Nehemiah did it, you can do it.
- ❖ If Ezra did it, you can do it.
- ❖ If it happened for Israel it can happen for you.

Are you ready for your floors to be full of wheat and your vats to overflow?

25 FASTING WILL UNSEAT THE BELLY-GOD

People can give many excuses for why they do not fast. Some have said, 'Since we are under grace there is no need for us to fast.' Actually they are wrong, considering Jesus, Paul and the early church fasted. The chief reason why people do not fast is because of the belly-god. We get this term from Paul:

For many walk, of whom I have told you often, and now tell you even weeping, that they are the enemies of the cross of Christ. Whose end is destruction, whose God is their belly, and whose glory is in their shame, who mind earthly things.

PHILIPPIANS 3:18-19

Our bellies govern our lives. Some of us feed the belly-god more than three meal-offerings daily and an untold amount of drink-offerings. Some of us, as soon as the belly-god groans, we run to the altar of the kitchen and prepare the fatted calf.

As Paul did, we need to learn to keep our bodies under control. Fasting is a great way to unseat the belly-god. Paul said these words to the Corinthians:

'Meats for the belly, and the belly for meats: but God shall destroy both it and them'

1 CORINTHIANS 6:13

You see, if your belly controls your life then you will be a victim of circumstances. Esau lost his birthright because he could not unseat the belly-god. Adam lost his position of authority because he ate what he should not have eaten; he could not keep his mouth shut. Many are losing their birthright simply because they do not know how to take authority over their mouth and belly. Fasting gives your spirit ascendancy over your flesh. It will bring discipline to your life and dethrone the belly-god.

CHAPTER 9
101 BENEFITS OF FASTING

Section 2: Benefits 26-50

WE are looking at the multiple benefits of fasting and by now I am hoping that, like the apostle Paul, you will give yourself to much fasting. Develop in you the habit and force of fasting; it will be a catalyst for greatness in your life.

26 FASTING IS ANOTHER FORM OF RESISTANCE TO THE WORKS OF THE DEVIL

We resist the devil with the Word and through our prayer and confession. However another way you can successfully resist the devil or the unseen powers is through fasting. Daniel was unaware that he was being resisted in the spirit realm and as he continued to fast, the Prince of Persia, which was the principality over Persia, had to relinquish his resistance. Jesus deployed fasting as a preemptive weapon on the Mount of Temptation. Fasting is building the bricks and wall of resistance to the flaming missiles of Satan.

(Scripture References: James 4:7, 1Peter 5:9, 2 Chronicles 20:29).

27 FASTING IS CHANGING THE UNSEEN FROM THE SEEN

We all know that faith is changing the seen from the unseen but fasting is changing the unseen from the seen; Daniel fasted in the seen realm and the unseen was being changed without his knowledge. When you fast you are in the visible and tangible world, provoking the unseen or spirit world to change for the better and to your advantage. This is so important to grasp: fasting affects the invisible realms. You may not realize it but as you fast, things are moving, shifting and rearranging for the better for you. As you fast you are making dents in the unseen realm, provoking your speedy answers. Many times we are looking for the seen realm to change without ever shifting the unseen realm. If Daniel and Paul can teach us anything it is that before things shift in the seen they have to be shifted in the unseen. Fasting changes the unseen from the seen.

(Scripture References: Daniel 10, Luke 4, Acts 27).

FASTING POSSESSES GREAT POWER. IF PRACTICED WITH THE RIGHT INTENTION IT MAKES ONE A FRIEND OF GOD – TERTULLIAN

---

28   FASTING BRINGS PROTECTION FOR YOUR CHILDREN

When Ezra and Israel were going back into the land to rebuild the temple, they needed to cross a dangerous path in the wilderness to go to their destination. They needed the protection of God rather than the protection of the king. Therefore they sought God for protection by fasting:

> *Then **I proclaimed a fast there**, at the river of Ahava, that we might afflict ourselves before our God, **to seek of him a right way for us, and for our little ones, and for all our substance.** For I was ashamed to require of the king a band of soldiers and horsemen to help us against the enemy in the way: because we had spoken unto the king, saying, The hand of our God is upon all them for good that seek him; but his power and his wrath is against all them that forsake him. **So we fasted and besought our God for this: and he was intreated of us.***
>
> Ezra 8:21-23

29   FASTING PAVES THE WAY FOR A SAFE CROSSING INTO OUR DESTINY

Fasting not only gives protection but gives a safe crossing into your promised land. Once again we can draw from Ezra's experience: he was on his way to rebuild the temple of God. That was his purpose and destiny. He also had families and young ones under his care. How was he going to get to his destiny without casualties of war? He sought God in fasting. It is a shame today that many are entering into their destiny but at a great cost. Some have lost families, homes, monies, marriages and children. The life of Ezra teaches us to embrace fasting, faith and God's Word to protect our coming-in and our going-out. Your family, your home and your health do not need to be the casualties of war. Many have entered their Promised Land without certain facets of their life that were important for them. This is why we must draw from the lesson of Ezra and Nehemiah.

(Scripture References: Ezra 8:21, Judges 20:26-28).

30   FASTING INVOKES AND ACTIVATES THE HAND OF GOD OVER YOUR LIFE

Ezra and company were crossing the desert with huge amounts of gold, silver and other precious offerings to build the temple of God. They were concerned that bandits and terrorists would hijack them and take all that they carried. How would they cross safely with such a precious cargo? We are talking of billions of dollars worth of gold in today's currency. Ezra had enough sense to fast. See the amount of gold, silver and monies they were carrying with them:

So we fasted and besought our God for this: and he was intreated of us. Then I separated twelve of the chief of the priests, Sherebiah, Hashabiah, and ten of their brethren with them, And weighed unto them the silver, and the gold, and the vessels, even the offering of the house of our God, which the king, and his counsellors, and his lords, and all Israel there *present, had offered: I even weighed unto their hand six hundred and fifty talents of silver, and silver vessels an hundred talents, and of gold an hundred talents; Also twenty basons of gold, of a thousand drams; and two vessels of fine copper, precious as gold. And I said unto them, Ye are holy unto the Lord; the vessels are holy also; and the silver and the gold are a freewill offering unto the Lord God of your fathers. Watch ye, and keep them, until ye weigh them before the chief of the priests and the Levites, and chief of the fathers of Israel, at Jerusalem, in the chambers of the house of the Lord. So took the priests and the Levites the weight of the silver, and the gold, and the vessels, to bring them to Jerusalem unto the house of our God. Then we departed from the river of Ahava on the twelfth day of the first month, to go unto Jerusalem: and the hand of our God was upon us, **and he delivered us from the hand of the enemy, and of such as lay in wait by the way.***

EZRA 8:23-31

Word had gotten out that they were carrying billions of dollars worth of gold and monies. The thieves, terrorists and hijackers laid in wait but all their plans failed; they could not get their hands on the stuff because God's hand was on them. Fasting provoked the hand of God and removed the hand of Satan.

Nehemiah went on a fast after he heard that the walls of Jerusalem had been destroyed. After Nehemiah's time of fasting, the King willingly obliged and donated all kinds of materials to rebuild the walls. Letters were given to Nehemiah in order to procure materials from different departments. Now look at the words of Nehemiah:

*'And a letter unto Asaph the keeper of the king's forest, that he may give me timber to make beams for the gates of the palace which appertained to the house, and for the wall of the city, and for the house that I shall enter into. And the king granted me, **according to the good hand of my God upon me.**'*

NEHEMIAH 2:8

When the good hand of God is upon you the bad hand of the devil is removed. Learn to fast today and see the good hand of God.

WHEREFORE LET US FORSAKE THE VAIN DOING OF THE MANY AND THEIR FALSE TEACHINGS, AND TURN UNTO THE WORD WHICH WAS DELIVERED UNTO US FROM THE BEGINNING, BEING SOBER UNTO PRAYER AND CONSTANT IN FASTINGS, ENTREATING THE ALL-SEEING GOD WITH SUPPLICATIONS THAT HE BRING US NOT INTO TEMPTATION, ACCORDING AS THE LORD SAID, THE SPIRIT IS INDEED WILLING, BUT THE FLESH IS WEAK – POLYCARP

---

31 FASTING EMPOWERS US TO TASTE AND SEE THAT THE LORD IS GOOD

Fasting is abstaining from the tasting of natural food, in order to taste the Lord. When you taste Him you will have tasted of His goodness. Letting go of natural food to engage in spiritual food from heaven will sustain and propel your wellbeing and future. Ezekiel ate the scroll that God told him to eat before he could speak to the nation and the taste of the scroll had the taste of honey. When Elijah was fed by an angel – who baked a cake for him – he went in the strength of that baked cake for forty days without eating natural man made food. The tasting of the Lord is sweet as the honeycomb and gives strength to your life.

32 FASTING AVERTS JUDGMENT

Wicked King Ahab, who was married to the evil Prophetess Jezebel, did much wickedness and abominable acts in the land. This evil couple were into witchcraft, idolatry and murder. Therefore when Elijah pronounced judgment over him, his wife and his sons, he quickly proclaimed a fast and humbled himself before God. The judgement pronounced over him and his family were not light and in his fear he turned to God. Look at what God then said to Elijah.

And the word of the Lord came to Elijah the Tishbite, saying, Seest thou how Ahab humbleth himself before me? because he humbleth himself before me, I will not bring the evil in his days: but in his son's days will I bring the evil upon his house

1 KINGS 21:28-29

Ahab averted judgment in his days through fasting.

Jonah was sent by God to deliver the word of judgment to the city of Nineveh. The wickedness of Nineveh was full and had come up to God. After initially refusing to go to Nineveh, Jonah finally made his way there to deliver the word of the Lord:

And Jonah began to enter into the city a day's journey, and he cried, and said, Yet forty days, and Nineveh shall be overthrown. So the people of Nineveh believed God, and proclaimed a fast, and put on sackcloth, from the greatest of them even to the least of them. For word came unto the king of Nineveh, and he arose from his throne, and he laid his robe from him, and covered him with sackcloth, and sat in ashes. And he caused it to be proclaimed and published through Nineveh by the decree of the king and his nobles, saying, Let neither man nor beast, herd nor flock, taste any thing: let them not feed, nor drink water: But let man and beast be covered with sackcloth, and cry mightily unto God: yea, let them turn every one from his evil way, and from the violence that is in their hands. Who can tell if God will turn and repent, and turn away from his fierce anger, that we perish not? And God saw their works, that they turned from their evil way; and God repented of the evil, that he had said that he would do unto them; and he did it not.

JONAH 3:4-10

Judgement was due for the Ninevites. However through fasting and prayer they averted judgement. All over the Scriptures you will see the people of God averting judgement by fasting. Through the book of Joel we see that when judgement was imminent, God said this:

Therefore also now, saith the Lord, turn ye even to me with all your heart, and with fasting, and with weeping, and with mourning: And rend your heart, and not your garments, and turn unto the Lord your God: for he is gracious and merciful, slow to anger, and of great kindness, and repenteth him of the evil. Who knoweth if he will return and repent, and leave a blessing behind him

JOEL 2:12-14

Fasting invokes the mercy of God to reverse judgement; God is ever merciful and kind. That is His nature and if we fall before Him in humility and fasting then the judgement that was due to us will be reversed.

33   FASTING WILL ENFORCE 'THY KINGDOM OF GOD AND THINE WILL BE DONE ON EARTH AS IT IS IN HEAVEN'

Esther had been on a three-day fast to appear before the King, who hadn't called her in thirty days. She gave these instructions:

Go, gather together all the Jews that are present in Shushan, and fast ye for me, and neither eat nor drink three days, night or day: I also and my maidens will fast likewise; and so will I go in unto the king, which is not according to the law: and if I perish, I perish

ESTHER 4:16

Esther was totally aware that anyone who went before the King without being summoned was in danger of losing his life unless the King held out his golden scepter. What did she do?

On the third day during her fast, Esther put on her royal robes and stood in the inner court of the palace, in front of the King's hall. The King was sitting on his royal throne in the hall, '*over against the **gate** of the house*' (Esther 5:1). Gates in the Old Testament were places where transactions took place, be it spiritual or physical. When the King saw Queen Esther standing in the court, he was pleased and held out the golden scepter of favor that was in his hand. So Esther approached and touched the tip of the scepter.

Now please notice the response of the king:

> *What wilt thou, queen Esther? and what is thy request? it shall be even given thee to the half of the kingdom.*
>
> ESTHER 5:3

We know the kingdom of Persia at the time stretched over 127 provinces from India all the way to Ethiopia. To be given half of that is a massive piece of real estate and riches. All that Esther did was fast and the kingdom was handed to her. However Esther was not so much interested in an earthly kingdom but to the kingdom of God as it pertained to Israel; her fasting stopped the kingdom of darkness from advancing and obliterating Israel, allowing the kingdom of God to be established in the lives of the Jewish people in 127 provinces. This is why, when you fast and pray, call for the kingdom of God to be established in your home, finances, cities, churches and ministries.

> **One important point to bear in mind**

In what is commonly known as the Lord's Prayer, Jesus said: "*Thy kingdom come. Thy will be done in earth, as it is in heaven*" (Matthew 6:10). Jesus did not say: 'Thy **will be done** and thy kingdom come.' No, it was the other way around! You may ask, 'What's the difference?' There is a big difference. In order for the will to be done, the kingdom has to be operational first; whatever kingdom is prevailing in the heavenlies is what will permeate in the earth.

'Kingdom' is a combination of two words, 'king' and 'domain'. Therefore the kingdom is the domain or dominion of the king. Wherever the domain of the king stretches to is the domain where his will can be enforced and executed. If he wanted his will to be exerted in another piece of real estate or land, he would have to annex it into his kingdom. Most of the time this was done by military conquest, by the king sending his troops in with weapons to annex the land and its people. *If the kingdom did not come thus far the will cannot be done.* Our weapons to bring the kingdom of God into place are fasting and prayer.

Many times the will of God in a place is subverted because the kingdom in residence sets the rule of law and operation. For example, if you look at countries in Asia or the Middle East where the kingdom of darkness, idolatry and anti-Christ religion are prevalent, you will not see the freedom or springing-up of churches like you would see in other parts of the world. What you will see in such places are the persecution of believers, prohibition of conversions, and restrictions imposed upon the church; we see the most powerful entity in the earth, the church, being stifled and persecuted by the kingdom of darkness. Looking back at Esther chapter 3, Haman had succeeded in legislating the killing of all Jews as the law of the land but it was through fasting, prayer and Queen Esther presenting herself to the King that new, superseding legislation was enacted; through fasting she pulled down the authority and kingdom of darkness, brought in the kingdom of God and established the goodness of the will of God for all Jews throughout the 127 provinces.

Whatever kingdom is in power is what makes the rule. We want the kingdom of God over our vicinity and we establish that with fasting and prayer. Trying to legislate without first having an invasion of the kingdom of God is like trying to legislate to build churches in certain countries in the Middle East. What is the likelihood of that happening? Very unlikely! Although it looks like a violation of human rights, nonetheless it is a reality in such nations. In order for this phenomenon to change, things have to change in the spirit and this can only be done by fasting and prayer. Fasting and prayer are the weapons that remove darkness and bring in the kingdom of God. Remember in the great sixth chapter of the book of Matthew – where Jesus unveiled the unbeatable trinity of prayer, giving and fasting – He finishes by declaring this:

But seek ye first the kingdom of God, and his righteousness; and all these things shall be added unto you.

MATTHEW 6:33

It is through fasting, prayer and giving that we are seeking and establishing His kingdom and when we do, all the rest will follow.

34 FASTING IS AGGRESSIVE FAITH IN ACTION TO DO VIOLENCE IN THE KINGDOM OF DARKNESS AND TAKE WHAT IS YOURS

Jesus told us that the violent takes it by force (Matthew 11:12). We know that we do not wrestle against flesh and blood, so how do we release aggressive and violent faith? After all the confession and praying, fasting adds a dimension of aggressiveness to our faith. In the ninth chapter of Mark we see a father whose son was grievously tormented by the devil; he had approached the disciples for help but they were powerless. Therefore he went to Jesus and asked Him, *'If you can do anything, please have compassion and help us,'* to which Jesus replied, *'If you can believe, all things are possible to him that believes.'* Faith makes all things possible! Then after having delivered the boy from the tormenting spirit, the disciples asked Jesus in private the cause of their ineffectiveness. Jesus replied, *'This kind can come forth by nothing, but by prayer and fasting'* (Mark 9:23-29). Jesus had already fasted and was coming down from a prayer retreat; aggressive faith was running through Him and He restored the son back to his father. When you fast you are increasing the intensity and aggression of your faith against the devil to reclaim what he has stolen from you.

35 FASTING WILL CAUSE THE GOLDEN SCEPTER OF FAVOR TO BE STRETCHED OVER YOUR LIFE. IT GIVES YOU FAVOR WITH GOD AND FAVOR WITH MAN

Esther had been on a three-day total fast and went before the King. No one was allowed to go before the King without an invitation. Only if the golden scepter was extended can one approach the King, otherwise, death was inevitable. Esther took a great risk to go before the King but she had made up her mind, 'If I perish, then I perish'. However she had been seeking the Lord with Mordecai and others, pressing into God on a three-day total fast. When she stepped before the King to plead her case, the King stretched forth the golden scepter of favor; in a place of death, favor was released. Favor simply means **preferential treatment**. As you embark on a life of fasting, the golden scepter of favor will be stretched out to you, resulting in you having favor with God and with man.

(Scripture references: Esther 5:1, 2, Esther 8:4,
Nehemiah 2:4-8, Daniel 1:8, 9).

36 FASTING WILL FORCE THE HAND OF THE ENEMY TO RELENT AND LET GO

So we fasted and besought our God for this: and he was intreated of us... Then we departed from the river of Ahava on the twelfth day of the first month, to go unto Jerusalem: **and the hand of our God was upon us, and he delivered us from the hand of the enemy,** *and of such as lay in wait by the way.'*

EZRA 8:23, 31

You can clearly see from the words of Ezra that fasting invokes the hand of God, which forces the hand of the enemy to move back from his plans.

37 FASTING ENABLES YOU TO TAP INTO THE SPIRIT OF REVELATION AND UNDERSTANDING

I am sure you remember the story of Daniel and his three Hebrew friends when they first were deported to Babylon: knowing that the food in Nebuchadnezar's school of Art were offered to idols, Daniel purposed in his heart that he would not defile himself with the King's portion. Therefore he requested of the eunuchs that he would only eat pulse. The latter was nervous as he realized that his head was on the line if Daniel and his friends looked malnourished. Daniel assured him that all would be well and asked him to prove them for the next few days. After ten days on the pulse fast, they looked better than those on the king's portion of wine and meat. Therefore Daniel stayed on that fast for three years because this was the term they had to finish before standing before Nebuchadnezar. Having stayed on that fast for three years, we notice a remarkable statement:

*As for these four children, **God gave them knowledge and skill in all
learning and wisdom: and Daniel had understanding in all visions and
dreams.** Now at the end of the days that the king had said he should
bring them in, then the prince of the eunuchs brought them in before
Nebuchadnezzar.*

DANIEL 1:17-18

Notice they walked in supernatural knowledge and revelation after the
fast. If it was not for the spirit of revelation, Daniel and his three colleagues
would have died with all the wise men and soothsayers of Babylon. He told
Nebuchadnezzar of the dream which the latter had, but had himself forgotten.
Now that is serious revelation! As you begin to fast you will receive fresh
revelations from the Word. You will also receive supernatural revelations
as you go through life's complicated situations. As ministers, when you
begin to fast, the spirit of revelation will unveil to you the utterance and
revelation gifts.

(Scripture references: Daniel 1:12-20, Daniel 9:3, 21, Daniel 10).

A HOLY AND LAWFUL FAST HAS THREE ENDS IN VIEW.
TO MORTIFY AND SUBDUE THE FLESH, THAT IT MAY NOT
WANTON, OR TO PREPARE THE BETTER FOR PRAYER AND
HOLY MEDITATION; OR TO GIVE EVIDENCE OF HUMBLING
OURSELVES BEFORE GOD – JOHN CALVIN

---

38   FASTING WILL DESTROY GENERATIONAL CURSES

What do we mean by generational curses? We mean a trait that is prevalent
in your lineage and recurs over and over again from previous generations to
the present generation. The only reason it is called a generational curse is
because it has been allowed to fester through from one generation to the next
without anyone breaking it. If you make a generational decision to break it by
the Word, the blood, prayer and fasting, whatever it is can be broken. Certain
families have particular traits, weaknesses and proclivities in their lives.

Some are good but when we talk about generational curses, we are talking about something negative, something detrimental. A curse is an invisible tracking device and a time-bomb that will detonate at some period in someone's generation. There are people who know that come what may, diabetes will eventually catch up with them because it runs rampant in their family. So diabetes is like a ticking time-bomb that will eventually detonate in their lives. For others it could be heart disease or mental illness.

How is this possible then? The key word is 'generational' from which we get the word 'genes' and 'genetic'. Something in their genetics has been programmed to act in a particular manner. So how does fasting destroy that? I want to bring to your attention the time when Jesus came down from the Mount of Transfiguration; an interesting event took place where a man brought his son – who was a lunatic – to be healed, but the disciples could not do it. This means that the disciples tried but the result was not a success. The man came to Jesus and said, '*I brought my son to your disciples and they could not cure him.*' Jesus then dealt with the situation, rebuked the devil and the boy was delivered. After seeing what had transpired, the disciples took Jesus aside privately and asked him, '*Why couldn't we cast the devil out?*' Jesus replied, '*...this kind goeth not out but by prayer and fasting*' (Matthew 17:21). I want you to notice the word, 'kind' which in Greek is 'genos' from which we get the English words, 'genes', 'genesis' and 'genetics'. The reason the disciples could not cure or cast the devil out of the son was because something was in his genes and genetics.

So many times we have prayed for people and they leave our presence, helplessly knowing that nothing has changed. Why? Because there is something in their genesis and genes that requires power to be dislodged. We see in the Scriptures that everything reproduces after its kind. If you want to reproduce another kind then you must be connected to another kind: the son of the father came in contact with the Son of the Father and a new genetic line started for this young man. We need to understand there are infirmities which are lodged in some people's genesis, genes and generation which can only be destroyed through fasting, prayer and standing on the Word.

In the book of Esther, we see a man by the name of Haman who was an Agagite. He made much trouble for the Jews. The question we have to ask ourselves is, 'How in the world, was there still an Agagite, after God told Saul to kill all the Amalekites, which would include Agag the king?' Well Saul did not kill them all: he spared Agag. We see generations later he came to be a stumbling block for the Jews, putting them under a death sentence all the way from India to Ethiopia. It was through the fasting of Mordecai and Esther that this generational problem was rooted out. All the sons of Haman were executed so that they could not be a problem generationally again:

...and the decree was given at Shushan; and they hanged Haman's ten sons.

ESTHER 9:14

Every genetic disease or every generational calamity tracking you will be destroyed as you learn to fast.

(Scripture References: Mark 9:17-29, Esther 7:10).

39 FASTING WILL APTLY PREPARE YOU FOR MINISTRY PROVING TO YOU THE POTENCY OF YOUR CALLING, GIVING EVIDENCES TO THE WORLD AND THE DEVIL OF THE VALIDITY OF YOUR COMMISSION

When Paul was an old man, he spoke to Timothy as a son in the faith. He uttered these instructions to him, which we also take to heart:

*But watch thou in all things, endure afflictions, do the work of an evangelist, **make full proof of thy ministry**.*

2 TIMOTHY 4:5

In other words, 'Timothy, your ministry must have evidences'. There has to be outward workings of the inward call. The purpose of evidence is to stop the mouth of the accuser. Too many Christians today have a title but little proof; the titles are big but the evidences are very small. We must be proof-producers in our ministry. According to the dictionary, evidence means:

❖ The available body of facts or information indicating whether a belief or proposition is true or valid.

❖ In regards to the Law it is information given personally, drawn from a document, or in the form of material objects, tending or used to establish facts in a legal investigation.

❖ Information presented in testimony that is used to persuade the fact finder (judge or jury) to decide the case for one side or the other.

❖ Signs, indications.

Without evidence, your ministry is not valid. Does that sound hard? It is the truth nonetheless. Without proof and evidence, your commission is nothing but cheap words. To make full proof of your ministry you must provide evidence on three levels:

❖ To the world – to validate your call.

❖ To the devil – to shut him up.

❖ To yourself – to boost your confidence.

⟩ Jesus had proof

*Ye men of Israel, hear these words; Jesus of Nazareth, **a man approved of God among you by miracles and wonders and signs, which God did by him in the midst of you, as ye yourselves also know***

ACTS 2:22

⟩ Paul had proof

For I will not dare to speak of any of those things which Christ hath not wrought by me, to make the Gentiles obedient, by word and deed, Through mighty signs and wonders, by the power of the Spirit of God; so that from Jerusalem, and round about unto Illyricum, I have fully preached the gospel of Christ.

ROMANS 15:18-19

And God wrought special miracles by the hands of Paul: So that from his body were brought unto the sick handkerchiefs or aprons, and the diseases departed from them, and the evil spirits went out of them.

ACTS 19:11-12

> Peter had proof

Insomuch that they brought forth the sick into the streets, and laid them on beds and couches, that at the least the shadow of Peter passing by might overshadow some of them. There came also a multitude out of the cities round about unto Jerusalem, bringing sick folks, and them which were vexed with unclean spirits: and they were healed every one.

ACTS 5:15-16

Where are your evidences? Jesus was a man approved of God by miracles as were Peter, Paul and others. How do we get this kind of proof and approval? Paul tells the Corinthian saints that one of the ways to commend or approve ourselves as ministers is through fasting:

But in all things approving ourselves as the ministers of God, in much patience, in afflictions, in necessities, in distresses, In stripes, in imprisonments, in tumults, in labours, in watchings, in fastings.

2 CORINTHIANS 6:4-5

Therefore there is a degree of preparation for ministry that comes with fasting; if you do not fast as a minister, then the results that you experience will be limited. You might think you have results but it will not be to the fullness of what God has for you. When Paul was called by Jesus to be the minister to the Gentiles on the road to Damascus, he immediately went on a three-day total fast (Acts 9:1-14). Paul and Barnabas were further set apart and commissioned for the great work and next phase of their ministry after a period of fasting and ministering unto the Lord:

Now there were in the church that was at Antioch certain prophets and teachers; as Barnabas, and Simeon that was called Niger, and Lucius of Cyrene, and Manaen, which had been brought up with Herod the tetrarch, and Saul. As they ministered to the Lord, and fasted, the Holy Ghost said, Separate me Barnabas and Saul for the work whereunto I have called them. And when they had fasted and prayed, and laid their hands on them, they sent them away. So they, being sent forth by the Holy Ghost, departed unto Seleucia; and from thence they sailed to Cyprus.

ACTS 13:1-4

As great as Bible schools, theological degrees and hermeneutics are, they are limited in their preparation if that is all you have had; you need spiritual power to deal with spiritual problems and spiritual entities that will come against you. The Lord Jesus received the testimony from heaven that He was the Son of God, was full and led by the Spirit and yet did not return in the power of the Spirit until after He had fasted and won the battle against Satan in the wilderness:

And Jesus returned in the power of the Spirit into Galilee.

LUKE 4:14

Even Nehemiah, on his way to rebuild the broken walls of Jerusalem did not do so without the aid and preparation of fasting, '*And it came to pass, when I heard these words, that I sat down and wept, and mourned certain days, and fasted, and prayed before the God of heaven*' (Nehemiah 1:4).

Ministry is rebuilding the broken walls of people's lives. If Nehemiah constantly fasted to rebuild the broken walls, you and I should imitate him in order to help mend the broken lives of people today. Books prepare you mentally, mentorship prepares you experientially, Bible school prepares you ministerially but fasting prepares you spiritually. There are some depths in God that you will only access when you fast.

(Scripture references: Luke 4:1-14, Acts 9:1-9, Acts 13:1-4, Nehemiah 1:4).

FASTING WILL PROVE TO YOU, THE WORLD AND THE DEVIL THE VALIDITY OF YOUR CALLING AND COMMISSION

40 FASTING IS DECLARING WAR ON THE SPIRIT OF UNBELIEF AND SHARPENING YOUR FAITH

When Jesus was asked by His disciples why they could not cast the devil out of the lunatic son, He replied, *'Because of your unbelief... howbeit this kind cometh not out but by prayer and fasting.'* Fasting also declares war on the unbelief that is lodged in a believer and hones our faith to obtain results.

(Scripture reference: Mark 9:17-29).

41 FASTING IS MAKING DEMANDS UPON THE SUPPLY OF THE SPIRIT

The supply of the Spirit is always available but our problem is a lack of demand upon that limitless supply. If there is no demand there will not be any supply. When we fast we are aggressively making demands upon the power supply of the Spirit. Jesus did this constantly and aggressively, which is why there was a constant flow of the miraculous in His ministry. If you want a constant flow of high-voltage power flowing through your ministry to the world then you have to make aggressive demands in fasting. A lackadaisical attitude in regards to fasting and prayer will not aid you in releasing high-voltage power. The Scripture says of Jesus:

*And straightway **the fountain of her blood was dried up;** and she felt in her body that she was healed of that plague. And Jesus, **immediately knowing in himself that virtue had gone out of him...***
MARK 5:29-30

*And they that were vexed with unclean spirits: and they were healed. And the whole multitude sought to touch him: **for there went virtue out of him, and healed them all.***
LUKE 6:18-19

If virtue did not go out of Jesus then all those who came with their infirmities would have left with their infirmities. The reason why they were healed is because of the virtue that left His body. Fasting enables you to be a carrier of virtues; it renders your spirit man as a conductor and your body as the cable through which Holy Ghost electricity can flow and bring light to those in darkness. I don't know about you but I want to be the cable and conductor that brings power to people.

(Scripture references: Mark 9:17-29, Philippians 1:19).

FASTING IS HANDS OFF, SATAN! AND HANDS ON, GOD!

42 FASTING IS PREPARING THE WAY OF THE LORD TO MOVE

John the Baptist, a man acquainted with a fasting lifestyle, prepared the way for Jesus. Your faith and your prayer prepares the way for a move of God. Equally important is your fast, as it prepares the way for a move of the Spirit. We see this prior to Pentecost when the disciples had gathered in praying and fasting: all of a sudden the Holy Spirit came in as a rushing mighty wind. Fasting is the catalyst to propel the wind of the Spirit.

❖ Anna fasted and prepared the way for the incarnation of Jesus to become a reality.

❖ John the Baptist fasted and prepared the way for the grand entry of the ministry of Jesus.

❖ The early church fasted and prepared the way for the grand entry of the Spirit on the day of Pentecost.

❖ Cornelius and Peter fasted, preparing the way for the grand entry of the Gospel to the Gentile world.

(Scripture references: Isaiah 40:3; Malachi 3:1; Matthew 3:3).

43 FASTING WILL BRING REST AND QUIETNESS TO YOUR REALM

After Jehoshaphat had fasted, because of the great multitude that was coming against him, God fought for him and gave him the victory. The ripples of this victory went a long way and brought the fear of God over the enemies of Judah. Thus the children of Judah had rest and quietness:

And the fear of God was on all the kingdoms of those countries, when they had heard that the Lord fought against the enemies of Israel. So the realm of Jehoshaphat was quiet: for his God gave him rest round about.

2 CHRONICLES 20:29-30

44 FASTING EMPOWERS YOU TO MAINTAIN YOUR CUTTING EDGE

There is an interesting event that took place with Elisha and the sons of the prophets who wanted a bigger place for themselves. They came to Elisha and told him, '*The place where we are is too small for us. Let's go to Jordan and get ourselves some beam in order to build this bigger premise.*' After some convincing, Elisha went with them. As they were busy cutting down wood, one of the sons of the prophets lost his axehead and lamented to Elisha, '*Alas, this axehead was borrowed!*' (2Kings 6:1-5). If the man lost his axehead this would mean he lost his cutting edge.

I want you to notice that the sons of the prophets had expansion and growth in mind. It is a noble thing to want to expand, as the Scripture clearly teaches us to '*enlarge the place of your tent*' (Isaiah 54:2). There are four very important points for you to learn as you embark on growth and expansion in your life:

❯ 1. Anointing

In order to expand, they went to the River Jordan, which symbolizes the anointing. This is where Elisha got his double portion and Jesus was baptized.

> 2. Structure

They went to the river to cut down beams. The cutting of beams speaks of structure. This is equally important to the anointing; you can have the anointing but without structure you will not go far.

> 3. Sharpness

Many times, ministers in their pursuit of growth and expansion lose their cutting edge. The man lost his axehead; he lost his cutting edge. How about you? Have you still got your cutting edge?

Why do many lose their cutting edge in their quest for growth?

Looseness – For the axehead to fall in the river it had to be loosed from the handle, a consequence of:

❖ Looseness in lifestyle.
❖ Looseness in prayer.
❖ Looseness in fasting.
❖ Looseness in the Word.

Looseness is a result of broken focus, skewed priorities and an element of pride: you think you can get away with looseness and no one will notice.

Precedence – Focus and priorities are keys to maintaining your cutting edge. As you embark on the expansion of your life and ministry never forget the things which are focal points: God must always be first; the Word, fasting, prayer and cultivating our relationship with the Holy Spirit must always be the focal point. The man was busy cutting beams next to the river but was not in the river. The structure became more important than the river.

Temperance – His axehead flew off the handle. 'To fly off the handle' is an English idiom meaning to lose one's temper, to lose control. Anger and rage will short circuit the anointing in your life, eventually. Lack of self-control and a violent temper are detrimental to your call and will lead to immorality of all sorts. Paul said, '*But I keep under my body, and bring it into subjection: lest that by any means, when I have preached to others, I myself should be a castaway*' (1 Corinthians 9:27). This is where fasting plays an important role since it is the crucifying of your flesh.

Appearance – The moment he lost the axehead the man cried, '*Alas master, it was borrowed!*' Many times we lose our cutting edge because we have borrowed someone else's axehead, pretending we are the rightful owner. Nobody knew it was borrowed until he lost it. Are you doing what God told you to do or are you doing something that you saw a minister friend do? Can you say, like the apostle Paul, '*I was not disobedient unto the heavenly vision*'? (Acts 26:19). Have you borrowed your vision or is it a heavenly vision? Many times we borrow other people's vision in order to keep up appearances; this is very dangerous. Safety is doing what God tells you to do.

> **4. Mentor**

The moment he lost the axehead, he cried, '*Alas master, it was borrowed!*' To regain his axehead he talked to Elisha, the mentor, the man of God, the prophet and spiritual father. One of the key things that will help you maintain your cutting edge is your close connection to your spiritual father or mentor. Elisha was crucial for this man to regain his axehead; having a man or woman of God as a mentor in your life is crucial for you to maintain or regain your cutting edge.

I totally believe in fasting as a tool to keep sharpening your spiritual and ministerial edge. Like Paul we must approve ourselves in fasting.

(Scripture references: 2 Kings 6:1-7, 2 Corinthians 6:4-5).

BOOKS PREPARE YOU MENTALLY, MENTORSHIP PREPARES YOU EXPERIENTIALLY, BIBLE SCHOOL PREPARES YOU MINISTERIALLY BUT FASTING PREPARES YOU SPIRITUALLY

---

45   FASTING SHARPENS YOUR FAITH AND EMPOWERS YOUR CONFESSION TO BE AS A DOUBLE-EDGED SWORD AS WELL AS A LASER BEAM TO CUT THROUGH THE ENEMY'S LINE OF DEFENSE

People look at what Jesus did on the Mount of Temptation and nonchalantly assume that if Jesus simply spoke the Word and won the victory over Satan then we can do the same thing too. Today we have many people confessing the Word but not seeing the results that Jesus had. Why was the confession of Jesus so potent in cutting down the enemy? Because Jesus confessed under the influence of fasting. Remember, He was led by the Spirit to be tempted of the devil and He fasted, eating nothing for forty days. The first thing He told Satan was, 'Man shall not live by bread alone but by every word that proceeds out of the mouth of God.' At that place, Jesus was literally living not on bread but on the Word. Fasting is living on the Word, the true bread from heaven, which is life-giving, powerful and sharper than a double-edged sword. Therefore the confessions of the Word from the lips of Jesus, under the influence of fasting did major damage to the works of the devil.

(Scripture References: Luke 4:2-13, Hebrews 4:12, 2 Chronicles 20:27).

46   FASTING DOWNLOADS THE WILL OF GOD INTO PHYSICAL MANIFESTATIONS

The will of God for our lives is always the best thing and the path of victory. Paul tells us, '*Wherefore be ye not unwise, but understanding what the will of the Lord is*' (Ephesians 5:17). It is our responsibility to discover and know the will of God and plan of God for our lives. This is revealed from two sources:

The Logos – the Bible, the voice of the Word, giving the general or standard will of God for all believers;

The Rhema – the voice of the Spirit, or the breathed Word, unveiling the specific will of God for a believer.

However, just because we know the will of God, it does not mean that it is automatically activated in our lives. We see a lot of things in the Scriptures concerning the will of God for victory in regards to His people and yet they tasted failure and calamity over and over. You can mentally know the will of God yet physically not experience it; many know it is God's will for them to be healed and yet they remain sick; many know it is God's will for them to prosper and yet are broke. Israel and Saul knew it was the will of God for them to defeat Goliath but they were living in fear of him. The will of God is not automatic: you have to know how to download it. The disciples knew that the will of God was '*to tarry at Jerusalem for the Holy Spirit to be endued with power from on high*'. So did they just hang around and kill some time. No! They were assembled in one place in one accord, in prayer and fasting. We've already seen that the disciples were fasting until the day of Pentecost; Daniel, in captivity in Babylon, is another great example of how to download the will of God:

> *In the first year of Darius the son of Ahasuerus, of the seed of the Medes, which was made king over the realm of the Chaldeans; In the first year of his reign **I Daniel understood by books the number of the years, whereof the word of the Lord came to Jeremiah the prophet**, that he would accomplish seventy years in the desolations of Jerusalem. And I set my face unto the Lord God, to seek by prayer and supplications, with fasting, and sackcloth, and ashes.*
>
> DANIEL 9:1-3

Daniel happened to be reading the book of Jeremiah and discovered that God's people were only meant to be in Babylon for seventy years; after that period, the will of God was for them to be free and back in Jerusalem. Have you ever read something in the Bible and then looked at your life, only to see a discrepancy between what you have read and what you are experiencing? Often this is where so many believers are! There is a difference between the *revealed* will of God and the *manifested* will of God; it is possible to know the revealed will of God and not see that will manifested. Ask Moses!

Ask the ten spies! So what did Daniel do? He set himself to seek the Lord in prayers and fasting. The question to ask is, 'If the will of God was already revealed in the book why did he have to pray and fast?' Because it is not automatic! God's will must be downloaded to the earth through faith (standing upon and believing his Word), praying and fasting.

Are you following the example of Daniel and Anna the prophetess who fasted and downloaded the already-revealed will of God?

(Scripture references: Daniel 9, 2 Chronicles 20, Mark 9:17-29, Judges 20).

THERE IS A DIFFERENCE BETWEEN THE REVEALED WILL OF GOD AND THE MANIFESTED WILL OF GOD

47 FASTING FORCES FOCUS

When you fast you are focusing on the Lord for specific answers to specific problems. Many times, because we are so busy in life we do not invest the time to obtain the answer to our problems. Then, because we do not have the answer we feel flustered and ruffled. However when we are fasting, we are putting ourselves in a place of focus, making a demand upon our spirit man to search the inward parts of our innermost being for the answer from the Holy Spirit. Fasting will shut down the many voices of the world, clamoring for our attention and sensitize us to the Lord.

FASTING IS FOCUSING UPON THE LORD FOR SPECIFIC ANSWERS TO SPECIFIC PROBLEMS

48 FASTING MAKES A DEMAND UPON YOU TO SEARCH THE INWARD PARTS OF YOUR INNERMOST BEING FOR THE ANSWER FROM THE HOLY SPIRIT

Everything that you need to know is already inside of you; whether you realize it or not you are already carrying the answer that you are looking for. Unfortunately, many are running helter-skelter, looking, searching for an answer that's already within their reach. The Psalmist said, '*...I commune with mine own heart: and my spirit made diligent search*' (Psalm 77:6). Fasting is like shining a torch in your inner man, lighting up the chambers to see the answer that is hidden there. If you are to search anywhere, search within yourself, a spiritual being, inhabited by the Holy Spirit Himself. Job tells us that God has put '*wisdom in the inward parts*' (Job 38:36); connect this with: '*The spirit of man is the candle of the Lord, searching all the inward parts of the belly.*' (Proverbs 20:27).

Fasting, therefore is a deliberate act on your part to stop running in search of an answer and to search the already-given answer from within; it is slowing down in order to *shine the torch*:

Behold, thou desirest truth in the inward parts: and in the hidden part thou shalt make me to know wisdom.

PSALM 51:6

FASTING IS PUTTING OURSELVES IN A PLACE OF FOCUS MAKING A DEMAND UPON OUR SPIRIT MAN TO SEARCH THE INWARD PARTS OF OUR INNERMOST BEING FOR THE ANSWER FROM THE HOLY SPIRIT

---

49 FASTING AMPLIFIES YOUR PRAYERS AND SUPERCHARGES YOUR PRAYER LIFE INTO A RICHER AND MORE EXPLOSIVE EXPERIENCE

In the Bible, humility is synonymous with fasting; the Psalmist said, 'I humbled my soul with fasting'. With that thought in mind, God himself tells us, *'If my people, which are called by my name, shall humble themselves, and pray, and seek my face, and turn from their wicked ways; then will I hear from heaven, and will forgive their sin, and will heal their land'* (2 Chronicles 7:14). This simply means if we fast and pray we will experience the healing virtues of God in our lands and communities. God also told the people, in the book of Isaiah that if they fasted with the proper motives here is what they can expect: *'Then shalt thou call, and the Lord shall answer; thou shalt cry, and he shall say, Here I am..."* (Isaiah 58:9). Truly, fasting will amplify your prayer life to be more productive.

(Scripture references: Psalm 35:13; 2 Chronicles 7:14; Isaiah 58:9).

UNDER SPECIAL DIFFICULTIES, OR WHEN IN GREAT
NEED OF, OR GREAT LONGINGS AFTER, ANY PARTICULAR
MERCY, FOR YOURSELF OR OTHERS, SET APART A DAY
FOR SECRET PRAYER AND FASTING BY YOURSELF ALONE
– JONATHAN EDWARDS

---

50 FASTING EXHIBITS YOUR TOTAL DEPENDENCE UPON THE HAND OF GOD RATHER THAN YOUR OWN HANDS

Jehoshaphat and Judah were in big trouble: their enemies had formed a conglomerate and were intent on destroying them. Jehoshaphat knew his soldiers and arsenal of weapons were no match for the assembly gathered against him. Therefore he called for the whole of Judah to fast and pray. In his prayer during the fast, he stated, *'O our God, wilt thou not judge them? for we have no might against this great company that cometh against us; neither know we what to do: but our eyes are upon thee'* (2 Chronicles 20:12).

Please note these words carefully: '*we do not know what to do but our eyes are upon you.*' Fasting is exhibiting your total dependence on God for deliverance, breakthrough and victory; it is knowing that there is nothing you alone can do to remedy the situation and only a move of God can bring about a positive change. We see the same attitude in the lives of Esther and Mordecai. When Israel was under a death assignment – concocted by Haman and signed by the King – they knew there was nothing that could be done in the natural to deliver Israel. Therefore they went on a fast, evidencing their dependence upon Jehovah to deliver them, and He did so. Many times in life you will face dire situations for which you have no answer: how will you respond? Do so by depending solely upon Him.

(2 Chronicles 20:12, Esther 4:12-16, Hebrews 12:2).

CHAPTER 10
101 BENEFITS OF FASTING

Section 3: Benefits 51-75

WE are now in the third part of the benefits of fasting. If you would only take up this tremendous weapon, like a man going through the jungle using a sword to cut through and make a path for himself, you will also cut through the blockages that are in your way to your desired destination.

51 FASTING WILL ENABLE YOU TO SAY, 'NOT BY MIGHT NOR BY POWER BUT BY MY SPIRIT, SAYS THE LORD'

It is not enough for you to shout over other people's victory: you need to have your own testimonies that will give hope to you and others in the future. You must come to the place where you can say, 'God did it before and He will do it again.' This is one benefit that fasting will give you – a testimony from your test. You will know it is not by your hand, your mind or your expertise that you were delivered but by pressing into God through fasting that the Almighty came out swinging on your behalf.

52 FASTING WILL CAUSE YOU TO TAP INTO THE WISDOM OF GOD AND MAKE YOU TEN-TIMES WISER THAN THOSE WHO COMPETE WITH YOU

We see this marvel in the lives of the Hebrew boys that were taken and deported from Judah to Babylon. Daniel had purposed in his heart that he would not defile and partake of King Nebuchadnezzar's daily portion of meat and wine because they were offered unto his idols. His three friends, who were renamed Shadrach, Meshach and Abed–nego (Daniel 1:7) also purposed to be on the chosen partial fast of Daniel.

They stayed on that fast for three years and after these three years they stood before Nebuchadnezzar to be evaluated for their knowledge, understanding, wisdom and skills. The outcome was:

> *Now at the end of the days that the king had said he should bring them in, then the prince of the eunuchs brought them in before Nebuchadnezzar. And the king communed with them; and among them all was found none like Daniel, Hananiah, Mishael, and Azariah: therefore stood they before the king. **And in all matters of wisdom and understanding, that the king enquired of them, he found them ten times better than all the magicians and astrologers that were in all his realm.***
>
> DANIEL 1:18-20

The wisdom of fasting gave them ten-times more wisdom than their contemporaries. It is not as if their contemporaries were unlearned. No, they all had the same indoctrinations and were being groomed to be the leaders and mighty men of the time:

> *Wisdom strengtheneth the wise more than ten mighty men which are in the city.*
>
> ECCLESIASTES 7:19

What set these Hebrews apart was that they were on a three-year partial fast, honoring God. He, in turn, gave them ten-times more wisdom than the most erudite scholars and politicians of the time: no one could compete with them, as mighty as others were; they were no match for the Hebrew boys.

53 FASTING WILL PROMPT THOSE WHO HAVE FORGOTTEN OR NEGLECTED YOU TO REMEMBER YOU AND HONOR YOU

On the third day of the total fast that Esther and Mordecai were on, the Bible says that the King could not sleep:

*On that night could not the king sleep, and he commanded to bring the book of records of the chronicles; and they were read before the king. And it was found written, that Mordecai had told of Bigthana and Teresh, two of the king's chamberlains, the keepers of the door, who sought to lay hand on the king Ahasuerus. And the king said, What **honour and dignity** hath been done to Mordecai for this? Then said the king's servants that ministered unto him, There is nothing done for him.*

ESTHER 6:1-3

During the fast, God caused the King to lose sleep and to remember the good deed that Mordecai did in the past. Sometimes we feel that our good deeds have not been rewarded and a sense of unfairness is lodged in our minds. I want to tell you that God will keep some people awake with your face and name on their mind. As you fast a shifting happens and people will remember to bless you; God will speak to people on your behalf! Those who have forgotten you will get a sudden jolt in their memory and remember you; they will not be able to sleep until they bless and remunerate you.

54 FASTING WILL CAUSE YOUR ENEMIES WHO PLANNED YOUR DESTRUCTION TO PARADE YOUR VICTORY

Haman was not satisfied that he was honored and preferred by the King. He wanted to see the end of Mordecai and the Jewish people:

*Haman said moreover, Yea, Esther the queen did let no man come in with the king unto the banquet that she had prepared but myself; and to morrow am I invited unto her also with the king. Yet all this availeth me nothing, so long as I see Mordecai the Jew sitting at the king's gate. Then said Zeresh his wife and all his friends unto him, **Let a gallows be made of fifty cubits high,** and to morrow speak thou unto the king that Mordecai may be hanged thereon: then go thou in merrily with the king unto the banquet. And the thing pleased Haman; and **he caused the gallows to be made.***

ESTHER 5:12-14

167

Haman is then summoned by the King who, upon his arrival, asks him a particular question that he believes can apply to none other but himself:

> *So Haman came in. And the king said unto him, What shall be done unto the man whom the king delighteth to honour? Now Haman thought in his heart, To whom would the king delight to do honour more than to myself? And Haman answered the king, For the man whom the king delighteth to honour,* **Let the royal apparel be brought which the king useth to wear, and the horse that the king rideth upon, and the crown royal which is set upon his head: And let this apparel and horse be delivered to the hand of one of the king's most noble princes, that they may array the man withal whom the king delighteth to honour,** *and bring him on horseback through the street of the city, and proclaim before him, Thus shall it be done to the man whom the king delighteth to honour. Then the king said to Haman, Make haste, and take the apparel and the horse, as thou hast said, and do even so to Mordecai the Jew, that sitteth at the king's gate: let nothing fail of all that thou hast spoken.* **Then took Haman the apparel and the horse, and arrayed Mordecai, and brought him on horseback through the street of the city, and proclaimed before him, Thus shall it be done unto the man whom the king delighteth to honour.** *And Mordecai came again to the king's gate. But Haman hasted to his house mourning, and having his head covered.*
>
> ESTHER 6:6-12

Haman, the enemy of Mordecai, who had erected gallows to hang him on, is now putting the King's garment on Mordecai. He put him on the royal horse and had him paraded in the city, heralding his greatness. Fasting will cause those who were planning your destruction to sing your praise and victory. They will hate every minute of it but they will have to do it because the hand of God is over your life as you fast. Mordecai went back to the King's place; Haman went to his home with his head covered in shame. Every shame that was meant for you will be upon those who hate you. As you fast you will no longer roam the streets of shame and disregard; instead, you will make your way to the royal court while your enemy dwells in shame.

55   FASTING BRINGS PROMOTION AND THE ELEVATION OF YOUR STATUS

Daniel led a life of fasting and was promoted; his three friends were also on a three-year partial fast and they were also promoted over the affairs of the Province of Babylon. Do you understand that when you are operating in ten-times more wisdom than your nearest competitor the battle is already won? Those who oppose you will be no match for you just as all the magicians were no match for the three Hebrew boys:

> Then **the king made Daniel a great man, and gave him many great gifts, and made him ruler over the whole province of Babylon,** and chief of the governors over all the wise men of Babylon. Then Daniel requested of the king, and he set Shadrach, Meshach, and Abed–nego, **over the affairs of the province of Babylon: but Daniel sat in the gate of the king.**
>
> DANIEL 2:48-49

> And all the rulers of the provinces, and the lieutenants, and the deputies, and officers of the king, helped the Jews; because the fear of Mordecai fell upon them. **For Mordecai was great in the king's house, and his fame went out throughout all the provinces: for this man Mordecai waxed greater and greater.**
>
> ESTHER 9:3-4

Those who are devoted to God and a life of fasting will wax greater and greater, just as Mordecai did: he looked to be a 'yesterday's forgotten man' but when God was through with him, he became the man of the hour.

56   FASTING WILL CAUSE THE WEAPON OF DESTRUCTION FASHIONED TO DESTROY YOU TO BE USED IN THE DESTRUCTION OF YOUR ENEMIES

And Harbonah, one of the chamberlains, said before the king, Behold also, the gallows fifty cubits high, which Haman had made for Mordecai, who had spoken good for the king, standeth in the house of Haman.

*Then the king said, **Hang him thereon. So they hanged Haman on the gallows that he had prepared for Mordecai.** Then was the king's wrath pacified.*

ESTHER 7:9-10

The gallows, which he had erected to hang Mordecai, became the means of his own destruction. Fasting has a way of causing ambushment, confusion and a reversal of situations.

57   FASTING WILL SHUT THE MOUTHS OF LIONS

When Daniel was unjustly thrown into the lion's den due to an evil plot, the King sought for ways to retract and deliver him. However the evil men who had devised the cunning plan reminded the King, *'Know, O king, that the law of the Medes and Persians is, That no decree nor statute which the king establisheth may be changed'* (Daniel 6:15). After exhausting all avenues and looking for loopholes, none were found and the King had no alternative but to command that Daniel be thrown into the lion's den. The evil men rubbed their hands together with glee knowing that this was the end of Daniel; they expected the lions to tear Daniel's body apart. However, although all loopholes were blocked, the King still had another card up his sleeve:

*Then the king went to his palace, and **passed the night fasting**: neither were instruments of musick brought before him: and his sleep went from him.*

DANIEL 6:18

What was the end result?

*Then the king arose very early in the morning, and went in haste unto the den of lions. And when he came to the den, he cried with a lamentable voice unto Daniel: and the king spake and said to Daniel, O Daniel, servant of the living God, is thy God, whom thou servest continually, able to deliver thee from the lions? Then said Daniel unto the king, O king, live for ever. My God hath sent his angel, and hath **shut the lions' mouths, that they have not hurt me**: forasmuch as before him innocency was found in me; and also before thee, O king, have I done no hurt.*

DANIEL 6:19-22

Fasting shut the mouths of the lions and they could not hurt Daniel in any way. I submit to you that fasting is another way of resisting and shutting the mouth of the devil. Heed the words of Peter, '*Be sober, be vigilant; because your adversary the devil, as a roaring lion, walketh about, seeking whom he may devour: whom resist stedfast in the faith...*' (1 Peter 5:8-9). If the King's fast could shut the mouth of the lion, your fast will also shut the mouth of the lion so that he will not devour your life, your health, your family or your finances.

58   FASTING WILL REVERSE EVIL PLOTS OF DESTRUCTION AGAINST YOUR LIFE

Every intended desire of the enemy against God's people backfired and became their own evil portion as the people of God fasted. We see this as a reality in the life of Daniel: the men who had planned his death to be a devouring in the lion's den were themselves eaten by the lions that could not eat Daniel. In another situation, Haman met his death on the gallows he erected for Mordecai; instead of Israel being wiped out, it was his generation that was totally cut off. The men who threw Shadrach, Meshach, and Abed-nego in the fiery furnace were themselves consumed by the fire. The evil conglomerate of enemy nations that came against Jehoshaphat's Judah turned on one another and killed each other:

> *For the children of Ammon and Moab stood up against the inhabitants of mount Seir, utterly to slay and destroy them: and when they had made an end of the inhabitants of Seir, every one helped to destroy another. And when Judah came toward the watch tower in the wilderness, they looked unto the multitude, and, behold, they were dead bodies fallen to the earth, and none escaped.*
>
> 2 CHRONICLES 20:23-24

All that was left to do for Judah was to pick up the blessings and the loot. It took them three days to collect it all because of the great abundance. The same will be applicable to you as you fast unto the Lord.

I really like how the New International Version explains what happened between the Jews and evil Haman:

For Haman son of Hammedatha, the Agagite, the enemy of all the Jews, **had plotted against the Jews to destroy them** *and had cast the pur (that is, the lot) for their ruin and destruction. But when the plot came to the king's attention, he issued written orders that the evil scheme Haman had devised against the Jews should come back onto his own head, and that he and his sons should be impaled on poles.*

ESTHER 9:24-25 NIV

May every enemy of your life, seeking your destruction be impaled! May every sickness and every curse seeking your obliteration be impaled. Even as the King issued written orders for the plot to fall back on the head of Haman, your King – the Lord Jesus – will release an executive decree on your behalf to reverse every plot against your life.

59 FASTING TAKES YOU FROM THE GENERIC TO THE SPECIFIC

Many have received the initial plan of God only to try to make it happen in their strength or as they deem it right in their eyes. This is one of the dumbest things you can do! Hannah warned us, '*For by strength shall no man prevail*' (1 Samuel 2:9). We must also heed the warning in Isaiah, '*Then I said, I have laboured in vain, I have spent my strength for nought, and in vain...*' (Isaiah 49:4).

Once I was doing a jigsaw puzzle with my little girl Jodie. I was fascinated watching her trying to put all the pieces together. Since this was a children's puzzle, the pieces had numbers to enable the child to complete the puzzle. I was amazed at how she completely ignored the number sequences and tried to do it by herself. She made some of the pieces fit together but after all was done, it was nothing like the puzzle picture. So I said to her, 'Follow the number sequence, they are there for a reason'.

This is how many live their lives: they have heard just enough from God to know what the picture is supposed to look like but then they get all kinds of pieces that do not match and force them to fit. The end result is frustration and failure. It is not because God does not want them to succeed, it is that they did not find the respective pieces to place them where they should go. On the road to Damascus, Paul encountered Jesus, who gave him the overall picture that he was called. It was as he fasted for three days right after his conversion that more of the pieces were given to him. Then in Acts 13, when he got together with certain prophets and teachers to minister to the Lord in fasting, he discovered the specific person he was to travel with and which regions he should specifically go to. The more you fast the more accurate you will be in your actions. It is through fasting and waiting upon the Lord that the missing pieces of the plan will be unfolded to you. Fasting and knowing all the right pieces will save you from doing a number of wasteful things.

(Scripture references: Acts 9:15-16; Acts 13:1-4; Acts 26:14, 16-18).

60 FASTING PREPARES YOU FOR NEW WINE, NEW OIL AND NEW ANOINTING

Jesus said, '*And no man putteth new wine into old bottles: else the new wine doth burst the bottles, and the wine is spilled, and the bottles will be marred: but new wine must be put into new bottles*' (Mark 2:22). This was His response to the question posed by the disciples of John in respect to fasting. Notice Jesus refers to new wine. In the same token when Joel was talking about a national fast, he mentioned, '*Yea, the Lord will answer and say unto his people, Behold, I will send you corn, and wine, and oil, and ye shall be satisfied therewith*' (Joel 2:19). Both referred to wine in connection to fasting. New wine is symbolic of the intoxicating anointing and glory of God.

In the olden days they would not put new wine in an old bottle because if they did the old bottle made out of leather would burst from the new fermentation. One of the ways they would renew the life of the bottle is through applying oil on the exterior of the leather, making it more supple, allowing it to expand from within. Then it would be like a new bottle, which would not burst from the content within. Fasting prepares us to be able containers of new wine, new oil and new anointing. Many want to be carriers of the new wine but have never been renewed with fresh oil. Are you ready to be used afresh by God? Do you want new oil, new wine and new anointing? Then it is time to fast! The world is ready for your manifestation as a child of God, anointed to bring the power of God to this generation. Will you fast and step into your destiny?

(Mark 2:18-22, Joel 2:21-24).

61 FASTING IS THE TIMING BELT OF THE SPIRIT AND WILL SYNCHRONIZE YOUR STEPS WITH THOSE OF GOD THUS ENSURING VICTORY

Fasting gives you the divine timing of the strategy to take the land and move into our destiny.

Many times even though we have heard or known of divine strategies we fail because we do not know divine timing. This is a very important point to grasp: it is one thing to know divine strategies but altogether a different matter to know divine timing. Without divine timing, you can still miss God even though you have divine strategies. Divine strategy without divine timing can still cause you to miss your destiny or add something to your destiny that causes you long-distance pain. You can see that with Abraham and Ishmael. Israel is still paying heavy consequences to a miss of divine timing from Abraham and Sarah. Every time a bomb is directed toward Israel from her hateful neighbors, it indicates the necessity of divine timing with divine strategy.

If Abraham had waited for the right timing none of the Middle East conflicts would be happening today. There is a disturbing event in the Old Testament that demonstrates this principle. In Judges chapter 19 we read of a Levite who had a concubine who was unfaithful to him and went away from his home to her father's house. She was away from her husband for four months.

In spite of her unfaithfulness the Levite went to fetch his wife. When the father-in-law saw that the Levite had come to fetch his wife he was thrilled to bits and the Levite stayed with his father-in-law for three days. On the fourth day when he was getting ready to leave, his father-in-law implored him to stay one more day. Again on the fifth day he pressed him to stay one more day but the Levite had already made up his mind that it was time to move on. He did so and as they went on their journey, it became late and they decided that it would be safer to spend the night in a city which belonged to Israel rather than a place which is unfriendly towards God's people. They stayed at a place called Gibeah which belonged to the children of Benjamin.

Then a terrible event took place that night: some men of Gibeah raped the Levite's wife all night long and the man found her dead in the morning. He then proceeded to cut her body in twelve pieces and sent it to the twelve respective tribes of Israel. This was an abomination that was never seen in Israel before, therefore they gathered together to see how to bring justice for this atrocious crime. After a time of counsel they demanded that the Benjamites hand over the men of Gibeah who had committed this great evil but they refused and instead set themselves to war against the rest of Israel. At this point, Israel set themselves in array against the men of Benjamin. The Benjamites numbered twenty six thousand soldiers facing four hundred thousand soldiers of Israel. The men of Israel did the right thing in inquiring of the Lord:

> *And the children of Israel arose, and went up to the house of God, and asked counsel of God, and said, Which of us shall go up first to the battle against the children of Benjamin? And the Lord said, Judah shall go up first. And the children of Israel rose up in the morning, and encamped against Gibeah.*
>
> JUDGES 20:17-19

Notice they enquired and received instruction from God. They had the right strategy from God and you would think that victory would have been inevitable.

And the men of Israel went out to battle against Benjamin; and the men of Israel put themselves in array to fight against them at Gibeah. And the children of Benjamin came forth out of Gibeah, and destroyed down to the ground of the Israelites that day twenty and two thousand men.

JUDGES 20:20-21

Look at that! They heard from God and still suffered defeat. They lost twenty two thousand men on the day that they heard from God. How is it that they heard from God and were still defeated? That does not make sense! Unfortunately this is where so many are in life today. So what did they do next?

And the people the men of Israel encouraged themselves, and set their battle again in array in the place where they put themselves in array the first day. (And the children of Israel went up and wept before the Lord until even, and asked counsel of the Lord, saying, Shall I go up again to battle against the children of Benjamin my brother? And the Lord said, Go up against him.) And the children of Israel came near against the children of Benjamin the second day. And Benjamin went forth against them out of Gibeah the second day, and destroyed down to the ground of the children of Israel again eighteen thousand men; all these drew the sword.

JUDGES 20:22-25

They encouraged themselves in the Lord. Like many of us who taste a setback, we psych ourselves up and say things like, 'Well, I'm not moved by what I see. I may have lost a battle but I have not lost the war', then we go again to the battle only to come back a second time heavily defeated, like Israel, who lost a further eighteen thousand men. So in the space of two days they lost forty thousand men. That is a heavy loss and yet they had heard from God. Eventually they went back to the temple and sought the face of God again but this time added an offering and fasting. God responded to them, '...*And the Lord said, Go up; for to morrow I will deliver them into thine hand*' (Judges 20:28). This time not only did they know the plan and strategy but they knew the timing of God. They stepped ahead of God by 72 hours which cost them heavily. Fasting enabled them to be synchronized with God which secured their victory.

62   FASTING ENABLES YOU TO KNOW THE RHYTHM OF GOD'S HEART

It is said that David was a man after God's heart. What does that mean? Does that mean he loved God? While I'm sure this is implied, can we say that David loved God more than Abraham? Did David love God more than Moses or Paul? The problem we have is that we think that when it says that *'David was a man after God's heart'* that it is talking about David's heart. The heart of God is the reference here. What does it mean to be after God's heart? Heart has a rhythmic beat. When we are a people after God's heart, it simply means that we follow the rhythm of his heart. This was said of David because God had rejected Saul. The reason why Saul was rejected was because he did not want to wait for the time for Samuel to come, which was ordained of God; Saul wanted to do things according to the rhythm of his own heart and his own timing and consequently missed his destiny. Although David's moral failure was worse than Saul, he could keep in sync with God because he had the sons of Issachar, who enabled him to know the timing and rhythm of God. David was also a man given to much fasting hence the reason he knew the rhythm and cycle of God's heart.

63   FASTING RENEWS YOUR STRENGTH, AS THE EAGLE, WHICH WAITS UPON THE LORD

It is not in our nature to stand still and do nothing when we face crises. In fact, on many occasions the stories of the Bible show that waiting patiently for God to act is one of the most difficult things to do. Human nature dictates that we have a tendency to take matters into our own hands and create all kinds of problems because they were acts of the flesh. Fasting is deliberately weakening the flesh in order to strengthen the spirit man. It is the molting of the flesh in order to release the renewal of the spirit. Although the Bible metaphorically likens God to an eagle in describing Him as a parent stirring and protecting the nest, it also uses the eagle to illustrate a believer's growth, one who waits upon the Lord for rejuvenation and renewal. Just as an eagle is not afraid of the storm or the serpent so should it be the case for the believer. However an eagle goes through a painful phase as it gets older and its vision, strength and physical attributes are no longer the same.

An eagle may live up in years but in order to do that, sometime at the age 30 or 40 it has to go through a life-threatening renewal called molting. The build up of calcium deposits on the eagle's talons and beak renders the king of the air – according to experts – to walk like a penguin or turkey. Some even say that the eagle, at such a stage of its life, is in a state of depression and if it wants to renew and prolong its life it is imperative that it goes through the molting process. Actually not all eagles survive the molting process but the fascinating fact is that those which survive this gruesome transformation come out on the other side stronger and sharper than they were in their youth. When the molting process begins the eagle has no strength and keenness of vision to hunt. At the beginning they fast! They do not eat, and later they become dependent upon other eagles – which have already gone through this process and survived – that fly above the valley where the eagle is and drop fresh food to strengthen him. Once some strength has been regained, the eagle climbs the mountain onto a rock and beats its beak on the rock, removing the calcium build up. Now with the beak looking new it begins to pluck the calcium off its talons. Although it is a very slow and painful process, it must be done. Then with its new beak it will begin to pluck the old feathers off and wait for new feathers to show up. With a new beak, new talons, new wings and fresh vision, the majesty of the air is fit to hunt again. During molting it looked like the prey but after the molting process it is once again the predator. The eagle had to go through the molting process, which included fasting and waiting.

Waiting upon the Lord in fasting is not wasting time! In the Old Testament there were several words in Hebrew for 'wait' and they have different meanings. In Isaiah 40:31, *'But they that wait upon the Lord shall renew their strength; they shall mount up with wings as eagle...'*, the Hebrew word is 'qavah' meaning to 'bind together by twisting' as in braiding and 'to expect'. We are also aware that the same word qavah is employed in Jeremiah's Lamentations:

> *The Lord is good unto them that wait for him, to the soul that seeketh him. It is good that a man should both hope and quietly **wait** for the salvation of the Lord.*
> LAMENTATIONS 3:25-26

When you fast you are interweaving your spirit with the Spirit of God and the Word to make a threefold cord that Satan cannot break. From this place your strength will be renewed.

64 FASTING GIVES REST TO YOUR DIGESTIVE SYSTEM, REBUILDS THE IMMUNE SYSTEM, REVERSES THE AGING PROCESS AND INCREASES YOUR LIFESPAN

When we abstain from food we give our digestive system a rest, giving our body time to be serviced. Just like your vehicle needs servicing to keep it operating at an optimum level so does your body. Your immune system will be strengthened. Too many are on the slow path of destruction by being continually on a three-meals-a-day eating habit. Fasting will make you healthier and look better. After Daniel and his friends had fasted ten days they looked better than those who were on the king's portion of meat and wine. It is a well-known fact that fasting will also increase your lifespan and the quality of your life by helping to prevent diseases.

65 FASTING WILL LOOSE THE BONDAGES OF WICKEDNESS AND MAKE STRAIGHT THAT WHICH IS TWISTED

From Isaiah 58, the Scripture gives us a list of the benefits that fasting will provide and I want to go through them with you for your understanding. *'Is not this the fast that I have chosen? to loose the bands of wickedness...'* (Isaiah 58:6).

The chosen fast is to loose the bands of wickedness. If you look around the world we live in, wickedness abounds; there are people whose lives have been ravaged by curses and crippling diseases from which there are no medical cures. A curse is an invisible tracking device following a person's movement in life and will detonate at a certain time, bringing failure. When it detonates, the full effect of the curse manifests: for some people it may not be a sickness but a recurring event that takes place in all the family line; Some people have mental problems in their family line;

another family is ravaged with miscarriages and loss of children; for others, untimely death and a proclivity for accidents seem to be familiar with their generations. These are bands of wickedness. If you do not deal with a curse then it becomes a principality in your life; it becomes a prince ruling in a place. Notice God called it a '*band of wickedness*'. The dictionary defines a band as:

* A range of frequencies or wavelengths in a spectrum (especially of radio frequencies).
* A thing that restrains, binds, or unites.

A *band of wickedness*, therefore, is a range of frequencies or a wavelength of wickedness. Just like we have airwaves over us and frequencies that pick up certain stuff, when we live under an air-wave of wickedness then things affect us and play out in us. Anything that disturbs the peace and wellbeing of your life is wickedness. It can be sicknesses or other things that affect you, your locality or your family. Secondly a band of wickedness is something that restrains, binds and unites you with wickedness. Remember, unless you deal with a curse it becomes a principality.

Fasting is one effective weapon that we have at our disposal to deal with such matters. Every principality or territorial devil in your city or family will be forced to bow the knee before you. Whatever band has twisted and restrains you will be loosened as you fast.

66 FASTING WILL UNDO HEAVY BURDENS AND LET THE OPPRESSED GO FREE

You will not carry any more 'heavy loads' of the enemy. Jesus' burden is light and His yoke is easy. As you fast you will exchange burdens with Him. Fasting is the casting of your burdens upon Him and taking His light burden upon you.

For my yoke is easy and burden is light.

MATTHEW 11:30

In Greek, the word for 'easy' means 'goodness'. Jesus was saying, *'my yoke is goodness'*. Once you are yoked with Him, you become His partner and the burden is light. The word 'burden' here is 'forteeon' meaning 'invoice'. When you structure these words, Jesus was saying:

'Come unto me all who have worked tirelessly but still have an unpayable heavy invoice and I will give you an exemption. My yoke is goodness and my invoice is light.'

In salvation, what you couldn't pay, Jesus paid in full and you were exempted. As you fast, the invoices that are unpayable and heavy, are taken care of by the Lord and you are exempted.

The Word also says, *'you will let the oppressed free'*. Often times as we roam the streets of our city and go through the churches, a sense of hopelessness is in the air as millions are bound and helpless. Even as ministers we feel impotent because we know the power of God is real and yet we cannot deliver and let the oppressed go free. What an indictment against the modern church! It is written that:

❖ Peter's shadow healed the sick on the streets.
❖ Paul's handkerchief healed the sick.
❖ Paul's hands had special and unusual miracles.
❖ By the hands of the apostles were great signs and wonders done.

What about you? The same will be written of you as you devote yourself to a sacrificial life of fasting and prayer. When you do, the oppressed will no longer be oppressed as you become a tool in the hand of your Heavenly Father to a hopeless world.

67   FASTING WILL CAUSE YOU TO BREAK EVERY YOKE

Fasting enables you to tap into the anointing which God said will destroy yokes (Isaiah 10:27). The devil's yoke – which means something that he imposed upon your neck – will be reduced to nothing and obliterated. Please mark these words: '*You will break every yoke*' implies if you've done it once, broken through and tasted sweet victory, you now have the experience and you will do it again and again. Fasting brings you to a place where you have the access point to the power of God. You do not have to rely upon someone else to be the conductor; you can tap into the power directly.

68   FASTING WILL CAUSE YOUR LIGHT TO BREAK FORTH AS THE MORNING

No more dark days for you! For some people even when it is daylight they are experiencing darkness. But for you, it is a new day and a new season; dark days and days of obscurity, languishing in mediocrity are over!

(Scripture References: Isaiah 58:8).

69   FASTING WILL SPEEDILY UNLEASH DIVINE HEALING, DIVINE HEALTH AND DIVINE LIFE

Your body will have a fresh lease of life. In the olden days, doctors prescribed fasting as a medicine. They understood, even as man's best friend the dog understands, when you are not feeling at your optimum level, give yourself over to fasting. As you make it a habit of weekly fasting, your health will be the better for it. A lot of what ails you now will begin to subside. Many of our ailments can be traced to too much food consumption and excess body weight. God has promised that our health shall spring forth speedily as we become wise to the force of fasting.

(Scripture Reference: Isaiah 58:8).

70   FASTING WILL CAUSE YOUR RIGHTEOUSNESS TO GO BEFORE YOU, AND THE GLORY OF THE LORD SHALL BE YOUR REARGUARD

Protection is given in the front and at the back so that there is no intrusion from the enemy. Just as Egypt could not creep behind Israel when they were on the march to the Promised Land, because of the pillar of fire, God will provide you the same defense and safekeeping.

71   FASTING IS THE RELEASE OF THE GLORY OF GOD IN YOUR LIFE

Fasting and glory go together. Anna the prophetess and the old man Simeon were intercessors who waited upon the coming of the Lord in constant fasting and prayers. When Jesus finally made his entrance in the earth, Simeon uttered these words:

> *For mine eyes have seen thy salvation, which thou hast prepared before the face of all people; A light to lighten the Gentiles, and the glory of thy people Israel.*   LUKE 2:30-32

Your eyes will see the glory of God as you press into fasting.

72   FASTING IS THE WARRANTY OF ANSWERED PRAYER. AS YOU CALL UPON GOD, HE WILL SAY, 'HERE I AM'

You will no longer struggle for answered prayer. No longer will you feel like saying, 'It does not seem like my prayer has gone above the roof.' No! No! No! Those days are over my friend! No sooner do you call to God, He will say 'Here I am!' What a thought! Answered prayer triggers glory in your life. From today, you will taste the glory of God like you have never tasted before.

73 FASTING WILL SECURE CONTINUOUS GUIDANCE, CAUSE YOUR SOUL TO BE SATISFIED IN DROUGHT, AND YOUR BONES TO BE MADE FAT

As you fast, you will experience divine guidance and receive divine direction that you need to keep you on track and in safety. Ezra experienced this and we have already mentioned it. Isaiah said:

And they thirsted not when he led them through the deserts: he caused the waters to flow out of the rock for them: he clave the rock also, and the waters gushed out.

ISAIAH 48:21

FASTING WILL PROTECT YOUR FRONT AND BACK, YOUR COMING IN AND YOUR GOING OUT

For the Lord's portion is his people; Jacob is the lot of his inheritance. He found him in a desert land, and in the waste howling wilderness; he led him about, he instructed him, he kept him as the apple of his eye.

DEUTERONOMY 32:9-10

Whatever desert that you are trekking through and whatever waste howling wilderness of a city that you find yourself in, you can still taste total satisfaction because He has promised to give you guidance continually. God found Jacob in a desert land and made him to ride upon the high places of the earth. This is what is going to happen to you. Some people think that they will only make it if they go to America or Europe but I know people who are in America and they are poorer than a church mouse. There are people living in the finest cities and their lives are a wreck. That does not need to be your reality. God promised that as long as you seek Him in fasting and prayer, putting Him first, He will continuously guide you and make you number one in the city.

(Scripture References: Isaiah 58:11, Isaiah 48:17-21, Romans 8:14, Deuteronomy 32:12).

74 FASTING WILL MAKE YOU TO BE LIKE A WATERED GARDEN, AND LIKE A SPRING OF WATER, WHOSE WATERS FAIL NOT

No more dry seasons for you! Fasting will fully irrigate your life. As your garden needs water to cause the plants to bloom, fasting will bring fresh water on the seeds that you have sown and cause you to see the fruit of your garden. No more dry, arid and cracked ground in your garden but a lush scene awaits you.

(Scripture References: Isaiah 58:11, Psalms 1).

FASTING WILL IRRIGATE AND GIVE YOU A LUSH LIFE

---

75 FASTING WILL CAUSE YOUR PROGENIES TO BUILD THE OLD WASTE PLACES

Whatever was broken down will be rebuilt. The God of restoration, restitution and recompense will re-erect what the enemy destroyed. After Nehemiah went on a fast he rebuilt the broken walls of Jerusalem in fifty-two days. That which had been laid in ruins for years was speedily reconstructed and restored. The old waste places will once again become a new solid fort.

(Scripture References: Isaiah 58:12, Ezra 8:21, Nehemiah 3:1-32).

CHAPTER 11
101 BENEFITS OF FASTING

Section 4: Benefits 76-101

As we come to the final part of the 101 benefits, you should realize that men and women who have shaken the earth have been those who were devoted to prayer and fasting. As Moses, Paul, Derek Prince, A.A Allen and T.L Osborne, you too can leave an imprint upon the earth. The time has come for you to eradicate powerlessness from your existence and be the power house that you were meant to be.

76   FASTING WILL ENABLE YOU TO RAISE UP THE FOUNDATIONS OF MANY GENERATIONS; AND YOU SHALL BE CALLED THE REPAIRER OF THE BREACH, THE RESTORER OF PATHS TO DWELL IN

The Scripture says, '*If the foundation be broken what can the righteous do?*' (Psalm 11:3). Well the righteous can fast and seek God! The Bible says that as we fast, we are raising up the foundations of many generations. Have you seen our generation lately? It is like the world has gone upside down and society now calls that which is good, evil and that which is evil and senseless, good. When could we have ever imagined that what our former generations fought for would be demonized and what they fought against would be considered the proper way of life? Today socialism is being heralded as the answer to America. God forbid! Socialism has never worked and will never work because man is evil and therefore will seek to control his peers. Today, alternative lifestyle is being taught in schools as normality. Our modern society is returning to a godless society. What is the answer? No matter how much money we invest on Gospel television and billboards, our communities seem to be getting darker and darker. May we be like Mother Elizabeth Dabney, who gave herself to prayer and intercession and changed her community. This dear mother wrote a book called **The Power of Praying through** which I highly recommend. In the midst of lawlessness, we can fast and see our communities change. We don't have to be subject to immoral laws legalized by senseless politicians: we can call upon God and become the repairer of the breach and the restorer of a godly path to dwell in.

(Scripture References: Isaiah 58:12,Nehemiah 3:1-32).

FASTING WILL RESHAPE OUR COMMUNITIES AND REBUILD THE FOUNDATION OF GENERATIONS

---

77 FASTING WILL ENABLE YOU TO DELIGHT YOURSELF IN THE LORD AND HE WILL CAUSE YOU TO RIDE UPON THE HIGH PLACES OF THE EARTH

Your Christianity will no longer be tasteless but sweet and you will partake of the more abundant life – the high life – which was ordained for you all along. You will land and rest in your wealthy place. Your days of lowliness will be over as you ride the high places of the earth, matching your position in Christ.

(Scripture References: Isaiah 58:14, Deuteronomy 32:13, 2 Samuel 22:33-34, Isaiah 41:18, Isaiah 58:14, Habakkuk 3:19, Ephesians 6:12).

78 FASTING WILL FEED YOU THE HERITAGE OF JACOB YOUR FATHER

For the Lord's portion is his people; Jacob is the lot of his inheritance. He found him in a desert land, and in the waste howling wilderness; he led him about, he instructed him, he kept him as the apple of his eye. As an eagle stirreth up her nest, fluttereth over her young, spreadeth abroad her wings, taketh them, beareth them on her wings: So the Lord alone did lead him, and there was no strange god with him. He made him ride on the high places of the earth, that he might eat the increase of the fields; and he made him to suck honey out of the rock, and oil out of the flinty rock; Butter of kine, and milk of sheep, with fat of lambs, and rams of the breed of Bashan, and goats, with the fat of kidneys of wheat; and thou didst drink the pure blood of the grape.

DEUTERONOMY 32:9-14

The heritage of Jacob was:

- ❖ God found him in a desert land and in the waste howling wilderness. God will not leave you to die in the wilderness.
- ❖ God led him about, instructed him, and kept him as the apple of His eye. You have a right to be led by God and be preserved as the apple of His eyes.
- ❖ God protected him as an eagle would bear its young on its wings. The same will be said about you.
- ❖ God will lead you and there will no foreign God with you.
- ❖ You will ride the high place of the earth. Promotion and elevation will be yours.
- ❖ You will eat the increase of the fields; the fields will produce for you. Your work will produce for you.
- ❖ You will suck honey out of the rock. The rock, which is the Word will be sweet to you. You will draw sweetness and anointing from the Word.
- ❖ You will spend your days in blessings.

79 FASTING WILL EXPOSE THAT WHICH IS HIDDEN AND REVEAL THE PROBLEM TO YOU

Fresh from their conquest of Jericho, Israel was now facing the tiny enemy population of Ai. After surveying the potential of their enemy, Israel came to the conclusion that this would be an easy victory. They were full of confidence but oblivious to the fact that Achan had defied and broken the specific instruction of not taking anything from Jericho, thus defiling Israel before God.

What should have been an easy victory turned into a nightmare as they lost thirty six men and disgracefully ran away from the men of Ai. Joshua and the elders of Israel were stupefied by what transpired, as the people's heart melted like wax in fear. In total shock, Joshua and the elders tore off their cloaks, threw ashes in the air, (which is connected to fasting because of national disaster) and set themselves before the Lord for the whole day until evening. They could not explain this defeat. Had God abandoned them? Did God bring them through Jericho only to be disgraced by a tiny nation? These were all questions they were asking God. After bombarding the Lord of questions, He spoke:

> And the Lord said unto Joshua, Get thee up; wherefore liest thou thus upon thy face? Israel hath sinned, and they have also transgressed my covenant which I commanded them: for they have even taken of the accursed thing, and have also stolen, and dissembled also, and they have put it even among their own stuff. Therefore the children of Israel could not stand before their enemies, but turned their backs before their enemies, because they were accursed: neither will I be with you any more, except ye destroy the accursed from among you.
>
> JOSHUA 7:10-12

After their consecration before the Lord for the whole day through fasting, the Lord unveiled to them the hidden crime that was committed. They discovered that Achan had taken that which was forbidden. Joshua would not have known this without getting before the Lord in consecration of fasting. The hidden became the revealed as they pressed into God through fasting. They discovered where Israel missed it and rooted out the problem.

> Nebuchadnezzar and Daniel

King Nebuchadnezzar dreamt some dreams and he wanted the interpretations so he summoned all the wise men, astrologers and sorcerers to interpret his dreams. The only problem was that he had forgotten the dreams and yet insisted that they gave him the interpretations! The men told Nebuchadnezzar that his request was illogical, and in a fit of rage he decreed an executive order to have all the wise men of the land executed; Daniel and his three friends found themselves implicated in this decree. There seemed to be no way out, but Daniel had been living a fasted life and subsequently requested some time from the king. After seeking God the hidden or unknown was revealed, which saved his life and the lives of all the wise men.

Too many times, when we experience a setback we lose even more because we do not go before God to enquire as to what caused the problem. What God told Joshua and Daniel has become an illustration for us. Today you do not have to rend your garments with your fasting to discover the problem but you do have to rend your hearts, fast and ask where you are missing it. The Holy Spirit, who is the Spirit of truth and revelation will unveil to you where the problem lies.

80   FASTING WILL TAKE YOU TO THE SECRET PLACE OF THE MOST HIGH TO ENCOUNTER THE REVEALER OF SECRETS

After the executive order to have all the wise men killed, the Scripture revealed that Daniel asked for time. Why do you think he did this? To seek God in prayer and fasting. He and his three friends sought God and the secret was revealed to Daniel, the hidden was revealed as he pressed through in fasting:

*Then was the **secret revealed** unto Daniel in a night vision. Then Daniel blessed the God of heaven.*

DANIEL 2:19

Notice these words, '*Then was the secret revealed...*' When? After he took time to seek God in prayer and fasting! Daniel then went before the king, who asked him, 'Are you sure you can do this?' to which Daniel replied:

*The secret which the king hath demanded cannot the wise men, the astrologers, the magicians, the soothsayers, shew unto the king; But there is a **God in heaven that revealeth secrets**...*

DANIEL 2:27-28

Once more, please notice these words, '*the secret which the king had demanded... there is a God in heaven that revealeth secrets*'.

He that dwelleth in the secret place of the Most High, shall abide under the shadow of the Almighty.

PSALMS 91:1

The secret of the Lord is with them that fear him; and he will shew them his covenant.

PSALM 25:14

Shall not God search this out? for he knoweth the secrets of the heart.

PSALM 44:21

Three things are in place here:

❖ Secret place of the Most High.
❖ Revealer of secrets.
❖ Secret of the Lord.

I want to remind you of the words of Jesus:

'*...appear not unto men to fast, but unto **thy Father which is in secret**: and thy Father, **which seeth in secret**, shall reward thee openly.*'

MATTHEW 6:18

From these Scripture verses, we can deduce that there is a secret place that we can go into and when we do we will have a divine encounter with God the Father –who is the revealer of secrets – who will then give you the secrets of the Lord, which will trigger an open reward.

How do we enter into this secret place to meet the revealer of secrets for the secrets of life? **Through the secret of fasting**. Moses entered into that secret place and received the tablets written by the finger of God.

I don't know about you but I crave to be in that secret place to meet the revealer of secrets. 'Help us, O Lord!'

81 FASTING ENABLES THE BELIEVER TO DEAL AND BE VICTORIOUS OVER THE SIN THAT SO EASILY BESETS US

Fasting gives you self-control and allows you to break addictive behavior; it is ascetic by practice. According to the dictionary, 'asceticism' means 'radical self-discipline and avoidance of all forms of indulgence, typically for religious reasons'. Therefore fasting is the quintessential way to crucify the flesh and present your body as a living sacrifice.

There is so much temptation around: we live in a world which is obsessed with sex. Television commercials have sexual innuendos and the comedy shows – even children's programs – depict alternative lifestyles. The world celebrates debauchery and we are being bombarded from all sides to the point where sexual sins are a commonality in the church, just as in the world. What was frowned upon a few years back is now considered to be cool and open mindedness. The Apostle Paul helps us with our quest to be holy:

But I keep under my body, and bring it into subjection: lest that by any means, when I have preached to others, I myself should be a castaway.
1 CORINTHIANS 9:27

Fasting is one way to take control over the flesh. For some of us, our flesh has gone wild; there are no limits. I am not talking about sinners but saints who are uncontrollable in their appetite for food, sex, drugs and other destructive habits. The one thing that fasting will help you with is to curb your hunger or desire for such things. Just like a drug addict goes 'cold turkey' when he is being weaned off drugs, fasting is like putting yourself through a 'cold turkey' process, to break certain cravings of the flesh.

(Scripture References: Isaiah 58:6, Hebrews 12:1, Romans 7:5,15-24).

FASTING IS TO ABSTAIN FROM SURFEITING, OR OVERMUCH
EATING, FROM DRUNKENNESS, AND CARE OF THE WORLD (AS
THOU MAYEST READ LUKE XXI) AND THE END OF FASTING
IS TO TAME THE BODY THAT THE SPIRIT MAY HAVE A FREE
COURSE TO GOD, AND MAY QUIETLY TALK WITH GOD
– WILLIAM TYNDALE

---

82 FASTING REMOVES PHYSICAL, MENTAL AND SPIRITUAL OBSTACLES TO YOUR CHRISTIAN GROWTH

Fasting is like a bomb that removes obstacles in your life. The man whose son was a lunatic and possessed by a devil became a spiritual stumbling block for the disciples. Jesus told them, *this kind can only come out by prayer and fasting.* The boy's mental problem was removed when Jesus dealt with him. The spiritual, physical and mental obstacles mentioned in Isaiah 58 are dissolved as we go on God's chosen fast; any kind of embargo imposed on your life by Satan can be revoked by tapping into the power of the chosen fast.

(Isaiah 58:6-12, Matthew 17:19-21).

FASTING REVOKES SPIRITUAL, PHYSICAL
AND MENTAL EMBARGO ON YOUR LIFE

---

83 FASTING GIVES YOU THE OPPORTUNITY TO RECALIBRATE YOUR SPIRITUAL LIFE

There are some instances in life where we lose our bearings and seem to be getting further away from our destination. There are times it seems that we are going through the motions and the results are not there; we go to church as we are supposed to but nonetheless our Christianity is tasteless and without wonders. What is the point of Christianity without wonders? It is a form of godliness without power. It is noble to walk in godliness but we've been called to power and an adventure with God.

In those times we need to put ourselves before the Lord in order to recalibrate our lives. There is no greater way to recalibrate your life and be on track with the Lord than separating yourself before the Lord in fasting and prayer, giving yourself to Him in the Word to find direction. Paul was on the road to Damascus with papers to kill believers when he had an encounter with Jesus. So what was his next step? In order to recalibrate his life, Paul went on a three-day fast and discovered more of his calling. Cornelius was a good, praying man, who feared God and gave much to the cause of God, but he was not saved. He went on a four-day fast and his life and the Gentile world was recalibrated.

Once again, if we refer to the life of Paul we will discover from his conversion in Acts 9 that he went along doing what he needed to do:

And straightway he preached Christ in the synagogues, that he is the Son of God. But all that heard him were amazed, and said; Is not this he that destroyed them which called on this name in Jerusalem, and came hither for that intent, that he might bring them bound unto the chief priests? But Saul increased the more in strength, and confounded the Jews which dwelt at Damascus, proving that this is very Christ... And when Saul was come to Jerusalem, he assayed to join himself to the disciples: but they were all afraid of him, and believed not that he was a disciple. But Barnabas took him, and brought him to the apostles, and declared unto them how he had seen the Lord in the way, and that he had spoken to him, and how he had preached boldly at Damascus in the name of Jesus. And he was with them coming in and going out at Jerusalem. And he spake boldly in the name of the Lord Jesus, and disputed against the Grecians...

ACTS 9:20-22, 26-29

Right after his conversion, Paul went straight into preaching and proving that Jesus was the very Christ; there is no mention of miracles, signs and wonders. He was in Jerusalem, going in and out among them. Notice these words, '*disputed against the Grecians*'. This means 'to reason and be controversial'. No wonder they sought to kill him. From the Acts 9 conversion record to

Acts 12 we hear nothing about Paul; then Acts 13 begins with certain prophets and teachers, among whom were Paul and Barnabas, getting together to minister to the Lord in fasting. What was the end result?

The Holy Ghost said, Separate me Barnabas and Saul for the work whereunto I have called them.

ACTS 13:2

Their lives were recalibrated. What happened next? They spent some more time fasting for clearer directions, hands were then laid on them and they were sent on their mission:

And when they had fasted and prayed, and laid their hands on them, they sent them away. So they, being sent forth by the Holy Ghost, departed unto Seleucia; and from thence they sailed to Cyprus.

ACTS 13:3-4

The rest is history, as they say! There was an explosion of signs, wonders and persecutions. If you want to recalibrate your life then give yourself to a life of fasting and prayer.

FASTING RECALIBRATES AND RE-ORIENTATES YOUR LIFE

84 FASTING IS THE COVERING OF THE MOUTH AND THE EMPTYING OF THE BELLY IN ORDER TO PUT SOMETHING IN YOUR HANDS AND ENLARGE YOUR MOUTH OVER YOUR ENEMIES

Hannah was married to Elkanah and he also had another wife called Peninnah. Although Hannah was loved by Elkanah, her problem was that she was barren. Peninnah, on the other hand, was a baby factory machine. When Peninnah saw that she had many children and that Hannah was barren, she mocked her. Fruitlessness makes you the object of mockery; when your life, business and ministry are not producing it attracts mockery from your adversary. Here is what you need to know about mockery: it is your enemy enlarging their mouth against you. Evidently Peninnah's mockery of Hannah affected her, crushing her emotions. What did Hannah do? She went on a fast:

> *And as she did so year by year, when she went up to the house of the Lord, **so she provoked her;** therefore she wept, **and did not eat**. Then said Elkanah her husband to her, Hannah, why weepest thou? and why eatest thou not? and why is thy heart grieved? am not I better to thee than ten sons?*
>
> 1 SAMUEL 1:7-8

How do you shut the mouth of your enemies when they open their mouths against you? It is not by retaliating in the flesh with some smart-aleck comment. What did Hannah do? She went on a fast! She stopped eating and prayed at the temple. What was the end result?

> *And Hannah prayed, and said, My heart rejoiceth in the Lord, mine horn is exalted in the Lord: **my mouth is enlarged over mine enemies;** because I rejoice in thy salvation. There is none holy as the Lord: for there is none beside thee: neither is there any rock like our God. **Talk no more so exceeding proudly; let not arrogancy come out of your mouth:** for the Lord is a God of knowledge, and by him actions are weighed.*
>
> 1 SAMUEL 2:1-3

If you do not stop the mouth of your enemy they will keep enlarging it against you. Victory belongs to the one whose mouth is enlarged. In other words whoever has the biggest mouth wins:

> *Therefore **my people are gone into captivity, because they have no knowledge:** and their honourable men are famished, and their multitude dried up with thirst. **Therefore hell hath enlarged herself, and opened her mouth without measure:** and their glory, and their multitude, and their pomp, and he that rejoiceth, shall descend into it.*
>
> ISAIAH 5:13-14

If you do not enlarge your mouth you can be sure that hell will enlarge its mouth to swallow you up. You know Goliath enlarged his mouth against David but David also enlarged his mouth against Goliath and destroyed him. Hannah enlarged her mouth against Peninnah by fasting. Won't you enlarge your mouth against the naysayers of your destiny by fasting? Fasting will shut the mouth of your enemy.

(Scripture references:1 Samuel 1, 1 Samuel 2:1-3, Isaiah 5:13-14).

85   FASTING IS ADDING VIRTUE TO YOUR FAITH

Peter told us to add virtue to our faith. Many times our faith needs a virtue shot; it is like drinking coffee and adding a caffeine shot to give it a bit more kick. Sometimes your faith needs a virtue or power shot; you do this by fasting. Many times, when I am standing by faith and feel like it is waning I just add a little fasting to it, with a dig in the Word and I find my faith is recharged. I am sure you remember a while ago when Duracell came up with a battery that allowed us to see how much power was in the battery? Sometimes when we look at our faith gauge whilst we are in the process of moving a mountain, we discover a waning in its potency. Your faith needs a shot of power: the best thing to do is to plug into the Word, mix it with fasting and keep going.

86   FASTING CAUSES THE NATURAL MAN TO PLAY SECOND FIDDLE TO THE SPIRITUAL MAN

Fasting is not a diet nor is it going on a hunger strike: it is a deliberate attempt to leave the flesh and get into the Spirit realm; it is fine-tuning your spirit with the Holy Spirit, giving you ascendancy over the lustful demands of your flesh. Peter's response to Jesus in the Garden of Gethsemane when asked to pray, was *'The spirit is willing but the flesh is weak.'* Many can identify with Peter and the disciples whose flesh dominated them in spite of the willingness of their spirit. The more you fast the more you will be placing your spirit man above your flesh. The weaker your flesh is (through the discipline of fasting) the stronger you will be; the stronger your flesh is (through feasting and indulgence) the weaker you will be.

FASTING IS THE QUINTESSENTIAL WAY TO CRUCIFY THE FLESH AND PRESENT YOUR BODY AS A LIVING SACRIFICE

---

87   FASTING WILL RESTORE TO YOU WHAT THE ENEMY STOLE FROM YOU

The first chapter of the book of Joel gives us a grim look at what God's people were going through:

That which the palmerworm hath left hath the locust eaten; and that which the locust hath left hath the cankerworm eaten; and that which the cankerworm hath left hath the caterpiller eaten. Awake, ye drunkards, and weep; and howl, all ye drinkers of wine, because of the new wine; for it is cut off from your mouth. For a nation is come up upon my land, strong, and without number, whose teeth are the teeth of a lion, and he hath the cheek teeth of a great lion. He hath laid my vine waste, and barked my fig tree: he hath made it clean bare, and cast it away; the branches thereof are made white. Lament like a virgin girded with sackcloth for the husband of her youth. The meat offering and the drink offering is cut off from the house of the Lord; the priests, the Lord's ministers, mourn. The field is wasted, the land mourneth; for the corn is wasted: the new wine is dried up, the oil languisheth. Be ye ashamed, O ye husbandmen; howl, O ye vinedressers, for the wheat and for the barley; because the harvest of the field is perished. The vine is dried up, and the fig tree languisheth; the pomegranate tree, the palm tree also, and the apple tree, even all the trees of the field, are withered: because joy is withered away from the sons of men.

                                        JOEL 1:2-12

They were going through great depression, recession, inflation, desolation, destruction and devastation, all at the same time. It was a grim and sad picture. Then Joel called for a national fast because of the catastrophic situation, and God made these promises:

199

And I will restore to you the years that the locust hath eaten, the cankerworm, and the caterpiller, and the palmerworm, my great army which I sent among you. And ye shall eat in plenty, and be satisfied, and praise the name of the Lord your God, that hath dealt wondrously with you: and my people shall never be ashamed.

JOEL 2:25-26

Fasting reinvigorated, rejuvenated, revitalized, regenerated and restored their years, their lives, their economy and their country.

88   FASTING STIRS GOD TO BE JEALOUS OVER YOU

Then will the Lord be jealous for his land, and pity his people.

JOEL 2:18

When? After the solemn fast. Fasting causes God to be jealous over you. Have you ever seen a husband who is jealous over his wife? He won't allow any man to talk to her as he feels threatened. He then becomes over protective and possessive. I am sure that you have met people like that. That's jealousy! It is one thing for a man to be jealous over you but it is a totally different matter when you can stir God to be jealous over you. I want to stir God to be jealous over me. I like Webster's threefold definition of the word jealous:

1.   Intolerant of rivalry or unfaithfulness.
2.   Hostile toward a rival or one believed to enjoy an advantage.
3.   Vigilant in guarding a possession.

The jealousy of God over you causes you to be His prize possession; He won't let anybody touch you. The devil is in serious trouble. If anybody is going to be jealous over me, let it be God.

89   FASTING IS ANOTHER WAY OF MINISTERING UNTO THE LORD; IT IS ANOTHER EXPRESSION OF PRAYER AND WORSHIP

We read in Acts 13:2 that '*they ministered unto the Lord and fasted*'. Other translations use the word *worshipped* instead of *ministered*. So we can see that fasting is worshiping or ministering to the Lord. Fasting is worship; it is a way we can offer the quality time we generally spend in eating, to the Lord in prayer; it is waiting upon the Lord; it allows you to do what you would normally not do.

AND PRAYER NEEDS FASTING FOR ITS FULL GROWTH: THIS IS THE SECOND LESSON. PRAYER IS THE ONE HAND WITH WHICH WE GRASP THE INVISIBLE; FASTING, THE OTHER, WITH WHICH WE LET LOOSE AND CAST AWAY THE VISIBLE – ANDREW MURRAY

---

90   FASTING WILL BE THE CATALYST TO CHANGE YOU EXTERNALLY, INTERNALLY AND ETERNALLY

There is no doubt about that! Fasting is a catalyst for change. Any which way you look at it, once you start to fast you will not remain the same. For one, your body will realign and be healthy by permitting your body to be serviced, cleaning out your organs. True fasting will also bring a change of circumstances and what it sets in motion will be eternal. Anna fasted, prayed and brought through the coming of the Messiah in the earth; the repercussions and ripples are still felt 2,000 years later and it will be so eternally. Esther fasted and the nation of Israel was not wiped out; the Gentile world was changed forever as Cornelius' fast opened the door of salvation, through which you and I have walked.

(Scripture References: Luke 4:14, Acts 9:9-20, Acts 10:30, 44-48).

91   FASTING WILL BRING A THREE-DIMENSIONAL CHANGE IN YOUR SPIRIT, SOUL AND BODY; IT AFFECTS HEAVEN, EARTH AND HELL

Fasting affects the tripartite human: it will strengthen your spirit man, empower your will and weaken the fleshly pressures of your body; it affects the whole of your make-up. Fasting also affects the heavens, as we see when Daniel fasted and Michael fought the Prince of Persia moving against the hordes of hell, in order for the will of God to be established in the earth. As you read through the Scriptures you will see this phenomenon to be a reality on so many different levels: Jehoshaphat's Judah fast saved the nation from five nations; Esther's fast went through the 120 provinces, crossing international borders to save the Jews from genocide. Of course we see Paul, along with Barnabas, fasting and receiving personal direction for their ministry. Jesus fasted and His fame went throughout all the regions round about. As you live a life of fasting you will see your influence grow locally; you will be a hallmark for miraculous results. You do not have to necessarily be in the ministry to see this phenomenon. If you are in business you can apply the same principle to your life. Fasting works in every spectrum of life.

(Scripture References: Daniel 1:8-20, 2 Chronicles 20, Joel 1-2, Esther 1:1, Esther 3:8-15, Esther 3:1-3, 11-17, Esther 5:3-17).

FASTING WILL BRING BLESSING ON A PERSONAL, LOCAL, NATIONAL AND INTERNATIONAL LEVEL

---

92   FASTING WILL PROPEL A NEW SEASON AND A NEW DISPENSATION INTO YOUR STORY AND HISTORY

Whenever things looked bleak and destruction inevitable, the people of God fasted; they were then propelled into a new season of life. New stories were written and history reshaped, as fasting was engaged. You can change your present season of insignificance to a season of influence. From today, engage this great weapon of fasting and release a new dispensation in your life. Moses' fast released a new dispensation for Israel after they had left Egypt; they received fresh information from God for a new era. Paul's ministry went through a new level as he ministered unto the Lord with fasting. Cornelius' fast definitely released a new dispensation for the Gentiles. Something that never happened before became a reality. It was the beginning of a new day and a new season. Are you ready for a new season? I know I am! What about you?

(Scripture References: Exodus 34:1-35, Esther 8-10,
2 Chronicles 20, Acts 10).

93   FASTING IS LOBBYING HEAVEN TO CHANGE GODLESS LAWS OF THE LAND ESTABLISHED BY LAWLESS POLITICIANS AND IMMORAL JUDGES

We do not have to sit and watch helplessly as immorality is legalized in our nation: we can lobby God in fasting and prayer to change our society. Senseless politicians are in every nation of the world. These elected officials, who were meant to make the lives of people better, seek to establish their own secular agenda under the guidance of Satan. Why would you lobby your senators, congressmen and congresswomen who do not respect your beliefs? For the most part, they are interested in legislating laws that legalize debauchery in the name of freedom of choice. Today we have an anti-church, anti-God system in place. While they may not be cutting off our heads, they are cutting off our voices. It is now deemed ignorant to be someone who believes in creationism while some godless, pompous ignoramus (but academically-educated) buffoon can spew the baseless evolutionism doctrine as bona fide belief. Marriage is being redefined by certain segments of society who don't even believe in the sanctity of marriage.

So what are we to do? What did Esther do? When a law was legislated to legally kill off the Jewish people, she promptly fasted and changed the law. What did Daniel do when a law was legislated to kill anyone who called upon God? Fasting changed the law. Remember what I told you at the beginning of the book in defining fasting? I mentioned an old preacher who said, *'Fasting was to close the mouth in order to move the hand of the politicians or government on or off'*. We will achieve more in seeking God through fasting and prayer to change our community. Some of these politicians need to be prayed out and some good people need to be prayed in. Remember these words from the Psalmist:

> *When the righteous are in authority, the people rejoice: but when the wicked beareth rule, the people mourn.*
>
> PROVERBS 29:2

We understand that when wicked people are in governance, the righteous suffer. This is how we translate *'the people mourn.'* However, remember that in the Old Testament, 'to mourn' and 'to humble' were alternative, synonymous terms for fasting. Therefore this verse can be rendered as:

> *When the righteous are in authority, the people rejoice: but when the wicked beareth rule, the people have to fast.*

I am amazed at how national church leaders have remained motionless throughout certain administrations; it is time to fast and lobby the Almighty to bring change to our land. This promise is still true:

> *If my people, which are called by my name, shall humble themselves (fast), and pray, and seek my face, and turn from their wicked ways; then will I hear from heaven, and will forgive their sin, and will heal their land.*
>
> 2 CHRONICLES 7:14

FASTING IS LOBBYING GOD TO UNSEAT LAWLESS POLITICIANS WHO LEGISLATE IMMORALITY TO BE THE LAW OF THE LAND AND BRING ABOUT CHANGE THAT WE CAN BELIEVE IN

---

94 FASTING WILL CAUSE GOD TO TAKE OVER YOUR BATTLES. YOU WILL LEARN THAT THE BATTLE IS NOT YOURS BUT GOD'S

It was after a national fast that the promise of God fighting the battle was made. Whenever we fast, God shows up as Jehovah Sabaoth: the God who will defend you. He is the man of war who is the undisputed champion of the world. He has never lost a battle and He never will. When Jehovah Sabaoth fights, He decapitates the enemy; ask Goliath! Many times believers have the idea that God just sits there nonchalantly letting the world and the devil have their way. No! As you invoke Him in fasting, He will come out swinging and when He does, it is always knock-out time.

(Scripture References: Chronicles 20:15-17, 1 Samuel 17:47).

95 FASTING TURNS BREAKDOWNS INTO BREAKTHROUGHS; DEFEATS INTO DELIGHTS

As you go through the pages of the Bible you will discover that those who fasted turned what was meant to be their breakdowns into breakthroughs. Judah was outnumbered and fearful but through fasting their enemies were destroyed. Esther and Mordecai turned breakdowns into breakthroughs, as did the Ninevites. As you fast, you will turn whatever the enemy throws against you into a door of uncommon breakthroughs. Even as King David changed the name of the Valley of Rephaim to Baalperazim, the same will be your portion. The valley of Rephaim means 'the valley of giants'. But David turned the valley of giants into Baalperazim meaning 'Lord of the Breakthrough'. Hannah and Jehoshaphat were prime examples of turning what looked to be the enemy's plan to break them down into breakthroughs. Hannah was in despair due to her lack of fruitfulness and the constant mockery by Peninnah. In her despair she turned to the Lord in prayer and fasting and the Lord gave her Samuel. She eventually broke through as the Lord visited her and gave her more sons and daughters (1 Samuel 2:21). When all the odds were against Jehoshaphat, he called for a national fast and secured victory.

96 FASTING ELICITS THE COMPASSION, MERCY AND PITY OF GOD TO TERMINATE A CRISIS

When the Ninevites, who deserved judgment, fasted, it elicited God's compassion on them. He was merciful and terminated the crisis which was due. God is a God of compassion and pity and as we seek Him, He will lavish His mercy upon us. His mercies are new every morning and we can tap into that. If God had pity, compassion and mercy upon Nineveh, He will have mercy upon our land.

(Scripture References: Jonah 3:4-10, Joel 2:12-18).

97 FASTING BOLDLY BRINGS YOU INTO THE PRESENCE OF GOD, TO FIND GRACE TO HELP IN TIME OF NEED

Fasting always secures the presence of God in our lives. It is our deliberate act of drawing near to God and as the Word says, *'he will draw near unto us'* (James 4:8). Looking at the story of Esther and the king, I want to draw a picture of what transpires when one fasts:

> *Now it came to pass on the third day, that Esther put on her royal apparel, and stood in the **inner court of the king's house**, over against the king's house: and the king **sat upon his royal throne** in the royal house, over against the gate of the house. And it was so, when the king saw Esther the queen standing in the court, that she **obtained favour** in his sight: and the king held out to Esther the golden sceptre that was in his hand. So Esther drew near, and touched the top of the sceptre.*
>
> ESTHER 5:1-2

Please note that Esther went into the King's inner court after her fast. This is a type (Typology *) of the bride – which is a type of the church – going before her king – a type of Christ – with boldness, in the inner court or the throne of grace,

---

* Typology in Christian theology and Biblical exegesis is a doctrine concerning the predictive relationship of the Old Testament to the New Testament. Events, persons or statements in the Old Testament are seen as types pre-figuring or superseded by antitypes, events or aspects of Christ or his revelation described in the New Testament.

to obtain mercy and find grace to help in time of need. Esther's boldness brought her before the throne of her king, who stretched the scepter of grace towards her. That sounds like what the author of Hebrews said:

Let us therefore come boldly unto the throne of grace, that we may obtain mercy, and find grace to help in time of need.

HEBREWS 4:16

We know that Esther was bold because she said, '*so will I go in unto the king, which is not according to the law: and if I perish, I perish.*' (Esther 4:16). Fasting accesses the presence of God in order to receive the scepter of grace to find help in time of need.

98 FASTING ENABLES YOU TO STAND IN THE GAP AND ADD TO YOUR INTERCESSION BEFORE THE LORD

Then once again I fell prostrate before the LORD for forty days and forty nights; I ate no bread and drank no water, because of all the sin you had committed, doing what was evil in the LORD's sight and so provoking him to anger. I feared the anger and wrath of the LORD, for he was angry enough with you to destroy you. But again the LORD listened to me. And the LORD was angry enough with Aaron to destroy him, but at that time I prayed for Aaron too.

DEUTERONOMY 9:18 NEW INTERNATIONAL VERSION

By all accounts, Israel and Aaron merited death because of the transgression of worshiping the golden calf. Aaron, who should have known better, was responsible in the fashioning of the molten calf. God's anger was hot against them but Moses interceded with fasting and prayer. Now we know, according to God, that Moses and Samuel were the two of the greatest intercessors in the Old Testament (Jeremiah 15:1). What these two had going for them was great intercessory prayers, aided by fasting. Even when Saul was rejected by God, Samuel mourned for him. Remember in the Scriptures mourning and fasting were synonymous terms. The lives of 2.5 million Israelis and Aaron were spared because of the intercession and fasting of Moses.

Notice Moses said, '*The Lord listened to me.*' That is wielding some power with God! He did so because he was a man given to much fasting.

99 FASTING WILL RELEASE THE GREAT OUTPOURING OF THE FORMER AND LATTER RAIN

The former and latter rain will constitute as a double portion blessing. As we fast and press into God, there will be a launching of the former and latter rain that will provoke a supernatural outpouring of the Spirit, with great manifestations. The outpouring will be of the glory of the Lord:

> *But this is that which was spoken by the prophet Joel; And it shall come to pass in the last days, saith God, I will pour out of my Spirit upon all flesh: and your sons and your daughters shall prophesy, and your young men shall see visions, and your old men shall dream dreams. And on my servants and on my handmaidens I will pour out in those days of my Spirit; and they shall prophesy: And I will shew wonders in heaven above, and signs in the earth beneath; blood, and fire, and vapour of smoke: The sun shall be turned into darkness, and the moon into blood, before that great and notable day of the Lord come: And it shall come to pass, that whosoever shall call on the name of the Lord shall be saved.*
>
> ACTS 2:16-21

The results of the great outpouring are:

❖ **Spirit upon all flesh** – a national revival that will also cross boundaries and become international such as the Azusa Street Revival, the Welsh Revival and many other great revivals.

❖ **Sons and daughters will prophesy** – revival fire among the young people; they will be on fire for God.

❖ **Young men see visions, old men dream dreams** – young visionaries will arise; new blood in ministry; older generations will see the fulfillment of the dreams of their youth.

❖ **My servants and my handmaidens I will pour out in those days of my Spirit** – anointed vessels and vessels of glory will be common in the land.

❖ **They will prophesy** – there will be an outpouring of revelations of the Word of the Lord.

❖ **Wonders in heaven above and signs in the earth beneath** – miracles, signs and wonders will be prevalent. No longer will you read about the wonders of past revivals and wish that you were alive back then: you will live to and see them.

❖ **Whosoever shall call on the name of the Lord shall be saved** – there will be a great harvest of souls. This is what it is all about: souls, souls, souls! There will be an influx into the kingdom and the churches will be filled to capacity again.

100 FASTING WILL REVEAL WHAT YOU TRULY VALUE AND WHAT IS THE REAL TREASURE OF YOUR LIFE

Anything that you place value on and want in your life you will fast for. There are some things that will never come into your life unless you fast for them. When Jesus said, *'For where your treasure is, there will your heart be also'* (Matthew 6:21), He was speaking in the context of fasting. You can see this if you read a few verses before this one. You will only fast for what you truly treasure; if you do not treasure the anointing then you will not fast for it; if you really want the healing anointing of God over your life you will fast for it. This is what we mean when we say 'contend for the gift'.

(Scripture References: Matthew 6:16-21, Matthew 6:33).

101 FASTING ENABLES YOU TO FIGHT A GOOD WARFARE WITH THE PROPHECIES THAT YOU HAVE RECEIVED

Daniel understood, by reading the prophecies of Jeremiah, that God had a plan of return from Babylon to Jerusalem for His people. He discovered that after seventy years of captivity, they were due back. However Daniel did not just assume because there was a prophecy that it would happen automatically. Many have made the mistake of thinking that prophecies are deployed automatically, but Paul instructed Timothy to do warfare with the prophecies that were spoken over his life. The way that you do warfare with prophecies is to take them up before the Lord in prayer and fasting. Daniel did just that! He did not assume it would happen automatically.

> A prophet from Texas

Many years ago when I was a teenager, in a Sunday night service a prophet of God from Texas called me out and started to prophesy on me while he played the keyboard, his eyes closed. I can't tell you everything that he told me in this book, but let me share some points that were very specific. Under the inspiration of the Holy Spirit, he said, '*Young man, you will cross many waters. You will write many books and God will give you an anointing to make that which is complicated to become easy. When you teach, things will look easy!*'

At the time I received that prophetic declaration I was in my early teens. At that time of my life it was a struggle for me to even read a book and the man said that I would write *many* books. He also said that I would cross many waters. At that time traveling was no way near my mind; I hated the notion of traveling because my father was a chief chef on ships and he would be away for months at a time. So that did not appeal to me! It may not look like it now but I was timid as a teenager and the idea of preaching was daunting for me. However the night after I received that prophecy, after the service I went straight to the P.A / sound people and asked them if they had recorded the prophecy. Thankfully they had. So I bought the tape and played it over and over until it registered in my spirit. I have fasted over these prophetic words. There was a time when it did not look like anything was happening but I fought *for* and *with* these prophecies, through fasting and prayer. At the time of writing this book, I have written 30 books and I have traveled extensively crossing many waters.

Today I encourage you not to let go of your prophecies. For many of us, the day we received our prophecies we were elated but after a period of time, having seen no results, we just gave up. No! It is not the time to give up. Fight for your prophecies. Fight a good warfare with the prophecies by engaging fasting to see the fulfillment of them.

(Scripture References: Daniel 9, 1 Timothy 1:18, Nehemiah 1).

CHAPTER 12
POSITIONING YOURSELF FOR A SUCCESSFUL FAST

IT is important that as you embark on a fast you position yourself correctly to maximize the results of the fast. People fail in fasting because they simply do not know how to act or behave during a fast. It is a bit like going to the gym and seeing all the machines and equipment that can give you the body that you desire but without the proper use of the machines and weights you are liable to hurt yourself. Through the years I have failed many times in fasting because I did not know how to correctly position myself according to the Scriptures. For many people, because of a lack of knowledge, fasting feels more like dieting or a hunger strike. Thank God for His mercy and patience towards us! I have learnt and am learning more and more about the ins and outs of fasting. You must remember that fasting is a spiritual force on a physical level. Therefore it is imperative that you partake of spiritual things during a fast. It is not just abstaining from food: it is abstaining from physical food for spiritual nourishment. So how do we present ourselves on a fast? What do you do? As I mentioned earlier in the book while discussing the different genres of fasting, as a believer there are only two levels of fasting that you can be involved in: the *corporate* level and the *personal* level. I want to show you how to rightly position yourself for both.

There are many examples of people who fasted corporately in the Bible but I will take you through the tiny book of Nehemiah for our lessons. Nehemiah, a man accustomed to fasting, rebuilt the walls of Jerusalem in 52 days. His experience gives us seven major keys that will unlock the gateway to a successful fast both on a corporate and personal level:

*Now in the twenty and fourth day of this month the **children of Israel were assembled with fasting**, and with sackclothes, and earth upon them.*

*And **the seed of Israel separated themselves from all strangers**, and stood and **confessed their sins, and the iniquities of their fathers**. And they stood up in their place, and **read in the book of the law of the Lord their God one fourth part of the day**; and another fourth part they confessed, and **worshipped the Lord** their God.*

NEHEMIAH 9:1-3

1 ASSEMBLING TOGETHER WITH FASTING

> Corporate level

In a corporate and united fast it is important that the body of believers who are engaged in the fast are assembled together. It is a shame that many times when a church has a corporate fast, the people do not get together. I have seen instances where the senior pastor himself does not assemble with the members. That is totally ludicrous! See the words of God through Joel:

Gird yourselves, and lament, ye priests: howl, ye ministers of the altar: come, lie all night in sackcloth, ye ministers of my God: for the meat offering and the drink offering is withholden from the house of your God. Sanctify ye a fast, call a solemn assembly, gather the elders and all the inhabitants of the land into the house of the Lord your God, and cry unto the Lord.

JOEL 1:13-14

And all Judah stood before the Lord, with their little ones, their wives, and their children.

2 CHRONICLES 20:13

When a corporate fast has been called, the pastors, ministers, elders and members should actively gather together to pray; gathering for the purpose of prayer and intercession on behalf of the church is called a *solemn assembly*. Notice it said, '*Cry unto the Lord*', meaning 'gather together to pray and not talk to each other' Many times, I have seen people get together and all they do is pray for a few minutes and then talk about a problem for the rest of the prayer meeting. This defeats the object of corporate prayer. Whether the gathering is for one hour or all night prayer, there has to be a prayer leader to lead the meeting otherwise it will descend into people talking, sleeping or doing their own thing. In a corporate fast, prepare for the gathering. Don't assume when you get together that it will all flow. Have the worship, prayer points, order of service and pray-ers ready. The prayer leader must make sure that the service is well ordered; if there is an unruly person who wants to take over and starts talking, then kindly ask them to talk *after* the service. You are about the King's business. If the corporate fast is between a husband and his spouse then the two should get together to pray. Once again, when you gather, come prepared regarding what you will do and pray about. This is where the *prayer of agreement* comes into play as well. It is important to assemble together on a corporate fast whether it is just as a couple, business partners, ministry or a church for the purpose of prayer, intercession and agreement of faith. When people do not get together during the fast for prayer, it indicates that the goal does not have the same urgency for some of the party involved. We all make time for what we truly value.

> Personal level

Set yourself for your fast; organize yourself and go into the fast with specific goals. Know what are you fasting for and how long the fast will be. Is it going to be a normal 24-hour fast, a 9am-6pm fast or for a longer period of time? Make a quality decision! A quality decision is one that you make and will not bow to outside pressures to change. Remember, the intensity and length of your fast is determined by you. Know your capacity! I usually say or write down the specific purpose, goals and length of my fast. I call it my *fasting contract* with the Lord. Don't ever go into a fast with a lackadaisical attitude because at the first sign of hunger pain or the smell of food you will capitulate. This is the voice of experience speaking!. I failed in my fast when I came with a casual attitude, but God is gracious and taught me how to fast. I also learned a lot from other, successful 'fasters'.

2 THE SEED OF ISRAEL SEPARATED THEMSELVES FROM ALL STRANGERS

> ### Applicable to corporate and personal level

The purpose of fasting is to get away from life's daily affairs and set ourselves to seek the Lord. Nehemiah 9:2: *'the seed of Israel separated themselves from all strangers'*. How is this applicable to us today? During the fast, separate yourselves from people – especially unbelieving friends – who love their sinful ways. Some unbelieving friends can also be some 'believers' who do not believe anything about anything. They are believers but they do not believe in miracles or healing and most certainly cannot believe the breakthrough that you are believing for during your fast. You do not need to be around these 'strangers' who would surely sap your faith. Don't ever get into a corporate fast with someone who cannot believe what you are believing for. Remove yourself from the distractions of the world – and there are many: television, newspapers, Facebook, Twitter, the Internet and others that you know. Separate yourself from anything that would engage your mind towards sin, the flesh and failure. The notion here is consecration to the things of God and for the things of God; it is focusing upon the Lord. The purpose of separating is to hear the voice of the Lord. You are not going to hear the Lord with all kinds of noises around you. It is not that He is not speaking it is that there are too many interferences to heed His instructions. One of the greatest things to learn in order to hear the Spirit is the shutting off of things:

- ❖ Shut off the voices of fear.
- ❖ Shut off the television and radio.
- ❖ Shut off social media.
- ❖ Shut off the voices of the world.

3 STOOD AND CONFESSED THEIR SINS, AND THE INIQUITIES OF
THEIR FATHERS

There was time when this was strange to my mind but it is very important to grasp. We see this measure prominently in Nehemiah and Daniel who were dealing with the return of the political exiles of Babylon back to the Promised land. I understand confessing and repenting of personal sins but why in the world would anyone want to dig up and confess the sins of their forefathers?

The reason they went into exile was because of a particular sin of the fathers. To be exact, it said the *iniquity* of their fathers. There is a difference between sin and iniquity. Sin – in this case, 'harmatia', meaning 'to miss the mark' – mainly affects the person that has committed the act. Iniquity, on the other hand, is more than just missing the mark. In Hebrew it is 'avon' meaning 'perverseness'. It is from the root word 'avah' meaning 'a crook, make crooked, perverse, trouble and pervert'. Iniquity is a sin of perversion that makes the lineage of a generation crooked, troubling those who follow after with the proclivity to do the same perverted act. While regular hamartia is held accountable to the person, iniquity is unfairly passed on. Hence the word 'iniquity' from the Latin 'iniquitas', deriving from 'iniquus' and being the combination of 'in' – meaning 'not' – and 'aequus' – meaning 'equal, just.' The two combined means 'not fair', 'not equal' or 'not just'. Iniquity is therefore a proneness to sin a particular kind of sin due to the weakness or predisposition to yield to that particular perversion from the family line. It is a perversion with the legal entryway of a demon or spirit thus giving access to future generations. It can be idolatry, sexual perversion or other forms of crookedness.

Because Satan is a legalist, whatever past agreement or pact there was, he will make a demand on it. There are people who are saved but are struggling with particular issues that they cannot shake off. Like Lazarus, they are resurrected to life but are still bound. There are people who love God but are in bondage. There are generational issues that have latched on and have been passed down. Have you noticed how a particular issue afflicts certain families for generations? Madness, sexual perversion, divorce, heart disease, diabetes, cancer, crime, addictions, suicide, alcoholism and promiscuity are a few examples. These sins and inclinations become generational issues that Satan employs to keep a believer, family, people, city or nation in his evil grip. You may or may not be aware of these sins in your family but Satan does not care; all he knows is that a legal entry was given to him. You don't know what altar your forefathers raised or what kind of evil pact was made. The point to remember is that physically and genetically speaking we all come from a line of sinners – going all the way back to Adam. Thank God for Jesus, the Last Adam and through His precious blood, we can call for the reverse of any family iniquity, issues or curse. Daniel, the prophet, did this: he laid himself out before the Lord and confessed the sins or iniquities of his forefathers as if he had committed the sins himself.

Here's another important fact to look at: the iniquities of fathers may not necessarily be your own physical forefathers. When we talk of nations we talk about the founding fathers or the fathers of a city. We may not be related to them physically but they are called fathers because they founded the place where you reside. Some were fathers of cities and nations who were godly men but there were places where evil and wicked men founded the city with wickedness. There were sins of iniquity committed from the founding fathers, presidents, rulers, kings and queens which are still affecting certain nations and cities today.

> Corporately

Unless you are dealing with sins in and of the land, it would not apply to you as a couple, business or ministry fasting for a breakthrough, but as a church it may very well apply if there are hindrances to the move of God. In certain cities and nations the churches are barren and there has been no revival or move of God. Some nations – in their inception – made pacts and covenants with Satan and witchcraft. In order to break that curse and see fruitfulness, during the fast the church needs to ask forgiveness for these sins and break the hold.

> Personal

If you are dealing with a particular issue or recurring pattern in your life that has been present in your lineage, while on your fast, you have to close the door to whatever pact, legal entry and legal agreement was made. You simply do that by the application and confessing of the blood of Christ. The covenant blood of Jesus is more powerful than any other blood pact made with the enemy. However if all is normal in your life and you are looking for a particular breakthrough but prior to your fast you were involved in certain sin or sins, wisdom would dictate that you repent, confess and move on. God is faithful to forgive:

> *If we confess our sins, he is faithful and just to forgive us our sins, and to cleanse us from all unrighteousness*
>
> 1 JOHN 1:9

4 READ IN THE BOOK OF THE LAW OF THE LORD THEIR GOD ONE FOURTH PART OF THE DAY

> Corporate and Personal

During the fast, take the time to load up on the Word. Another rendition of this verse is, '*They read from the Book of the Law of the LORD their God for a quarter of the day*' (NIV). This means immerse yourself in the Word, read spiritual books, feed your spirit as you starve your flesh. Now unless you are in full-time ministry or have taken days off from work to fast, you may not be able to spend a quarter of your day reading and soaking in the Word. If you are fasting on your work day, use your lunch time to get into the Word. Why is it important to read and meditate the Word? Because the Word is God speaking to you. You will hear God through his Word. In fact reading your Bible when you are fasting is like reading the Bible in 3D: Everything becomes alive. The book becomes alive and revelations will spring into your spirit and mind. Reading and meditating the Word will trigger the Law of Receiving in your life:

*This **book of the law** shall **not depart** out of **thy mouth**; but thou shalt **meditate** therein **day and night**, that thou mayest **observe to do** according to all that is **written therein**: for then thou shalt **make thy way prosperous**, and then thou shalt **have good success**.*

JOSHUA 1:8

*My son, **attend to my words; incline thine ear** unto my **sayings**. Let them **not depart** from **thine eyes**; keep them in the midst of **thine heart**. For they are life unto those that find them, and health to all their flesh. Keep thy heart with all diligence; for out of it are the issues of life. **Put away** from thee a **froward mouth**, and **perverse lips** put **far from thee**. Let **thine eyes look right on**, and let **thine eyelids look straight** before thee. **Ponder** the path of **thy feet**, and let all thy ways be **established**. **Turn not** to the **right** hand nor to the **left: remove** thy **foot** from **evil**.*

PROVERBS 4:20-27

5 ANOTHER FOURTH PART THEY CONFESSED

Confess the Word. Confess God's promises over your life, your family, your business, your situation and your church. There is something powerful about confession done under the influence of fasting. Notice the quick results that Jesus got when He confessed the Word during His fast on the Mount of Temptations. It is imperative that you, like Israel, learn to confess the Word and the promises of God during your fast. Confession is simply the voicing of the Word to a given situation. In a church's corporate fast, make sure to speak the Word and promises over the church; speak what you desire to see. During the gathering time or the prayer meeting, have the congregation to speak the promises of the Lord. Your faith in God can only rise to your level of confession. During the fast, turbo-charge your life with the confession of the Word, which is simply declaring the end from the beginning. If you do not declare your end then Satan and others will declare your end. Jesus said, '*You can have what you say*' (Mark 11:23). What you confess with your lips dominates your inner being: nothing will establish you and build your faith as quickly as confession. God can be no bigger in you than what you confess Him to be. Declare the promises boldly; the Word of God spoken in boldness will defeat the devil every time. The voicing of God's promises is the lifting of the shield of faith, which will quench all the fiery darts of Satan. Raise up a hedge of protection and health around you with the Word fitted in your mouth. When you confess the Word you are simply applying the principle of the 'send and return Word' of Isaiah 55:

> *So shall my word be that goeth forth out of my mouth: it shall not return unto me void, but it shall accomplish that which I please, and it shall prosper in the thing whereto I sent it.*
>
> ISAIAH 55:11

❯ Returning God's Word to Him

God states that whenever a word goes out of His mouth it has been sent on a mission and He expects it to return to Him. That Word will not return to Him void but will accomplish what He has intended. So anytime He speaks, He expects His word to return to Him. When we speak the Word we are returning His Word back to Him by way of giving voice to it. God – who creates the fruit of our lips – will back-up our confession.

6 WORSHIPPED THE LORD THEIR GOD

❯ Corporate and personal

Worship God. Worship is important all the time but it is *very* important during a fast? Why?

> *Now there were in the church that was at Antioch certain prophets and teachers; as Barnabas, and Simeon that was called Niger, and Lucius of Cyrene, and Manaen, which had been brought up with Herod the tetrarch, and Saul. **As they ministered to the Lord, and fasted, the Holy Ghost said**, Separate me Barnabas and Saul for the work whereunto I have called them. And when they had fasted and prayed, and laid their hands on them, they sent them away. So they, being sent forth by the Holy*

Ghost, departed unto Seleucia; and from thence they sailed to Cyprus.

ACTS 13:1-4

Notice the words *minister to the Lord*. It means to *worship*. While they were fasting and worshiping the Lord, the Holy Spirit spoke. So worship opens you up to the voice of the Holy Spirit for instruction, guidance and direction. He will give wisdom and exact instructions for your secured victory. When Elisha needed to hear from God for King Jehoshaphat, the King had come to the Elisha with evil King Jehoram. When Elisha saw Jehoram, he was irritated, displeased and he made his feelings known. But in order for him to hear from the Lord, look what he asked for:

But now bring me a minstrel. And it came to pass, when the minstrel played, that the hand of the Lord came upon him. And he said, Thus saith the Lord...

2 KINGS 3:15-16

Worship is ministering unto the Lord and as you minister unto Him, He will minister back unto you. Many times, during my fast I worship the Lord with a worship CD or just singing to the Lord. Both are excellent but I love to worship from my own heart to God. Then after a while, I will simply say, 'God, what are you saying to me today?' or 'Holy Spirit, what do you have for me?' Then I listen within my spirit man because this is where He is. Also during those times of fasting, I will read my Bible extensively. Sometimes I get an inward nudge to read certain portions of Scripture and the Spirit of the Lord will highlight something for me and give me my answer. My Bible is very, very close to me when I am fasting. In a corporate scenario, after worship, give time to listen to the voice of God. A prophecy or tongues and interpretation of tongues can follow. The idea is to hear from God:

*Then **upon Jahaziel** the son of Zechariah, the son of Benaiah, the son of Jeiel, the son of Mattaniah, a Levite of the sons of Asaph, **came the Spirit of the Lord** in the midst of the congregation; And he said, Hearken ye, all Judah, and ye inhabitants of Jerusalem, and thou king Jehoshaphat, Thus saith the Lord unto you, Be not afraid nor dismayed by reason of* *this great multitude; for the battle is not yours, but God's. **To morrow** go ye down against them: **behold, they come up by the cliff of Ziz; and ye shall find them at the end of the brook,** before the wilderness of Jeruel.*

2 CHRONICLES 20:14-16

When the Spirit of the Lord spoke, He gave them the exact day, exact place and exact strategy to execute. It pays to worship in order to hear His voice to know what to do.

7 INTERCEDE

Lastly, as we are fasting corporately, we need to intercede for what we are fasting for: bring it before the Lord in prayer. Remember, fasting is making demands on the supply of the Spirit and forcing the enemy to relent and let go of his opposition towards you. You can pray without fasting but you cannot – or should not – fast without praying. If you recall, Paul, after his first encounter with Jesus, went on a three-day fast and Ananias was told by the Lord to, *'go into the street which is called Straight, and enquire in the house of Judas for one called Saul, of Tarsus: for, behold, he prayeth'* (Acts 9:11). Paul was clearly fasting and praying. It is interesting to note that Paul was in the house of Judas on Straight street while he was fasting and praying. This is what fasting and praying does: it causes you to dwell in the house of praise and make that which is crooked to become straight.

CHAPTER 13
THE 101 FASTING POWER LIST

My favorite 101 Fasting nuggets

WE have already looked at an exhaustive list of 101 benefits of fasting but here are my favorite 101 nuggets that I keep looking at when I am fasting; these are my motivational factors to keep me on track during a fast. These nuggets came to me when I was on a year of fasting; I started with 21-days in January, on the Daniel fast. After that I went on to a normal fast of water for a few days. After adapting for a while to the normal fast I took some days where I had total fast. Then, I reverted to the Daniel fast again, where I did not eat meat for a year. It was during this long fast that I saw major spiritual and financial breakthroughs. It was also during that time when the Bible became alive to me and God gave me these nuggets. They are here to keep you focused while you are fasting.

1. Fasting will trigger an open, physical reward and manifestation.
   (Matthew 6:16-19, Hebrews 11:6)

2. Fasting moves God the Father onto the scene.
   (Matthew 6:16-19, Nehemiah 6:16)

3. Fasting is a weapon of mass destruction for the pulling down of strongholds.
   (Luke 4:1-3, 2 Corinthians 10:4)

4. Fasting gives you dominion in the spirit.
   (Luke 4:14)

5. Fasting weakens spiritual opposition and wickedness.
   (Luke 4:14, Daniel 10)

6.   Fasting will precipitate the answer which has been delayed and
      obstructed. It is a blow to the spirit of delay.
      (Daniel 10)

7.   Fasting is the release of angels. It summons warring angels
      on warring assignments.
      (Daniel 10, Acts 10:1-5, 30, Acts 27:21-38)

8.   Fasting is the pathway of humility turning you towards the Lord
      and grants access into the grace of God.
      (Psalm 35:13, Psalm 69:10, James 4:6, 1 Peter 5:5-10)

9.   Fasting turns breakdowns into breakthroughs, defeat into delight.
      (2 Chronicles 20, 1 Samuel 1:1-19)

10.   Fasting will cause a divine shift in the realm of the spirit.
      (Luke 4:14, Daniel 10, Acts 2:1-4)

11.   Fasting will reverse death assignments and decrees of death
      against your life.
      (2 Chronicles 20, Daniel 6:18-22, Esther 9:1)

12.   Fasting will bring total confusion into the camp of the enemy
      and force the impossible to become possible.
      (2 Chronicles 20:22, Acts 27:21-38)

13.   Fasting breaks barrenness and releases a season of fruitfulness.
      (1 Samuel 1:1-19, Joel 2)

14.   Fasting will open you to the gifts of the Spirit.
      (2 Chronicles 20:13-16, Acts 10:5-30)

15.   Fasting opens you up to the voice of God.
      (Judges 20:26-28; 2 Chronicles 20:13-16, Acts 27:21)

16.   Fasting causes God to see and notice you.
      (1Kings 20:21-28, Isaiah 58:3)

17.   Fasting attracts God.

18.   Fasting gives you the exact strategy to take the land and move into your destiny.
(2 Chronicles 20, Judges 20:26-28, Acts 10)

19.   Fasting opens you to the realm of visions.
(Acts 10, Daniel 10)

20.   Fasting will release prosperity into your life.
(Joel 2:12-27, 2 Chronicles 20:24–27)

21.   Fasting will induce the birth and safe delivery of your destiny.
(Isaiah 66:7-9, Mark 9:29, Galatians 4:19, Genesis 25:21-26)

22.   Fasting will unseat the belly-god.
(1 Corinthians 6:13, Philippians 3:17-19, Galatians 5:17)

23.   Fasting is another form of resistance to the works of the devil.
(James 4:7, 1Peter 5:9, 2 Chronicles 20:29)

24.   Fasting is changing the unseen from the seen.
(Daniel 10, Luke 4, Acts 27)

25.   Fasting brings protection for your children.
(Ezra 8:21)

26.   Fasting paves the way for a safe crossing into your destiny.
(Ezra 8:21, Judges 20:26-28)

27.   Fasting invokes and activates the hand of God over your life.
(Ezra 8:31, Nehemiah 2:8, 1 Peter 5:6)

28.   Fasting is tasting and seeing that the Lord is good.
(Psalm 34:8)

29.   Fasting averts judgment.
(1 Kings 21:27, 1 Chronicles 33:1-18, Jonah 3:4-10, Joel 2:12-14)

30. Fasting is the quintessential way to crucify the flesh and present your body as a living sacrifice.
    (Romans 12:1-2)

31. Fasting is aggressive faith in action to do violence in the kingdom of darkness and take what is yours.
    (Matthew 11:12, Mark 9:23, 29)

32. Fasting will force the hand of the enemy to relent and let go.
    (Ezra 8:31)

33. Fasting will cause the golden scepter of favor to be stretched out over your life. It gives you favor with God and favor with man.
    (Esther 5:1-2, Esther 8:4, Nehemiah 2:4-8, Daniel 1:8-9)

34. Fasting enables you to tap into the spirit of revelation and understanding.
    (Daniel 1:12-20, Daniel 9:3, 21, Daniel 10)

35. Fasting will destroy generational curses.
    (Mark 9:17-29, Esther 7:10)

36. Fasting will aptly prepare you for ministry.
    (Luke 4:1-14, Acts 9:1-9, Acts 13:1-4, Nehemiah 1:4, 2 Corinthians 6:4-5)

37. Fasting is declaring war on the spirit of unbelief and sharpens your faith.
    (Mark 9:17-29, Matthew 4)

38. Fasting is making demands on the supply of the Spirit.
    (Mark 9:17-29, Philippians 1:19)

39. Fasting is preparing the way of the Lord to move.
    (Isaiah 40:3; Malachi 3:1; Matt 3:3)

40. Fasting will bring rest and quietness into your realm.
    (2 Chronicles 20:30)

41. Fasting is the maintaining of your cutting edge.
    (2 Kings 6:1-7, 2 Corinthians 6:4-5)

42. Fasting sharpens your faith and empowers your confession
    to be as a double edged sword as well as a laser beam to cut
    through the enemy's line of defense.
    (Luke 4:2-13, Hebrews 4:12, 2 Chronicles 20:27)

43. Fasting downloads the will of God into physical manifestation.
    (Daniel 9, 2 Chronicles 20, Mark 9:17-29, Judges 20)

44. Fasting forces focus.
    (Mark 9:29, Luke 4:2)

45. Fasting is the master key to operating in the supernatural.
    It gives a supernatural edge to your life and ministry.
    (Matthew 4:1-17, Luke 4:1-44, Acts 9:1-9)

46. Fasting amplifies your prayers and supercharges your prayer life
    into a richer and more explosive experience.
    (2 Chronicles 7:14, Isaiah 58:9)

47. Fasting exhibits your total dependence upon the hand of God
    rather than your own hands.
    (2 Chronicles 20:12, Esther 4:12-16, Hebrews 12:2)

48. Fasting will enable you to say, '*Not by might nor by power but
    by my Spirit, says the Lord.*'
    (Zechariah 4:6, Joel 2, Nehemiah 6:16)

49. Fasting brings promotion and the elevation of your status
    *(Nehemiah 1: 2:1, 5:14, Esther 6:1-11, Esther 9:3-4, Esther 10:1-3,
    Daniel 1:1-20, Daniel 2:48, Daniel 3:30, Daniel 6:1-4)*

50. Fasting will have those who have forgotten or neglected you to remember you and honor you.
    (Esther 6:1-3)

51. Fasting will cause your enemies who planned your destruction to parade your victory.
    (Esther 6:7-13)

52. Fasting will cause the weapon of destruction fashioned to destroy you to be the destruction of your enemies.
    (Esther 6:13, 7:9,10)

53. Fasting will reverse evil plots of destructions against your life.
    (Esther 7:9-10, Daniel 6:16-24, Esther 8:17, Esther 9:1-5)

54. Fasting will shut the mouths of lions.
    (Daniel 6:16-24, Hebrews 11:33, 1 Peter 5:6-8)

55. Fasting will cause God to talk to other people about your needs.
    (Esther 6:1-3, Daniel 6:16-24)

56. Fasting will cause you to tap into the wisdom of God and make you ten times wiser than those who compete with you.
    (Daniel 1:18-20)

57. Fasting prepares you for new wine, new oil and new anointing.
    (Mark 2:18-22, Joel 2:21-24)

58. Fasting gives you the right timing to make your move thus ensuring victory.
    (Judges 20:26-28, Acts 13:1-4, Acts 14:23)

59. Fasting is waiting upon the Lord to renew your strength as the eagle.
    (Isaiah 40:29-31, Psalm 103:5, Deuteronomy 32:9-13)

60. Fasting causes the natural man to play second fiddle to the
     spiritual man.
     *(Galatians 5:16-18, Romans 7:18-23, Romans 8:5-8,
     Romans 8:12-13, 1 Corinthians 9:25-27)*

61. Fasting cleanses the temple of God, gives rest to your digestive
     system, rebuilds the immune system, reverses the aging process
     and increases your lifespan.
     (Daniel 1:8-15, Deuteronomy 33:7)

62. Fasting will loose the bondages of wickedness and make straight
     that which is twisted.
     (Isaiah 58:6, Mark 9, Judges 20)

63. Fasting will undo heavy burdens.
     (Isaiah 58:6, Luke 4:18,19)

64. Fasting will break every yoke.
     (Isaiah 58:6, Isaiah 10:27)

65. Fasting will cause your light to break forth as the morning.
     (Isaiah 58:8)

66. Fasting will speedily unleash divine healing, divine health
     and divine life.
     (Isaiah 58:8)

67. Fasting will cause your righteousness to go before you.
     (Isaiah 58:8)

68. Fasting will protect your front and back, your coming in and
     your going out.
     (Isaiah 58:8)

69. Fasting is the release of the glory of God in your life.
     (Isaiah 58:8, Joel 2:21-24, Acts 2:16-20)

70. Fasting will secure continuous guidance, cause your soul to be satisfied in drought, and your bones to be made fat.
(Isaiah 58:11, Isaiah 48:17-21, Romans 8:14, Deuteronomy 32: 12)

71. Fasting will make you to be like a watered garden, and like a spring of water, whose waters fail not.
(Isaiah 58:11, Psalms 1)

72. Fasting will cause your progenies to build the old waste places.
(Isaiah 58:12, Ezra 8:21. Nehemiah 3:1-32)

73. Fasting will enable you to raise up the foundations of many generations; and you shall be called, the repairer of the breach, the restorer of paths to dwell in.
(Isaiah 58:12, Nehemiah 3:1-32)

74. Fasting will enable you to delight yourself in the Lord and He will cause you to ride upon the high places of the earth.
(Isaiah 58:14, Deuteronomy 32:13, 2 Samuel 22:33-34, Isaiah 41:18, Isaiah 58:14, Habakkuk 3:19, Ephesians 6:12)

75. Fasting will free you the heritage of Jacob your father.
(Isaiah 58:14, Deuteronomy32:9-14, Deuteronomy 33:4)

76. Fasting will expose that which is hidden and reveal to you the problem.
(Joshua 7:1-20, 1 Samuel 7:1-6)

77. Fasting enables the believer to deal and be victorious over the sin that so easily besets us.
(Isaiah 58:6, Hebrews 12:1, Romans 6:14)

78. Fasting removes physical, mental and spiritual obstacles to your Christian growth.
(Isaiah 58:6-12, Matthew 17:19-21)

79. Fasting gives you the opportunity to recalibrate your spiritual life.
    (Isaiah 43:19, Lamentations 3:22-24)

80. Fasting gives you self control and breaks addictive behavior.
    (Isaiah 58:6, Hebrews 12:1, Romans 7:5,15-24)

81. Fasting is adding virtue to your faith.
    (Mark 9:29, 2 Peter 1:5)

82. Fasting gives you a door of utterance.
    (Matthew 11:18, John 1:23, Matthew 3:1-6, 1 Corinthians 2:4-5)

83. Fasting will restore to you what the enemy stole from you.
    (Joel 2:25-26)

84. Fasting stirs God to be jealous over you.
    (Joel 2:17-18)

85. Fasting is a way of ministering unto the Lord, it is another expression of prayer and worship.
    (Luke 2:36-37, Acts 13:2)

86. Fasting will be the catalyst to change you externally, internally and eternally.
    (Luke 4:14, Acts 9:9-20, Acts 10:30, 44-48)

87. Fasting will bring blessing on a personal, local, national and international level.
    (Daniel 1:8-20, 2 Chronicles 20, Joel 1-2, Esther 1:1, Esther 3:8-15, Esther 3:1-3, 11-17, Esther 5:3-17)

88. Fasting will break the spirit of stagnation, restraint and constraint. No more plateau on a personal, professional, spiritual and ministerial level.
    (1 Samuel 1:7-20, Daniel 1:18-21, Daniel 2:48, Acts 13:1-4)

89. Fasting will propel a new season and a new dispensation in your story and history.
     (Exodus 34:1-35, Esther 8-10, 2 Chronicles 20, Acts 10)

90. Fasting will give a three dimensional change in your spirit, soul and body; It affects heaven, earth and hell.
     (Ephesians 3:16; 1 Corinthians 9:27; Luke 4:14)

91. Fasting will cause God to take over your battles; you will learn that the battle is not your's but God's.
     (2 Chronicles 20:15-17, 1 Samuel 17:47)

92. Fasting will cause you to confront and beat your fear and release joy.
     (2 Chronicles 20:3, Acts 27:21-25, Matthew 5:4, 2 Chronicles 20:27-28, Joel 2:15-23)

93. Fasting elicits the compassion, mercy and pity of God to terminate a crisis.
     (Jonah 3:4-10, Joel 2:12-18)

94. Fasting brings in the presence of God.
     (Luke 5:33-35, 1 Samuel 7:1-15)

95. Fasting turns your heart back to God thus rekindling your first love.
     (Joel 2:12)

96. Fasting will fuse exousia and dunamis thus releasing kratos. It puts you in a commanding position of dominion.
     (Luke 4:14, Ephesians 1:16-19)

97. Fasting will release the great outpouring of the former and latter rain.
     (Joel 2:21-24, Acts 2:16-20)

98. Fasting will reveal what you truly value and what is the real treasure of your life.
    (Matthew 6:16-21, Matthew 6:33)

99. Fasting enables you to fight a good warfare with the prophecies that you have received.
    (Daniel 9, 1 Timothy 1:18, Nehemiah 1)

100. Fasting is covering your mouth, emptying your belly to put something in your hands and enlarge your mouth over your enemies.
    (Exodus 34, 1 Samuel 1, 1 Samuel 2:1-3)

101. Fasting opens up the mission field.
    (Acts 13:1-4)

ABOUT THE AUTHOR

D R. Glenn Arekion is a uniquely gifted teacher and conference speaker. He conveys the Word of Truth in a simple, yet dynamic and motivational, way. With more than two decades' experience, he travels the globe mentoring leaders, equipping businessmen, and ministering to people, helping them to fulfill their purpose in life. He is a captivating and much sought-after speaker.

The author of thirty books, Glenn is dedicated to transforming lives from defeat into victory. His teaching materials are sold in many countries and are popular among those with a desire to grow strong in faith and experience great success.

Glenn is apostolic in his thrust of ministry. He believes in teaching and training pastors in their calling. His television program, *Faithlift*, airs twice a week on The Word Network. *Faithlift* is also a weekly television program on a number of networks that broadcast across the US, Africa, the U.K. and all over Europe.

Born in Mauritius, but raised and educated in London, Glenn holds a master's degrees and three doctorate degrees.

Glenn and his beautiful wife, Rosanna, have three children – Lisa, Ethan, and Jodie – and reside in Kentucky.

Author Contact

Glenn Arekion Ministries
P.O. Box 197777
Louisville, KY 40259, USA
mail@glennarekion.org
www.glennarekion.org

Further books by Dr Glenn Arekion...

Available online at glennarekion.org
Download eBooks and MP3 messages instantly

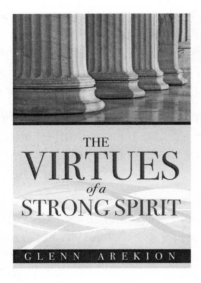

God created man with words of dominion and His original intent was for man to live from the inside out. This simply means to dominate the flesh from the spirit, and the natural from the spiritual. Since the fall of Adam, man has been living from his flesh, dominated by circumstances. Through the regeneration, our spirit man was reborn to win but the key is to know how to have a strong spirit. The stronger we are in our spirit the easier it will be for us to resist the attacks of the devil.

Living in the last days, it is imperative for the believer to be strong in spirit, to overcome the relentless attacks of the world, the flesh and the devil. Paul, the apostle, commanded the Ephesian believers to be 'Strong in the Lord'. How does one do that? He is not talking about our physical muscles. It is in the working out of our spirit man that we can truly be strong.

This book will unveil the secrets of spiritual strength and the consequences of having a weak spirit, such as:

- The stronger you are in your spirit, the more miracles and breakthroughs you will experience.
- The stronger you are in your spirit, the easier it will be for you to resist the attacks of the devil.
- The stronger you are in your spirit, the healthier you will be in your body.
- The stronger you are in your spirit, the less influence the world will have over you.

Further books by Dr Glenn Arekion...

Available online at glennarekion.org
Download eBooks and MP3 messages instantly

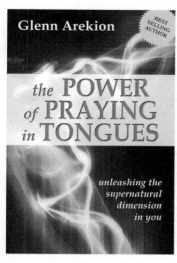

Are you ready for the supernatural?

Tired of mundane, dead Christianity and want to see Bible days in your life? Then this book is for you!

"I thank my God, I speak with tongues more than ye all" (1 Corinthians 14:18). Paul, the greatest apostle who ever lived, who wrote close to two-thirds of the New Testament and gave you your foundations for living an effective Christian life, uttered these words.
This founding father of the faith deemed "praying in tongues" of utmost importance and was grateful that he partook of such a great blessing.

Prayer is a command and calling of God. The Lord Jesus Christ specifically mentioned that His house is to be the house of prayer.
If you are born again, then you form part of the family of God, and prayer is your calling.

In The Power of Praying in Tongues, you will learn:

- The importance of praying in tongues
- Sixty expository benefits of praying in tongues
- The roots of negativism concerning tongues
- To develop partnership with the Holy Spirit
- To tap into supernatural Christianity

Also available in French and Spanish.

Further books by Dr Glenn Arekion...

Available online at glennarekion.org
Download eBooks and MP3 messages instantly

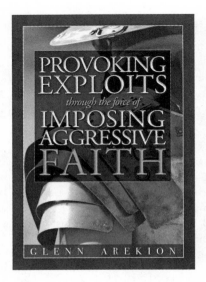

And such as do wickedly against the covenant shall he corrupt by flatteries: but the people that do know their God shall be strong, and do exploits – Daniel 11:32

The strength of your enemy is your ignorance. Those who are weak and ignorant will be exploited but those who are strong will have exploits. An exploit is a great feat that brings joy and every believer is called to a life of unlimited exploits – yet not every believer is experiencing this quality of life. Why? There are some key life-elements and attributes that are likely missing. Using Daniel 11:32 as the foundational verse, you will learn the prophecy and the history that this verse refers to. From the text, Glenn unravels five key attributes the believer must have in order to lead a life of exploits, specifically:

- Knowing God
- Being strong
- Having Imposing, aggressive faith
- Persistent and importunate prayer
- The leading of the Spirit

For many believers, the time span between exploits is too long. The Scripture says, *'Blessed be the Lord, who daily loadeth us with benefits...'* (Psalm 68:19).

Therefore we can have daily exploits. Many books have been written about faith but this book will open up another vista that will boost your faith for supernatural exploits. These five attributes – when implemented in your life – will set you up for exploits. No longer will you be exploited!

Further books by Dr Glenn Arekion...

Available online at glennarekion.org
Download eBooks and MP3 messages instantly

What you are about to read will revolutionize your life and take you to a higher dimension! The anointing is the most indispensable force in the life of the believer. With it, you will have the power and faith to do great exploits. Without it, life and ministry will be a constant source of frustration and irritation. Many have visions but simply do not know how to make the realities in their lives.

This book is full of answers to your most frustrating questions. The name of the game is results, and when you know how to purposely tap into the anointing and treasure of God, you will:

- Be transformed into a different person
- Be elevated into a new place in God
- Be the catalyst for positive change in the lives of suffering people
- See your dream become your destiny

Seven ways to increase your anointing will answer your heart's cry. It will show you how to remove the powerlessness and lack of influence in your life, while empowering you to do the mighty works of God.

Also available in French.

Further books by Dr Glenn Arekion...

Available online at glennarekion.org
Download eBooks and MP3 messages instantly

Jesus declared that healing is the children's bread. It is the divine right of every believer to walk in divine healing, divine health and divine life. However, as long as there are questions in your mind as to whether or not it is God's will to heal, your faith will be hampered from receiving what Jesus legally purchased for you.

Since Jesus Christ is the same yesterday, today and forever, He is still anointed to heal. The ministry of Jesus, today, is still a miraculous, healing ministry - as it was when he first walked the streets of Jerusalem and the shores of Galilee.

This book will answer the important healing questions and reveal God's thoughts towards your wellness. This book will eliminate doubts, banish fear and boost your faith to receive your inheritance. As you meditate upon the truths in these chapters, you will discover:

- Did healing pass away with the apostles?
- Is God glorified through sickness?
- Am I entitled to divine health in old age?
- How to resist sickness
- How to receive your healing
- 101 healing promises
- Daily healing confessions to cover your life

His Word is medicine to our flesh. He sent His Word and His Word healed them all. You are part of the "all" He sent his Word to heal. Receive your healing NOW!

Further books by Dr Glenn Arekion...

Available online at glennarekion.org
Download eBooks and MP3 messages instantly

The apostle Paul had an understanding of the new creation like no other authors of the New Testament. What was passed on in the first Adam is now passed away in the last Adam! A revelation of the new creation in Christ will revolutionize your life. New-creation realities will enable you to dominate the old creation, that is the old man. In this powerful book, Dr Glenn Arekion unveils the power of the new man over the old man and the mindset of Paul by the explanation of:

- The finished work of Christ
- The curse of the law
- The blessing of Abraham
- The believer's position
- The realities of the new creation

Break free from the fallen genetics of the first Adam passed down to the human race and live from your new identity in Christ. This book will enlighten your understanding to your position in Jesus Christ. No longer will you accept the lies of the devil as the norms in your life.

Enjoy your new status in Christ over all the works of the enemy and walk in victory.

Also available in French.

Further books by Dr Glenn Arekion...

Available online at glennarekion.org
Download eBooks and MP3 messages instantly

'I'm living the dream' is an expression that is often said but hardly ever experienced. Much has been said in the past years about the importance of dreams and visions for a fulfilled life and yet there are more dissatisfied people today than ever. This is because without wisdom, strategies and disciplines, visions remain grounded. Many have not reached the lofty positions that their dreams had for them due to a lack of these three fundamental forces.

Solomon, the most successful entrepreneurial king, knew the keys to success and he said in Ecclesiastes, 'For a dream cometh through the multitude of business...' Modern translations render this verse as, 'A dream comes through by much business, much activities and painful efforts.' Sitting down and merely having a dream without activities, strategies and certain disciplines implemented in your life will not trigger your dream to materialize.

This book explains the necessary wisdom strategies and the corresponding disciplines that you need to turn your dreams into realities. In this book you will learn:

- You are the number one enterprise that you need to build
- To destroy the excuses people use to abort their destiny
- The values of goals and diversities of goals
- Time management
- The ten characteristics of the diligent
- The million dollar habits you need to develop
- Wisdom secrets from the ants, the conies, the locusts and the spiders
- To turn your dreams into realities

Further books by Dr Glenn Arekion...

Available online at glennarekion.org
Download eBooks and MP3 messages instantly

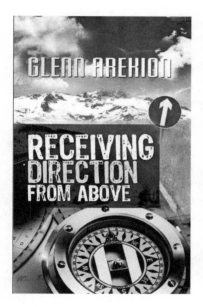

Whatever is troubling you is not troubling God. Whatever is disturbing you is certainly not disturbing God. Why? Because God knows what to do about your problem. The reason you are perturbed and troubled is due to the fact that you do not know what God knows. If you knew what he knew then you would be just like God: cool, calm and collected.

Having access to the voice of God is the right of every believer. He wants to speak to you.

In this powerful book, you will discover the secret of receiving direction from above. You will learn:

- How God speaks
- Why 'fleece' is not for the New Testament believer
- How God led the apostle Paul
- How to fine-tune your spirit man to pick up on the voice of God

This powerful book will change your life.

Further books by Dr Glenn Arekion...

Available online at glennarekion.org
Download eBooks and MP3 messages instantly

You are only as effective as the quality of the information you receive. As a believer, you will be empowered, enlightened and energized as the exciting truths become alive in your heart and mind.

This book is a toolbox for the believer and minister, equipping them to fix life's problems. Life and ministry without the Holy Spirit, the Supernatural and His gifts will be a cycle of frustration but with Him actively involved, Bible results will become your reality!

If you are tired of living your Christian life without results then you need this great tool in your hands TODAY.

Through this book, Dr Glenn helps you:

- To develop your relationship with the greatest partner – The Holy Spirit
- To attract an active partnership with the Holy Spirit
- To grasp the purpose and validity of the gifts of the Spirit
- How to activate the gifts in your life and ministry
- To know what Paul meant by 'the best gift'
- To understand what the supernatural means
- To release the supernatural in your life and ministry
- To delve into 101 benefits of praying Tongues
- To understand the efficacy of fasting for a supernatural ministry
- To keep the fire of God burning in your life

This book contains 13 powerful chapters that will help you in your walk with God.

Also available in French and Spanish.

Further books by Dr Glenn Arekion...

Available online at glennarekion.org
Download eBooks and MP3 messages instantly

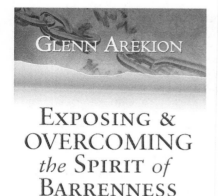

The first prophetic words ever spoken to humanity by Elohim were, "Be fruitful and multiply". Barrenness therefore is a direct assault, confrontation, violation and challenge to God's first decree to mankind. In this book you will discover that barrenness is not only a biological or a female problem and it operates on many different levels with different facets.

Barrenness is manifested:

- Biologically
- Territorially
- Financially
- Ministerially
- Generationally
- Mentally
- Professionally
- Spiritually
- Personally

When dealing with the spirit of barrenness, you are dealing with the spirit of stagnation and limitation. It seeks to curtail your life, your status, your ministry, your church, your family and your finances.

BUT IT CAN BE BROKEN!

In this book, Dr. Glenn gives you five powerful keys to destroy the spirit of barrenness and forbid it from ever operating in your life.

Further books by Dr Glenn Arekion...

Available online at glennarekion.org
Download eBooks and MP3 messages instantly

Does the sight of blood scare you? Make you shudder? Cause you to feel faint?

A childhood experience left Dr Glenn feeling this way for years – until he focused on the "precious blood of Christ" that provides eternal life and love.

Throughout time, the world has searched for the keys of protection and redemption. Every type of ritual, performance, and self-abasement imaginable has been attempted in this search while the true key has been overlooked.

The much neglected and noticeably overlooked subject of the blood of Christ trickling down the cross, which held captive His out-of-joint but unbroken body, is the answer that all of mankind has been waiting for. There are inexhaustible benefits of this uncommon blood; but before we can ever experience these benefits, we must first not only acknowledge them but also explore their possibilities.

This blood holds within it manifold blessings because of the covenant which it represents, whether it is approached for the salvation of a loved one, forgiveness of sin, or when the storms of life come upon us. This book will show you a step-by-step process to the victory in life that the precious blood of Christ holds. May Heaven kiss you and grant you its favor as you dig deeply into these anointed words.

PEOPLE LIKE YOU... MAKE PEOPLE LIKE ME... GO!

So two good things happen as a result of your gifts—those in need are helped, and they overflow with thanks to God. Those you help will be glad not only because of your generous gifts to themselves and others, but they will praise God for this proof that your deeds are as good as your doctrine. And they will pray for you with deep fervor and feeling because of the wonderful grace of God shown through you

2 CORINTHIANS 9:12-14 – LIVING BIBLE

EVERY major ministry making an impact in the world today is blessed with faithful financial and prayerful partners. Partnership with a ministry is a crucial way for the Gospel to go in all the world. Together, I am totally convinced that we can impact the world and accomplish great things to the glory of God.

I have a simple vision burning in my spirit and that is to unveil the Good News to sinners and saints that victory is available in life through Jesus Christ. Therefore partners are an important part of this ministry and their assistance enable us to accomplish the following:

❖ Globally preach the Gospel through the media: The Word Network;

❖ Travel and preach the Gospel to the nations;

❖ Author books anointed by the Holy Spirit, endowed with information that will radically transform the lives of believers;

❖ Healing crusades and conventions worldwide;

❖ Planting churches in different nations.

Partners help us to do what we cannot do by ourselves.

Not everyone is called to full time ministry but every one is called to reach our world. Everyone who actively participates in supporting Glenn Arekion Ministries with their finances and prayers will receive credit and rewards for whatever this ministry accomplishes.

So join me as a partner today and be part of this end-time harvest! Together, let's reach the millions who need to hear the gospel of Jesus Christ. Your partnership with me will give you the personal satisfaction of being part of a strong ministry that is doing its best to fulfill the Great Commission. You can have the confidence of sowing into a ministry of integrity, knowing that your support is accomplishing the work of the gospel.

Visit **glennarekion.org/partner** today and join us!